GIVE ME /

The Alphabetical Sayings of the Desert Fathers

ST VLADIMIR'S SEMINARY PRESS
Popular Patristics Series
Number 52

The Popular Patristics Series published by St Vladimir's Seminary Press provides readable and accurate translations of a wide range of early Christian literature to a wide audience—students of Christian history to lay Christians reading for spiritual benefit. Recognized scholars in their fields provide short but comprehensive and clear introductions to the material. The texts include classics of Christian literature, thematic volumes, collections of homilies, letters on spiritual counsel, and poetical works from a variety of geographical contexts and historical backgrounds. The mission of the series is to mine the riches of the early Church and to make these treasures available to all.

Series Editor
JOHN BEHR

Associate Editor
AUGUSTINE CASIDAY

Give Me a Word

THE ALPHABETICAL SAYINGS
OF THE DESERT FATHERS

Translated by

JOHN WORTLEY

ST VLADIMIR'S SEMINARY PRESS
YONKERS, NEW YORK
2014

Library of Congress Cataloging-in-Publication Data

Apophthegmata Patrum.

    Give me a word : the alphabetical sayings of the fathers / translated by John Wortley.

        pages cm. — (Popular patristics series, ISSN 1555–5755 ; number 52)

        In English; translated from Greek.

        Includes bibliographical references.

        ISBN 978-0-88141-497-4 (paper) — ISBN 978-0-88141-498-1 (electronic)

        1. Monasticism and religious orders—Early works to 1800. 2. Asceticism—Early works to 1800. 3. Christian life—Early works to 1800. 4. Apophthegmata Patrum. I. Wortley, John. II. Title.

        BR60.A54313 2014

        271.009'015—dc23

                         2014018460

COPYRIGHT © 2014 BY

ST VLADIMIR'S SEMINARY PRESS
575 Scarsdale Road, Yonkers, NY 10707
1-800-204-2665
www.svspress.com

ISBN 978-088141-497-4
ISSN 1555-5755

PRINTED IN THE UNITED STATES OF AMERICA

PIAM IN MEMORIAM

UXORIS NUPER OBITAE

Contents

(*Note that the names of the Fathers are in order
according to the Greek alphabet.*)

A—*Alpha*

B—*Beta*

Γ—*Gamma*

Δ—*Delta*

E—*Epsilon*

Abbreviations

APanon See N, below

APalph The Alphabetic series of Sayings of the Desert Fathers (*i.e.* the present volume).

APsys The Systematic series of Sayings of the Desert Fathers, ed. Jean-Claude Guy, *Les Apophtegmes des Pères: collection systématique, 3 vols, Paris* 1993, 2003, 205; *Sources Chrétiennes* 387, 474 & 498, tr. John Wortley, *The Book of the Elders,* Cistercian / Liturgical Press 2012.

HL Palladius of Hellenopolis, *Historia Lausiaca,* ed. Cuthbert Butler, *The Lausiac History of Palladius,* 2 vols, Cambridge 1898, 1904; ed. G.J.M. Bartelink, tr. Marino Barchiesi, *Palladio, La Storia Lausiaca,* Fondazione Lorenza Valla 1974; tr. John Wortley, forthcoming, Cistercian/ Liturgical Press 2015.

HME Anon., *Historia Monachorum in Ægypto,* edited by André-Jean Festugière, *Subsidia Hagiographica* N53, Brussels 1971. tr. ibid., *Enquête sur les Moines d'Egypte* in *Les Moines d'Orient* IV/1, Paris 1964; tr. Norman Russel, *The Lives of the Desert Fathers,* Oxford and Kalamazoo 1981, new tr. John Wortley *en chantier.*

N refers to Frédéric Nau, the first editor of this series, also designated as *APanon,* ed. & tr. John Wortley, *The Anonymous Sayings of the Desert Fathers, a select edition and complete English translation,* Cambridge University Press 2013.

OED *Oxford English Dictionary*. 2nd ed. 20 vols. Oxford: Oxford University Press 1989. Also available on line at *http://www. oed.com/* and on CD-ROM.

P&J Pelagius and John (Latin tr.) *Apophthegmata Patrum* ed. Heribert Rosweyde in *Vitae Patrum VI & VII*, Anvers 1615 & 1623, repr. in *PL* 73:851–1022, tr. B. Ward, *The Desert Fathers: sayings of the early Christian monks*, Penguin 2003.

PG *Patrologia Cursus Completus*. Series Graeca: I–CLXI, edited by J.-P. Migne, Paris 1857–66.

PS John Moschos, *Pratum Spirituale*, ed. J.-P. Migne (after Fronto Ducaeus and J.-B. Cotelier) with the Latin tr. of Ambrose Traversari, *PG* 87:2851–3112; tr. John Wortley, *The Spiritual Meadow*, Kalamazoo 1992, rpt 1996, 2001; tr. Jean Bouchet, *Fioretti des moines d'orient*, Paris 2006.

Synag Paul Evergetinos, *Synagogē* Venice 1783; 6th edition, 4 vols Athens 1980.

VA Athanasius, *Vie d'Antoine* ed. G.J.M. Bartelink, *SC* 400, Paris 1994, tr. Tim Vivian and A.N. Athanasakis, *The Life of Antony, the Coptic Life and the Greek Life*, Cistercian / Liturgical Press 2003.

Introduction

The Desert Fathers were the pioneers of Christian monasticism; men and women who, responding to Christ's summons to "leave all and follow me," abandoned "the world" for the wilderness, there to practice spiritual discipline (*askēsis*) in order to achieve that inner calm they called *hesychia*. Antony of Egypt (*c.* 250–356) has been called the founding father of a movement that engulfed Egypt in the fourth and fifth centuries of our era, creating major centers of monastic activity in the Wadi Natrun district of Northwest Egypt, at Scete, Nitria, The Cells and elsewhere.[1] Even larger monastic communities were also established in the Thebaid under the leadership of Pachomius (*c.* 290–346), but these are scarcely acknowledged in the literary remains now known as the *Sayings of the Desert Fathers*.

The earliest attempts to codify the oral tradition of those sayings and the tales with which they are interspersed are nearly all lost, but their existence is attested by the compiler(s)[2] of the present work in their prologue: "Many have set out these sayings and righteous deeds of the holy elders in narrative form from time to time, in simple and uncontrived language."[3] Those who wrote these words produced a compilation consisting of two parts, now known respectively as the Alphabetic Sayings of the Desert Fathers[4] (presented here) and

[1]See (most recently) Mario Cappozzo, *I monasteri del deserto di Scete* (Todi: Tau, 2009).

[2]It seems unlikely that one person could have accomplished the task alone.

[3]Prologue to *APalph*, PG 65:73A.

[4]The present translation is based on the Greek text: Jean-Baptiste Cotelier, ed. and trans., *Apophthegmata patrum, collection alphabetica, Ecclesiae Graecae Monumenta* 1 (Paris: Apud Franciscum Muguet, 1647), re-ed. Jacques-Paul Migne, PG 65:71–440, supplemented by Jean-Claude Guy, *Recherches sur la tradition grecque des Apophthegmata Patrum,* second ed. (Brussels: Société des Bollandistes, 1962);

the *Anonymous Sayings of the Desert Fathers*.[5] Together these parts
constitute the oldest extant major corpus of tales and sayings, probably compiled in and for a monastic community originally settled
perhaps at Scete and certainly in the Wadi Natrun. But that area
was subject to successive raids by Bedouin tribes. Scete, the most
exposed of the monastic settlements, was devastated in 407, and
434/444[6] by Mazics, its monks driven off or killed.

One group of monks found refuge somewhere in Palestine,
bringing with them little of value other than the oral tradition of
the teaching of the Fathers. Fully aware that this tradition was now
endangered by the disruption of the monastic communities, they
wisely sought to consolidate and preserve that legacy for posterity
by committing it to writing. Those charged with the task had also to
render the material more easily accessible, for, as they wrote of earlier attempts at codification: ". . . as the narrative of many is confused
and disorderly, it presented some difficulty to the reader's mind."[7]
Working (so far as we can tell) in the last decade of the fifth century,
they succeeded in imposing some sort of order on the confusing
mass of oral and written monastic lore then in circulation. In doing
so they created a sound and easily accessible literary basis for the
monastic endeavor, for they laid it all out in Greek, whereas Coptic
had been the language of the early monks.

Greek was still the most widely spoken language of the Mediter-
ranean in those days, and already by the end of the fourth century
Hellenism was entering the Desert. Due at least in part to the influ-
ence of Athanasius' *Life of Antony* (written between 356 and 373),
sophisticated Greek-speaking people from the Nile Delta and from

Jean-Claude Guy, trans. (partial), *Paroles de Anciens* (Paris: Seuil, 1976); Lucien
Regnault, trans., *Les Sentences des Pères du Désert, collection alphabétique* (Sablé-
sur-Sarthe: Solesmes, 1981); Benedicta Ward, trans., *The Sayings of the Desert Fathers*
(Kalamazoo: Cistercian, 1975).

[5]*APanon.* John Wortley, ed. and trans., *The Anonymous Sayings of the Desert
Fathers, a select edition and complete English translation* (New York: Cambridge
University Press, 2013).

[6]The precise date is uncertain.

[7]Prologue to *APalph*, PG 65:73BC.

even further afield began embracing the monastic life: Evagrius Ponticus (346–399) and Arsenius (354–449) are two outstanding examples. With the arrival of such people the tales and sayings of the Fathers began to circulate in Greek as well as in Coptic—and with them the first attempts to record the material were made (of which the only extant remnants are the ten "Sayings of the holy monks" in Evagrius' *Praktikos* § 91–100).

To what extent our compilers were also translators, who can say? It may be that some of the material was already available in Greek, some only in Coptic. That a variety of translators have been at work here is suggested (for example) by the fact that the Coptic word *thbbio* is sometimes translated by the Greek word for *humility,* sometimes by a similar word meaning *humble-mindedness*. But, however it was accomplished, a large amount of desert lore was recorded almost entirely in Greek.[8]

It was also arranged in an orderly manner; faced with the daunting task of imposing some sort of organization on the data, the compilers first gathered all the known sayings of each elder and the tales about him or her into a separate dossier. Then, by reference to the initial letter of each elder's name, they arranged the dossiers (more or less) in the order of the letters of the Greek alphabet. Thus the collection begins with the dossiers of Antony the Great, Arsenius, and Agathon, then (about a thousand items later) concludes with those of Cheremon, Psenthaisius, and Ōr (Χ,Ψ,Ω).

However, when *that* task was finally accomplished, it was found that there still remained a considerable amount of material. This the compilers assembled into a supplement or appendix, of which they say: "Since there are also other words and deeds of the holy elders that do not indicate the names of those who spoke or performed them, we have set them out under headings after the completion

[8] A few Coptic words were retained, e.g. *abba, amma.* A large amount of apophthegmatic material has been preserved in languages other than Greek. Identified by Dom Lucien Regnault, this will shortly appear in English as John Wortley, ed. and trans., *More Sayings of the Desert Fathers* (Kalamazoo: Cistercian; Collegeville, MN: Liturgical Press, 2015).

of the alphabetic sequence."[9] Thus they created what is now known as the *Anonymous Collection*,[10] partially organized by theme rather than by name—a classification system that would be far more rigorously applied maybe a generation later in yet another major collection of desert lore, now known as the *Systematic Collection*.[11]

Generally speaking, one can say of the so-called apophthegms[12] that while the sayings set out the theory of primitive desert monasticism, the tales (fewer in number but of greater length) illustrate something of how desert life worked out in practice. Many sayings begin with a junior approaching a senior monk with the request: "Tell me a saying," or maybe a question, often: "How am I to be saved?"—probably meaning: "How can I keep from failing in this monastic endeavor?"[13] The elder might (or might not) break his silence to utter a laconic original saying, or he might begin to recount how: "Abba so-and-so used to say . . ." More rarely a tale might be told, but no matter what response the visitor received, he would carry it away as a great treasure, repeating it to himself many times and (eventually) communicating it to others.

For the most part the earliest monks were not sophisticated people; indeed many of them were very simple *fellahin*, peasants with little or no education, speaking one or other of the Coptic dialects. Literacy would have been rare among them, books even rarer. Rote-learning and recitation appear to have been a frequent method for the transmission and dissemination of the Holy Scriptures. So too were the tales and sayings of the elders memorized, cherished,

[9]Prologue to *APalph*, PG 65:73BC.

[10]See note 2, above. *APanon* now contains almost 900 items, but at least a third of them are later accretions.

[11] Jean-Claude Guy, ed., *Les Apophtegmes des Pères: collection systématique*, SC 387, 474, & 498 (Paris: Éditions du Cerf, 1993, 2003, & 2005); John Wortley, trans., *The Book of the Elders, Sayings of the Desert Fathers: The Systematic Collection* (Kalamazoo: Cistercian; Collegeville, MN: Liturgical Press, 2012); henceforth cited as *APsys*.

[12]It may have been the compilers who first applied the less-than-adequate Greek word *apophthegm* ("A terse, pointed saying embodying an important truth in few words" OED s.v. "apophthegm") to both sayings and tales.

[13] See John Wortley, "What the Desert Fathers meant by 'being saved,'" *Zeitschrift für Antikes Christentum* 12 (2008): 322–343.

and passed on from generation to generation of successive would-be ascetics, an ever-increasing treasury that functioned both as a unique training manual for the neophyte and as a *vade-mecum* for the monk already proceeding along the Royal Way. Naturally, as surely as pebbles are polished in the sea, as with any other folklore, the tales (especially) and sayings were to a certain extent transformed in the process of transmission, but not so much that the authentic voice of the Fathers (and some Mothers) who first uttered them cannot still be heard in them. Hence the reader will discover in this collection both a consensus, but also considerable diversity regarding the theory and the practice of desert monasticism.

The reader will also discover that, while the sayings of the elders appear to have survived the process of oral transmission relatively unscathed, the tales have not. Large and even alarming discrepancies can be found between different versions of them, to the point that one is tempted to suspect that what eventually came to be written down was not (and was never intended to be) any more than a mere abstract or skeleton, which a narrator was to flesh out to the best of his ability. This would explain why, in spite of an extraordinary degree of variation, the tale nearly always succeeds in maintaining its essential structure, hence its "moral."

Furthermore, the reader will note that tales and sayings both run the gamut from the simple to the highly enigmatic, but all have this in common: they characterize the nature of the monastic *askēsis,* "spiritual discipline." That *askēsis* was the endeavor to translate the words of the gospel into real life. Real life "in the desert" that is, which means a life subject to varying degrees of loneliness. The word *monk* comes from *monos,* "alone"; it is something of a paradox that, while Jesus preached an essentially social gospel, the monastic movement was both a rejection of society and a turning away from it. Every monk was alone in the sense that he had renounced (or abandoned) wife and family together with anything else that smacked of "the world." Those who had advanced furthest in monastic discipline lived completely alone as hermits in solitary places, but these were few. Most monks lived in communities large or small, but life there was only partially communal. In many cases monks came together only for the Saturday-Sunday celebration and for the great feasts, considerable emphasis being placed on spending much of their time alone, working (physically and spiritually) in the cell. To this extent the tales and sayings are misleading: perforce, they all derive from a moment when there was actual contact between monks, otherwise they would not have come down to us. In reality such moments must have been far, far rarer than the texts suggest; but that only made them more memorable.

Monastic life was a lonely life, nevertheless it was not so far removed from our life today that these tales and sayings of those who tried to live that life do not have some very useful things to say to those who are trying to live the Christ-life "in the world," even in this twenty-first century. The insistence on a monk's staying quietly alone in his cell most of the time may not be pertinent for us,[14] nor may the practice of staying up all night and sleeping "hard" be very useful. The Fathers' attempts to "pray without ceasing"[15] and their quest for inner calm (*hesychia*) are exemplary, but there are three cardinal qualities on which they insist over and over again, three essential elements of the monastic (indeed of the Christian) life, which it is good to heed. These are not listed in order of importance, for they are equally important:

Humility/humble-mindedness, the antithesis of vainglory and pride, is the most frequently mentioned and most highly praised quality in a monk, in whom it is an absolute necessity. "Blessed are the *poor in spirit*," says the Lord. The Fathers had no doubt that by this he meant the humble-minded, and they took very seriously what he says of such people: "for theirs is the Kingdom of Heaven" (Mt 5.3), because "the Lord exalts the humble and meek" (Lk 1.52).

[14]Worldings can however profit from observing that injunction *some* of the time: "Go into a room by yourself, shut the door and pray to your Father in secret . . ." says the Lord, Mt 6.6.

[15]John Wortley, "Prayer and the Desert Fathers," *The Coming of the Comforter: when where and to whom? Orientalia Judaica Christiana* 3 (2012): 109–129.

Abba Antony said: "I have seen all the snares of the devil spread out on earth and I said with a sigh: 'Who can pass these by?' and I heard a voice saying to me: 'Humble-mindednness'" (Antony 7, 15.3).

Then there is concern about and caring for, and being in love and charity with one's neighbor. The teaching of the Gospel is categorical here (cf. Mt 25, etc.), and the elders echo it faithfully: "Life and death depend on our neighbor," said Antony the Great, "for if we win over our brother, we win over God, but if we offend our brother, we sin against Christ" (Antony 9, 17.2). One cannot escape one's duty toward other children of God by running off to lead a solitary life. At the very least your handiwork must produce enough profit to feed yourself *and any other person in need*, for that person is your neighbor and your neighbor is Christ himself.

Finally, everything must be done with discretion. "There are some who, after wearing their bodies away with *askēsis*, have become distant from God because they did not have discretion."[16] The gospel has little to say about discretion, but the elders spell it out by insisting that all things be done with discernment and in moderation. There is no shortage of cases in the desert lore in which the reader suspects that somebody went too far: too much fasting, too little sleep, not enough exercise, and so forth. Again and again the voice of reason prevails: everything in moderation, avoid the extremes of too much or too little. Of course this comes back to a matter of individual choice, hence such sayings as: "If you have a heart you can be saved" (Pambo 10) and "We do not need anything other than an alert intelligence" (Poemen 135).

In these and other ways the monastic lore remains pertinent to every Christian's life. Antony the Great was well aware that monks have no monopoly on holiness: "It was revealed to Abba Antony in the desert: 'There is somebody in the city like you, a physician by profession, who provides those in need with his superfluous income and is singing *Holy, holy, holy* with the angels of God all day long'"

[16]Antony 8, 10.1; cf. John Wortley, "Discretion: Greater than All the Virtues," *Greek, Roman, and Byzantine Studies* 51.4 (2011): 634–652.

(Antony 24, 18.1). This message is frequently repeated in the apo-phthegms: holiness can be attained, whoever and wherever you are, desert or city, and no matter what you are wearing.

It must never be imagined that there is any "stable text" of the so-called *Sayings of the Desert Fathers*. There is not, there never was, and it is therefore unlikely for there ever to be anything that can be truly labeled "definitive." The reason is simple: whereas there lies at the origin of most works a text that somebody sat down and wrote or dictated— and an editor's task is therefore to reconstruct that *Urtext* as far as possible—no such foundation underpins the tradition of the apophthegms. For not only do its roots lie buried in the shifting sands of oral transmission, but there is every reason to suppose that, far from its being silenced as soon as the matter was committed to writing, transmission by word of mouth continued in vigorous exis-tence for some centuries, thus contaminating the written tradition and vice versa.

This double transmission partly explains the further complica-tion that scribes, who would under normal circumstances reproduce the exemplar before them with the greatest possible accuracy, appear to have accorded themselves extraordinary editorial license when the matter was of an apophthegmatic nature. This may well have been because, when faced with a discrepancy between the dead letter of the exemplar on his desk and the living voice of some charismatic elder, the scribe preferred the latter. He might also have adjusted or augmented the text a little to clarify what he perceived to be its mean-ing. And if he recalled some tale or saying that seemed appropriate, he would not hesitate to include it in his copy or, on occasion, to omit an item he felt to be less than edifying. Hence the apophthegmatic texts survive in a bewildering array of manuscripts under a variety of names: *Patericon*, *Geronticon*, *Paradise of the Fathers*, *Book of the Elders*, and so forth, all consisting of tales and sayings, but all differ-ing from each other to a greater or a lesser extent: in the wording of the items, in the items they include or exclude, and in the order in which the items are presented.

Obliged to choose among a confusing variety of versions, for this translation we have mainly relied on the classic edition of Jean-Baptiste Cotelier, made in the seventeenth century from a small number of manuscripts at his disposal. The researches of Jean-Claude Guy have also been used to supply additional material (marked *S* in the text; see note 4, above). Where Cotelier gives alternative readings we have tried to select the one that makes the most sense. And where we have a later version of a saying or tale available to us (e.g. in *APsys*, or even in *Synagōgē*) we have used that when it supplied what seemed to be missing or defective in Cotelier's text. This does not for a moment mean that the present translation is any more "authentic" than the text in PG; what it does mean is that it is every bit as authentic as anything any early monastic scribe might have produced.

Let it also be added that the notion that there is such a thing as an adequate translation is wholly illusory. Those who would translate are caught on the horns of a cruel dilemma: no matter how well the original text be understood, it can only be expressed using the forms and the conventions of the second language. Moreover, it has to be expressed in a way that is at least inoffensive and at best pleasing to the reader; hence, inevitably, the meaning shifts a little to the left or to the right as one tries to adapt the thought to the angularity of the newer language. These considerations notwithstanding, in presenting this inaccurate translation of an unstable text, the present translator hopes to give the reader some impression of the amazing life and sound teachings of those pioneers who abandoned "the world" to live with Christ in the wilderness, and he further hopes that the reader will benefit from the experience as he too has benefitted.

* * *

A brief summary of what is known of each elder has been inserted into the text; where nothing is said, nothing is known. Much of that information has been derived from the various works of Dom Lucien Regnault (1924–2003), a monk of Solesmes who did the world an inestimable service by providing it with the entire (known) range of apophthegmatic literature in contemporary language. His careful work and vast experience have been a constant guide and an inspiration to the present translator, who hereby gratefully acknowledges his debt to Dom Lucien, and to his *confrères* at Solesmes and Bellfontaine; also to the late Jean-Claude Guy, SJ.

Glossary

Non-English words retained in the translation

Abba—Father; a senior monk but not necessarily an *old* one.

Accidie (akēdia)—"Sloth, torpor, especially as a condition leading to listlessness and want of interest in life" (*OED*); probably akin to depression.

Agapē—Literally "love"; used to designate a common meal shared by monks on special occasions (hence "love-feast") possibly originally made possible by some freewill offering (*agapē*); also a charitable donation.

Amma—Mother.

Anchorite (anachorētēs)—One who withdraws; one who has abandoned "the world" for the desert, or (more usually) has left a community to live alone.

Apatheia—Literally "unfeeling"; indifference to physical conditions, often translated *dispassion*. The word is rarely found in the *Apophthegms*, but it is common in later monastic writing.

Askēsis—Literally a formation, usually meaning the practice of asceticism; the discipline associated with the monastic way of life, often translated "spiritual discipline."

Askētēs—One who practices *askēsis*.

Coenobion (koinobion)—Literally "common life"; a place or a community in which monks live together with shared worship, meals, and responsibilities.

Dynamis—The healing "power" believed to be given off by holy persons and their relics, etc., as in Mk 5.30.

Higoumen (hēgoumenos)—The head of a monastic community.

Hesychia (hēsuchia)—Not merely (or necessarily) silence (σιωπή), but an interior silence characterized by a tranquil acquiescence in the will of God, producing a profound calm and great peace within.

Leviton (i.e. Levite's)—The monk's garment for prayer, usually white.

Logismos, pl. *logismoi*—This is a word of many meanings; it can simply mean one's thinking process, but it can also mean everything that goes on in that process—good, bad, and indifferent—from a mere whim to a serious temptation.

Porneia—Any illicit (therefore for monks *all*) sexual activity of body, mind, or spirit.

Synaxis (σύναξις)—Literally "a congregating"; an act of worship, either of one or a few monks (the "little synaxis," also called *liturgy*) or of an entire community (e.g. at weekends and festivals) at a central location. The Holy Eucharist ("Offering") is also called *synaxis*.

Monastery—"The name of a dwelling and means nothing more than a place, a lodging that is, for monks" (even for only one monk).[1]

English words used with specific meanings

Voluntary exile, Alienation, and *Expatriation (xeniteia,* Latin *peri-grinatio)*—Making oneself a "stranger and sojourner" (1 Pet 2.11), usually in an uninhabited place or in a foreign land.

Ascetic, -ism (askētēs, askēsis)—The practitioner and practice of monastic discipline, perceived as a training or formation in travelling the way to perfection.

[1]Cassian *Conferences* 18.10.

Backbiting (*katalalia*)—To speak ill of or to somebody is by far the most frequently mentioned offence against one's neighbor. To recriminate, rail, slander, detract, *calumniari, maudire,* and similar words are all comprehended in this one.

Burnt-faced-one, Aithiops (from which "Ethiopian")—A devil or demon.

Coenobion (*koinobion*; cf. *coenobitic*)—"Common life," meaning wherever persons live together in community (a convent) under the supervision of a *koinobiarch*, here translated "superior," or higoumen (see above).

Dried loaf (*paxamas*)—"Biscuit" named after the baker Paxamos; a bread-roll that has been sun-dried or baked hard.

Elder (*gerōn*)—Often misleadingly rendered "old man," age is not necessarily implied (cf. "elder" among North-American Indians). An elder is one advanced, not so much in age as in experience; hence a senior monk, as opposed to a junior (brother).

Expatriation—see *Alienation.*

Loose-talk (*parrhēsia*)—"Outspokenness," "familiarity," also in a good sense "freedom of access," e.g. to the Deity (cf. 1 Jn 2.28, etc.).

Lord-and-master (*despotēs*)—An appellation of Jesus Christ.

Poverty (inadequately translates *aktēmosynē*)—Literally "without possessions." In the *Apophthegms* the word means not only the voluntary abandonment of material possessions, but *a fortiori*, indifference to possessions even when they are accessible.

Sheepskin (*mēlōtē*)—Something every monk needed as a protection against the cold at night; the word is also used to mean all his portable possessions (cf. 2 Kg 2.8, etc.; also Mark the disciple of Silvanus 4).

Sorrow for sin (*katanyxis*)—Sometimes rendered "compunction."

Spiritual gift (*charisma*)—Cf. "charismatic," one endowed with such gifts.

Worldling—"One who is devoted to the interests and pleasures of the world" (*OED*). This obsolete English word has been resurrected to represent the Greek *kosmikos*, a person "of the world" as opposed to one "of the desert," i.e., a "non-monk"; sometimes translated "layman," "non-clergyman" (though very few monks were clerics), sometimes "secular," but that usually means a cleric who is not a monk; very few worldlings were clerics.

* * *

Words found in square brackets in the text are words that are not found in the Greek but are desirable to make the meaning clear.

Apophthegmata Patrum:
series alphabetica

Preface to the Book about the *Askēsis* of the Blessed Fathers

In this book are recorded the virtuous *askēsis*, the wondrous way of life, and the sayings of the holy, blessed fathers for emulation and instruction on the part of those who are desirous of achieving the heavenly way of life, and to be imitated by those who wish to travel the road that leads to the Kingdom of Heaven. It has to be known that the holy fathers who became devotees of this blessed monastic life and teachers [of it], once they were enflamed with this divine and heavenly desire, reckoning everything that is good and valuable to men as nothing, strove above all to do nothing by way of ostentation. They pursued the path of God in such a way, hiding themselves away and concealing the greater part of their righteous deeds by excessive humility so nobody has been able accurately to describe their virtuous way of life for us. Those who have diligently labored on their account have set down in writing a few of their righteous sayings and deeds, not to flatter them, but endeavoring to infuse those who came after with zeal. Most have set out these sayings and righteous deeds of the holy elders in narrative form from time to time, in simple and uncontrived language, with only this one end in view: to benefit many [folk]. But as the narrative of many is confused and disorderly, it presents some difficulty to the reader's mind—for the memory does not have the capacity to retain what is scattered throughout the book as his mind is drawn hither and thither. For that reason we have been moved to adopt this alphabetical exposition, which is able, by its orderliness, to provide a grasp that is very clear, and a [spiritual] benefit ready for those who want it. Thus in the first chapter are found matters pertaining to Abba Antony, Arsenius, Agathon, and those whose names begin with *A*; in the second those with *B*: Basil the Great, Bessarion, Benjamin, and so forth down to Ω.[1] Since however there are other sayings and deeds of holy elders where the names of those who pronounced or performed them do not appear, we have arranged those under headings after the completion of the alphabetical disposition. After we had investigated and searched in many books, we included whatever we could find at the end of the headings so that, deriving spiritual benefit from them all and delighting in the fathers' sayings, "sweeter than honey and the honey-comb" [Ps 18.11], having lived a life worthy of the calling with which we were called by the Lord, we might attain to his Kingdom. Amen.

[1]Omega, the last letter of the Greek alphabet.

Sayings of the Holy Elders

A—*Alpha*

Antony the Great

*Antony (c. 250–356), "the Great One" as he was known,[2] is gener-ally reckoned the first and foremost of the Christian monks, largely because Athanasius wrote a Life of him shortly after his death (*Vita Antonii*), from which Antony 10 is taken, while 8, 9, and 22 are from letters attributed to Antony.*

Antony 1 [7.1]   Once when the holy Abba Antony was residing in the desert, overcome by *accidie* and a great darkening of *logismoi*, he was saying to God: "Lord, I want to be saved and my *logismoi* do not leave me alone. What am I to do in my affliction? How am I to be saved?" Going outside [his cell] a little way, Antony saw somebody like himself, sitting working—then standing up from his work and praying; sitting down again, working at rope-braiding, then standing to pray once more. It was an angel of the Lord sent to correct Antony and to assure him. And he heard the angel saying: "Act like this and you shall be saved." He experienced much joy and courage on hear-ing this and, acting in that way, he went on being saved.

Antony 2 [15.1]   Contemplating the depths of God's judgments, the same Antony inquired: "Lord, how is it that some die after a short life while others grow very old? Why are some in penury and others affluent? How do the wicked become affluent while the righteous are

[2]*HL* 21.7–8

31

impoverished?" A voice came to him that said: "Antony, pay attention to yourself, for these are the judgments of God and it is not to your advantage for you to learn about them."

Antony 3 [1.1]   Somebody asked Abba Antony: "By observing which [precept] shall I be well-pleasing to God?" The elder answered: "Observe what I am telling you: Always have God before your eyes wherever you go. Whatever you are doing, have the testimony from Holy Scripture to hand. Wherever you are living, do not be in a hurry to move away. Observe these three [precepts] and you will be saved."

Antony 4 [15.2]   Abba Antony said to Abba Poemen: "This is the great task of a person: personally to take responsibility for his own shortcoming in the presence of God and to expect temptation until his last breath."

Antony 5   The same [elder] said: "Nobody who has not been tempted will be able to enter the Kingdom of Heaven, for take away temptations," he says, "and nobody is being saved."[3]

Antony 6 [1.2]   Abba Pambo asked Abba Antony: "What am I to do?" The elder said to him: "Have no confidence in your righteousness; have no regrets about a past action; get control of your tongue and your belly."

Antony 7 [15.3]   Abba Antony said: "I have seen all the snares of the devil spread out on earth and I said with a sigh: 'Who can pass these by?' and I heard a voice saying to me: 'Humble-mindednness.'"

Antony 8 [10.1]   He also said: "There are some who, after wearing their bodies away with *askēsis*, have become distant from God because they did not have discretion."

Antony 9 [17.2]   He also said: "Life and death depend on our neighbor: for if we win over our brother, we win over God, but if we offend our brother, we sin against Christ."

[3]cf. Evagrius 5.

Antony 10 [2.1]   He also said: "Just as fish die if they are on dry land for some time, so do monks who loiter outside their cells or waste time with worldlings release themselves from the tension of *hesychia*.[4] So we should hasten back to the cell (like the fish to the sea) lest while loitering outside we forget to keep a watch on the inner [self.]"

Antony 11 [2.1]   He also said: "He who stays in the desert in *hesychia* releases himself from the battle on three fronts: hearing, speaking, and seeing. He has only one more battle: with *porneia*."[5]

Antony 12 [10.2]   Some brothers visited Abba Antony to report to him some visions they were seeing and to learn from him whether they were genuine or from demons. They had an ass, but it died along the way. When they came to the elder, he anticipated them, saying to them: "How did it come about that the little ass died on the way?" "How do you know that, abba?" they said to him, and he said to them: "The demons showed me," and they said to him: "This is the reason we came to inquire of you because we are seeing visions and they are often genuine, but maybe we are being led astray." The elder convinced them, using the example of the ass, that [visions] are from demons.

Antony 13 [10.3]   There was somebody in the desert hunting wild animals and he saw Abba Antony jesting with the brothers. The elder wanted to convince the hunter that he had to come down to the level of the brothers from time to time. He said to him: "Put an arrow to your bow and draw it." He did so. He said to him: "Draw again," and he drew. Again he said: "Draw." The hunter said to him: "If I draw beyond its capacity my bow will break." Said the elder to him: "So it is too with the work of God. If we draw on the brothers beyond their capacity, they will quickly break.[6] So it is necessary

---

[4] cf. VA 85.3; Sozomen *Historia Ecclesiastica* 1.13.10.

[5] Instead of *porneia*, some manuscripts read *accidie* or *heart* (*kardias; akēdias*)— thus *PSsys* 2.1.

[6] Lit. "soon dash against [each other]."

to come down to the level of the brothers from time to time." The hunter was conscience-stricken when he heard this and went his way greatly benefitted by the elder. The brothers withdrew to their place strengthened.

Antony 14 [8.1]   Abba Antony heard about a younger monk who had worked a wonder on the road; how, when he saw some elders travelling and toiling on the road, he ordered some wild asses to come and carry the elders until they came to Antony. So the elders reported these things to Abba Antony and he said to them: "That monk seems to me like a boat filled with good things, but I do not know whether he will come into the harbor." Some time after, Abba Antony suddenly began to weep, to tear his hair and to lament. His disciples said to him: "Why are you weeping, abba?" and the elder said: "A great pillar of the church just fell" (he was speaking about the young monk). "But go to him," he said, "and see what has happened." So off went the disciples and found the monk sitting on a mat, weeping for the sin he had committed. On seeing the elder's disciples, he said to them: "Tell the elder to beg God to grant me just ten days and I hope to give an account of myself"—and he died within five days.

Antony 15 [8.2]   A monk was praised by some brothers to Antony, but he tested [the brother] when he visited, whether he could endure dishonor. Finding that he did not tolerate it, he said to him: "You are like a village that is all prettied up in front, but pillaged by robbers at the back."

Antony 16 [10.4]   A brother said to Abba Antony: "Pray for me," and the elder said to him: "Neither I nor God will take pity on you unless you yourself make an effort and petition God."

Antony 17 [15.4]   Some elders once visited Abba Antony and Abba Joseph was with them. The elder mentioned a verse from Scripture, wishing to put them to the test. He began to ask, starting with the least of them, what this verse was about and each one began to speak according to his own ability. But the elder said to each one:

"You have not discovered it yet." Last of all he said to Abba Joseph: "You then, what do you say this phrase is about?" "I do not know," he replied—so Abba Antony said: "Because he said: 'I do not know' Abba Joseph has indeed discovered the way."

Antony 18 [4.1] Some brothers from Scete visited Abba Antony. When they got into a boat to go to him they found an elder who wanted to go there too, but the brothers did not know him. While they were sitting in the boat they were speaking about statements made by the fathers and taken from the Scripture, then too about their own handiwork, but the elder remained silent. When they came to the anchorage it emerged that the elder was going to Abba Antony too. When they got to him he said to them: "You found in that elder good company," and he said to the elder: "You found good brothers with you, abba." The elder said to him: "They are good, but their courtyard has no gate. Whoever wishes comes into the stable and unties the ass." He was saying this because they were speaking whatever came into their mouths.

Antony 19 [16.1] Some brothers visited Abba Antony and they said to him: "Tell us a saying [indicating] how we are to be saved." The elder said to them: "Have you not heard the Scripture? That is good enough for you," but they said: "We want to hear [it] from you, father." So the elder said to them: "The Gospel says: 'If someone hits you on thy right cheek, turn the other one to him too'" [Mt 5.39]. "We cannot do that," they told him. The elder said to them: "If you cannot turn the other [cheek], at least patiently endure the one [blow]." "We cannot do that either," they told him. The elder said: "If you cannot do that either, do not return [the blow] you received," but they said: "Nor can we do that." So the elder said to his disciple: "Make them a little soup, for they are sick" and he said to them: "If you cannot do this and you will not do that, what am I to do for you? There is need of prayer."

Antony 20 [6.1] A brother who had renounced the world and distributed his goods to the poor, but kept back a little for himself, visited Abba Antony. When the elder learnt of this, he said to him: "If you want to become a monk, go to such and such a village, buy some meat, and put it on your naked body; then come here like that." When the brother did that, the dogs and the birds tore his flesh. When he came back to the elder, he inquired whether it had happened as he had counseled. When that [brother] showed his lacerated body holy Antony said: "They who have renounced the world and want to have money are lacerated like that by the demons doing battle with them."

Antony 21 [9.1]   A brother once experienced temptation in the coenobion of Abba Elijah. Expelled from there, he went to a mountain,[7] to Abba Antony. After the brother had stayed with him for some time, he sent him to the coenobion out of which he had come; but when they saw him, they expelled him again. Back he went to Abba Antony, saying: "They refused to receive me, father." So the elder sent [him] saying: "A vessel was wrecked on the high seas and lost its cargo but, with great effort, it came safely to land. But you want to sink that which has come safely to land!" When they heard that Abba Antony had sent him, they immediately received him.

Antony 22 [5.1]   Abba Antony said: "I think that the body has a natural impulse inherent in it, but it does not operate if the soul is unwilling; it merely indicates a passionless impulse in the body. There is another impulse that arises from feeding and warming the body with food and drink, from which the heat of the blood raises the body up for action. Thus the Apostle said: 'Do not get drunk on wine for that leads to dissipation' [Eph 5.18], and the Lord too, urging the disciples in the Gospel said: 'Watch out that your hearts be not weighed down with intoxication and drunkenness' [Lk 21.34]. There is a certain other impulse for those who are fighting the good fight, which arises from the onslaught and envy of demons. So it should be known that there are three impulses of the body:

[7] Whether the "exterior mountain" at Pispir by the Nile or the "interior mountain" three days' march to the east is not clear; see *VA* 10.4, 51.1, etc.

one natural, another from indiscriminate feeding, the third from demons."

Antony 23 [10.5]   He also said: "God does not allow there to be battles against this generation such as there were in the time of those of old; for he knows these are weak and cannot sustain it."

Antony 24 [18.1]   It was revealed to Abba Antony in the desert: "There is somebody in the city like you, a physician by profession, who provides those in need with his superfluous income and is singing Holy, holy, holy with the angels of God all day long."

Antony 25   Abba Antony said: "A time is coming when people will rave and when they see somebody who is not raving, they will attack him, saying: 'You are raving [mad]'; for he is not like them."

Antony 26   Some brothers visited Abba Antony and repeated to him a verse from Leviticus. The elder went out into the desert and, without his knowing, Abba Ammonas followed him, for he was aware of his habits. When he had gone a very long way, standing to pray, the elder called out in a loud voice: "O God, send Moses and he will teach me [the meaning of] this verse"—and there came a voice speaking with him. Abba Ammonas said: "I heard the voice speaking with him but did not comprehend the meaning of what was said."

Antony 27 [17.5]   Three of the fathers were in the habit of going to the blessed Abba Antony each year. Two of them would ask him about *logismoi* and the soul's salvation, but the third always remained silent, asking nothing. After some considerable time Abba Antony said to him: "Look, you have been coming here for such a long time and you ask me nothing." In reply he said to him: "It is enough for me just to see you, father."

Antony 28   They used to say that one of the elders asked God to see the fathers, and see them he did, but there was no Abba Antony. "Where is Abba Antony," he said to the one who was showing [them to] him, but he said to him: "He is there in the place where God is."

Antony 29   A brother in a coenobion falsely accused of *porneia* got up and came to Abba Antony. The brothers from the coenobion came too, to cure him and take him [back]. They began to reprove him, saying: "You behaved like that," but he defended himself: "I did nothing of the sort." Now Abba Paphnutius Cephalas was spending some time there and he told them a parable like this: "I saw a man at the river bank up to his knees in mud. Then some people came to give him a hand and immersed him up to the neck." Speaking of Abba Paphnutius, Abba Antony said to them: "Here is a man indeed, capable of healing and saving souls." So they were pricked in their consciences by what the elders said and they prostrated themselves before the brother. Encouraged by the fathers, they took the brother [back] to the coenobion.

Antony 30   There were those who used to say of Abba Antony that he was filled with the Spirit[8] but that he was unwilling to speak on account of people. He used to indicate what was happening in the world and what was going to come about.

Antony 31   Abba Antony once received a letter from the emperor Constantius[9] [instructing him] to come to Constantinople and he was pondering what to do. So he said to Abba Paul, his disciple: "Ought I to go?" He said to him: "If you go, you will be called Antony; if you do not go, Abba Antony."

Antony 32 [17.1]   Abba Antony said: "I do not fear God anymore: I love him, for 'love casts out fear'" [1 Jn 4.18].

Antony 33 [3.1]   The same [elder] said: "Always have the fear of God before your eyes. Remember him who gives death and life [1 Sam 2.6]. Hate the world and all that is in it. Hate all physical repose. Renounce this life so you may live for God. Remember what you promised to God, for he will be looking for it from you on the Day

---

[8]Lit. "Spirit bearing"; *pneumataphoros*, "inspired . . . united to the Spirit," Lampe ad loc.

[9]Constantius II, reigned 337–361.

of Judgment. Be hungry and thirsty, endure nakedness, keep watch; sorrow, weep, and groan in your hearts. Examine whether you are worthy of God. Despise the flesh in order to save your souls."

Antony 34 Abba Antony once visited Abba Amoun at the Mountain of Nitria and, when they had met with each other, Abba Amoun said to him: "Since, thanks to your prayers, the brothers have become numerous and some of them want to build cells far away so they may live in *hesychia,* how far from here do you bid The Cells to be built?" "Let us eat the ninth-hour meal," he said, "then let us set out and walk through the desert in search of the place." When they had travelled the desert until the sun was about to set, Abba Antony said to him: "Let us offer a prayer and set up a cross here so that they who want to build may build here; and so that when the [brothers] over there visit those here, setting out after taking their collation at the ninth hour, they may in that way make their visits—and those going the other way likewise. Thus they may remain undistracted in their visits to each other." The distance is twelve miles.[10]

Antony 35 [11.3] Abba Antony said: "He who is hammering a piece of iron first takes note in his *logismos* what he is going to make: a scythe, a sword, or an axe. So ought we to consider what kind of virtue we are seeking, so that we do not labor in vain."

Antony 36 He also said that submission with continence masters wild beasts.

Antony 37 [11.1] He also said: "I know some monks who fell after many labors and came to the point of losing their reason. This was because they had pinned their hopes on their own work and had ignored the commandment of him who said: 'Ask your father and he will tell you'" [Deut 32.7].

Antony 38 [11.2 adds N 370] He also said: "If possible, the monk ought to reveal to the elders how many steps he takes or how many

---

[10]Thus was established the community known as The Cells.

drops of water he drinks in his cell [to see] whether he does not transgress in those matters."

ARSENIUS

Born at Rome in the mid-fourth century, Arsenius rose to high office at Constantinople and may have been the tutor of the future emperors Arcadius and Honorius for a time. In 394 he fled to become a monk at Scete under the guidance of John Colobos. After the final devastation of Scete in 434/444 he spent the rest of his days just south of where Cairo stands today. A clear picture of him emerges from his apophthegms; he clearly made a great impression on his contemporary monks.

Arsenius 1 [2.3]   When Abba Arsenius was still in the palace, he prayed to God saying: "Lord, guide me as to how I can be saved," and there came to him a voice saying: "Arsenius, flee from people and you shall be saved."

Arsenius 2 [2.4]   When the same [person] had retired into the solitary life he prayed again, offering the same prayer, and he heard a voice saying to him: "Arsenius, take flight, keep silent and maintain *hesychia*, for these are the roots of sinlessness."

Arsenius 3 [15.5]   The demons once set upon Abba Arsenius in his cell and were afflicting him. When those who were looking after him came by and were standing outside his cell, they heard him crying out to God, saying: "O God, do not abandon me! I have done no good thing in your sight but, of your kindness, grant me to make a start."

Arsenius 4 [15.6]   They used to say of him that whereas nobody of the palace used to wear finer clothing than he did when he was in the palace, so in church nobody would wear [clothes] more shabby than he wore.

Arsenius 5 [10.7]   Somebody said to the blessed Arsenius: "How is it that we have gained nothing from so much education and wisdom, while these rustic Egyptian peasants have acquired such virtues?" Abba Arsenius said to him: "For our part we have gained nothing from the world's education, but these rustic Egyptian peasants have acquired the virtues by their own labors."

Arsenius 6 [15.7]   Abba Arsenius was once asking an Egyptian elder about his own *logismoi*. Another person, when he saw him, said: "Abba Arsenius, how is it that you, who have such a command of Greek and Roman learning, are asking this rustic about your *logismoi*?" But he said to him: "A command of Greek and Roman learning I have, but I have not yet learned the alphabet of this rustic."

Arsenius 7 [2.6]   The blessed archbishop Theophilus once visited Arsenius together with an official and he asked the elder if they might hear a saying from him. After remaining silent for a little, the elder answered him: "If I say something to you, will you observe it?" They agreed to observe it, then the elder said to them: "Wherever you hear Arsenius is, do not come near."

Arsenius 8 [2.7]   Another time the archbishop wanted to visit him again; first he sent to know whether the elder would open [the door]. [Arsenius] declared to him: "If you come, I will open to you; and if I open to you, I open to everybody—and then I am not staying here any longer." When he heard that, the archbishop said: "If I am coming there to chase him away, I am not coming to him any more."

Arsenius 9 [11.4]   A brother asked Abba Arsenius if he could hear a saying from him. The elder said to him: "As much as you are able, strive so that what goes on inside you be godly and you conquer your external passions."

Arsenius 10 [11.5]   He also said: "If we seek for God, he will appear to us and, if we hold him fast, he will remain with us."

Arsenius 11 [7.34, N 195]   Somebody said to Abba Arsenius: "[My] *logismoi* are afflicting me, saying: 'You cannot fast or labor; then visit the sick, for that too is charity.'" Recognizing the devices of the demons, the elder said to him: "Go: eat, drink, sleep, do no work— only do not be out of your cell"—for he was aware that remaining patiently in one's cell is what brings a monk into line. {When he had spent three days there, he had an attack of *accidie*. He found a few palm-leaves which he split and, [taking them up] again next day, began braiding them. When he got hungry, he said: "Here are some small palm-leaves, so I will eat," and when he had worked the palm-leaves, again he said: "I am going to read a little and then eat." When he had read, he said: "I shall recite the psalms of the little *synaxis* and then eat without concern." With the help of God, he began to make progress little by little, in this way, until he made the grade and, gaining confidence against his *logismoi*, he overcame them.}[11]

Arsenius 12 [10.8]   Abba Arsenius used to say: "Let a foreign monk in a strange land not meddle in anything and he will experience repose."

Arsenius 13 [2.5, 17.6]   Abba Mark said to Abba Arsenius: "Why do you run away from us?" The elder said to him: "God knows that I love you, but I cannot be with God and with people. The thousands and tens of thousands above have one will, but people have many wills, so I cannot forsake God and come among people."

Arsenius 14 [4.2]   Abba Daniel used to say of Abba Arsenius that he used to spend the whole night watching and toward dawn, when naturally he wanted to sleep, he would say to sleep: "Come on then, wicked slave," and he would snatch a little, sitting down, then get up straight away.

Arsenius 15 [4.3]   Abba Arsenius used to say: "It is enough for a monk to sleep one hour if he is a fighter."

---

[11]The passage { . . . } is not found in PG 65.

Arsenius 16 [15.8]   The elders used to say that a few dried figs were once given to Scete. As these were of no account, they did not send [any] to Abba Arsenius, so he would not be insulted. But when the elder heard, he did not come to the *synaxis,* saying: "You have excluded me by not giving me the donation God sent to the brothers, which I was not worthy to receive." They all heard and [all] benefitted from the humility of the elder. The priest went off and brought him the figs, then brought him to the *synaxis* with joy.

Arsenius 17 [4.4]   Abba Daniel used to say of him: "He stayed with us for so many years, and we used to make only one *thallion*[12] of grain a year for him and we would eat from it when we visited him."

Arsenius 18 [4.5]   He also said of the same Abba Arsenius that he only changed the water [for steeping] the palm-leaves once a year; he just added to it. He used to braid rope and stitch it until the sixth hour. The elders entreated him: "Why do you not change the water of the palm-leaves, for it stinks?" He said to them: "I have to accept that stench in place of the incense and myrrh I enjoyed in the world."

Arsenius 19 [4.6]   He [Abba Daniel] also said that when he [Abba Arsenius] heard that every manner of fruit was ripe, for his part, he would say: "Bring me [some]," and he would taste just a little of them all, once only, giving thanks to God.

Arsenius 20 [6.3]   There was a time when Abba Arsenius was ill at Scete and he did not have a thing, not even one sheet. As he did not have the wherewithal to buy one, he accepted alms from somebody, saying: "I thank you, Lord, that you considered me worthy to receive alms in your name."

Arsenius 21 [2.9]   They used to say of him that his cell was thirty-two miles away and he did not readily come out, for there were others who were looking after him. But when Scete was devastated,

---

[12]A dry measure of uncertain dimensions; a basket made of palm-fronds.

he came out weeping and saying: "The world has lost Rome, the monks Scete."

Arsenius 22 [10.9]   Abba Mark asked Abba Arsenius: "Is it good not to have any refreshment at one's own cell?—for I saw a brother who had a few vegetables and he was rooting them out." Abba Arsenius said: "It is good, but according to the ability of the person; for if he doesn't have the strength for such a way of life, he will plant others again."[13]

Arsenius 23   Abba Daniel, the disciple of Abba Arsenius recounted: "One day I was with Abba Alexander when pain seized him. He stretched himself out, looking upwards, because of the pain. The blessed Arsenius happened to be coming to speak with him and saw him stretched out. When he spoke, he said to him: 'Who then was the worldling I saw here?' Abba Alexander said to him: 'Where have you seen him?' and he said: 'As I came down from the mountain I turned my attention here, to the cave, and I saw somebody stretched out, looking upwards.' [Alexander] prostrated himself before [the elder] saying: 'Forgive me: it was I. Pain had gripped me.' The elder said to him: 'Was it indeed you? Very well then; I supposed it was a worldling; that is why I asked.'"

Arsenius 24 [14.2]   On another occasion the blessed Arsenius said to Abba Alexander: "Come and eat with me when you have cut your palm-fronds, but if some guests come, eat with them." So Abba Alexander worked away evenly and moderately; when the time came, he still had palm-fronds. Wishing to fulfill the elder's instruction, he stayed to complete the palms. When Abba Arsenius saw that he was late, he ate, thinking that [Abba Alexander] had guests, but Abba Alexander went [to him] when he had finished the palm-fronds in the evening and the elder said to him: "You had guests?" and he said: "No." "So why did you not come?" [the elder] said to him. "Because you said to me: 'When you have cut your palm-fronds, come then,'"

[13]cf. Poemen 22, 10.66.

he said, "and, observing your instruction, I did not come because I only completed [the task] just now." The elder was amazed at his scrupulosity and he said to him: "Break your fast earlier so you can perform your *synaxis* and partake of your water, otherwise your body will soon sicken."

Arsenius 25 [2.8]   Abba Arsenius once visited a place where there were reeds and they were moved by the wind. The elder said to the brothers: "What is that disturbance?" and they said to him: "It is the reeds." The elder said to them: "Naturally, if somebody is living in *hesychia* but hears the sound of a sparrow, his heart does not have the same *hesychia*; how much more so you who have the disturbance of these reeds!"

Arsenius 26   Abba Daniel used to say that some brothers were about to go to the Thebaid for linen thread and they said: "Maybe we might see Abba Arsenius too." Abba Alexander went in and said to the elder: "Some brothers have come from Alexandria and they wish to see you." The elder said: "Find out from them for what reason they are here." When [Alexander] found that they were going to the Thebaid for linen thread he reported it to the elder and *he* said: "They are certainly not going to see the face of Arsenius—because they did not come for my sake, but for their work's. Give them some refreshment and send them on their way in peace, telling them: 'The elder cannot meet with you.'"

Arsenius 27 [18.2]   A brother went to the cell of Abba Arsenius at Scete and, looking through the window, saw the elder as though he were all fire, for the brother was worthy to see [this.] When he knocked, the elder came out and saw the brother looking astounded. "Have you been knocking for long?" he said to him. "You didn't see anything here?" but he said: "No." [The elder] conversed with him and sent him on his way.

Arsenius 28 [2.10]   Once when Arsenius was living at Canopus, an exceedingly rich, God-fearing virgin of senatorial rank came from

Rome to see him. Archbishop Theophilus received her [as his guest] and she entreated him to persuade the elder to give her an audience. He went to him and entreated him, saying: "So-and-so of senatorial rank came from Rome and she wants to see you," but the elder would not agree to meet her. She, however, when this was reported to her, ordered beasts to be saddled, saying: "I am trusting in God that I shall see him, for I did not come to see a man. There are many men in our city, but I came to see a prophet." By divine providence, the elder happened to be outside the cell when she approached it. She fell at his feet when she saw him, but he angrily raised her up and looked her up and down, saying to her: "If you want to see my face, take a look," but she was ashamed to look him in the face. The elder said to her: "Have you not heard of my deeds? You should look to those. How dare you undertake such a voyage? Do you not realize that you are a woman and ought never to go out anywhere? Or was it so that you can say to the other women when you return to Rome: 'I saw Arsenius,' and they may turn the sea into a highway for women coming to me?" She said: "If it be the Lord's will, I will not allow anybody to come here; but do you pray for me and ever be mindful of me." In answer he said to her: "I am praying to God that he might expunge the memory of you from my heart," on hearing which she went away deeply troubled. When she came to the city, she fell into a fever from her grief. It was reported to Theophilus the archbishop that she was ill and he came to her, begging of her that he might learn what was the matter. Said she to him: "Would that I had not come here, for I said to the elder: 'Be mindful of me,' and he said to me: 'I am praying to God that the memory of you be expunged from my heart,' and here I am dying of grief!" "Are you not aware that you are a woman," the archbishop said to her, "and that it is through women that the enemy does battle with the holy ones? This is why the elder said [that], for he is praying for your soul all the time." In this way her *logismos* was healed; she went back to her homeland with joy.

Arsenius 29 [6.2]   Abba Daniel said of Abba Arsenius that there once came to him an officer[14] bringing him the testament of some senator related to him who had left him an exceedingly large inheritance. He took it and would have torn it up, but the officer fell at his feet, saying: "Do not tear it up I beseech you since my head will be struck off." Abba Arsenius said to him: "I died before he did just now," and he sent it back, accepting nothing.

Arsenius 30 [12.1]   They also used to say of him that on Saturday night when Sunday was about to dawn he used to put the sun behind him and stretch out his hands to heaven, praying until the sun shone on his face; and then he would sit down.

Arsenius 31 [8.3]   They used to say of Abba Arsenius and of Abba Theodore of Phermē that they hated the glory of men above all [shortcomings]. While Abba Arsenius would not readily meet anybody, Abba Theodore would—but he was like a sword.

Arsenius 32 [15.10]   Once when Abba Arsenius was living in the lower regions [of Egypt] and was being mobbed there, he decided to leave his cell. Taking nothing out of it he went like that to his own disciples, the Pharanites Alexander and Zoïlos. He said to Alexander: "Get up and sail away," which he did. To Zoïlos he said: "Come with me as far as the river and find me a vessel sailing to Alexandria and, in that way, do you too sail off to your brother." Zoïlos was troubled at the instruction but he kept silent and they separated from each other like that. When the elder came into the environs of Alexandria he fell seriously ill. His attendants said to each other: "Perhaps one of us grieved the elder and that was why he separated from us?" but they found nothing [offensive] among themselves, not even that they had ever disobeyed him. When the elder recovered, he said: "I am going to my fathers," and so saying, he sailed off and came to Petra where his attendants were. When he was near the river, a black serving wench came and touched his sheepskin, but the elder

---

[14]*magistrianos*, "a military messenger"; *agens in rebus.*

reprimanded her, so the wench said to him: "If you are a monk, get
to the mountain." Conscience-stricken by the remark, the elder said
to himself: "Arsenius, if you are a monk, get to the mountain," and
forthwith, there met him Alexander and Zoïlos. They threw themselves at his feet; the elder threw himself down too and both parties
wept. The elder said to them: "Did you not hear that I was ill?" "Yes,"
they said, and the elder said: "Then why did you not come and see
me?" Abba Alexander said to him: "Because your separation from
us did not take place plausibly and many were not edified, saying: 'If
they had not disobeyed the elder he would not have separated from
them.'" He said to them: "Now people are going to say again that the
dove did not find a resting place for her feet so she returned to Noah
in the ark" [cf. Gen 8.9]. In this way they were reconciled and they
stayed with him until his death.

Arsenius 33 [18.3]   Abba Daniel said that Abba Arsenius told us
as though he were speaking of somebody else (but it may well have
been he) that while an elder was residing in his cell, a voice came to
him that said: "Come, I will show you the works of folk." [The elder]
got up and went out; [the voice] brought him to a place and showed
him a burnt-faced-one cutting wood and making a great bundle.
He attempted to carry it but could not. But instead of taking away
from it, he cut some more wood then added it to the bundle—and he
was doing this for a long time. When he had gone a little further he
also showed him a person standing in a lake, drawing water from it
and pouring it into a receptacle with holes in it: the same water was
running out into the lake. He spoke to him again: "Come on, I will
show you something else;" then he saw a temple and two persons
on horseback carrying a piece of wood crossways, one beside the
other. They wanted to enter through the gate but could not because
the piece of wood was crossways. One would not humble himself
to carry the wood lengthwise behind the other; for that reason they
remained outside the gate. "These are they," he said, "who bear the
yoke of righteousness with pride and did not humble themselves to

put their house in order and to travel the humble way of Christ; so they remain outside the Kingdom of God. The one cutting wood is a man beset by many sins; instead of repenting, he adds other transgressions on top of his sins. And the one drawing water is a person who does good works but, because he has an evil mixture in him, for this he lost his good deeds too. So every one must keep a watch over his works, lest he toil in vain."

Arsenius 34 The same [elder] recounted that some fathers once came from Alexandria to see Abba Arsenius and one of them was the uncle of the former archbishop of Alexandria, Timothy, called "the poor"; he had one of his nephews with him. As the elder was unwell at that time he did not wish to meet them, for fear that others would come troubling him; he was then at Petra in Troe. They went back in sorrow. Then, as there happened to be an incursion of barbarians, he came and stayed in lower Egypt. On hearing this they came again to see him and he received them joyfully. The brother who was with them said to him: "Do you not know that they came to visit you at Troe and you did not receive them, abba?" and the elder said to him: "For your part you [pl] ate bread and drank water but naturally I, my son, tasted neither bread nor water; neither did I sit down, punishing myself until I figured you had reached your own place, as it was on my behalf that you were worn out; but forgive me, brothers"; and they went away comforted.

Arsenius 35 [11.6] The same [elder] used to say: "Abba Arsenius called me one day and said to me: 'Look after your father so that when he goes to the Lord he may personally intercede with him on your behalf—then it will be well with you.'"

Arsenius 36 They used to say of Abba Arsenius that once when he was sick at Scete, the priest came and brought him into church. He put him on a mattress with a little pillow under his head. And here one of the elders coming to visit him was offended when he saw him on the mattress with a pillow under him. "This is Abba Arsenius," he said, "lying on those things?" The priest took him aside and said to him: "What did you do in your village?" "I was a shepherd," he said. "And how did you live your life?" said [the priest.] "I lived it with great toil," he said and [the priest] said: "So how do you live now, in your cell?" "I am rather more comfortable," he said. Then [the priest] said to him: "You see this Abba Arsenius? He was the father of emperors when he was in the world; thousands of slaves all wearing golden insignia stood around him and there were valuable carpets beneath [his feet]. When you were a shepherd you did not enjoy the comfort in the world you now enjoy. But this man does not have here the luxury he knew in the world. Here you enjoy comfort and he is afflicted." He was conscience-stricken when he heard this; he prostrated himself saying: "Forgive me, abba, for I have sinned. There indeed is the true path, for he came to lowliness, I to comfort"—and he went his way edified.[15]

Arsenius 37   One of the fathers came to Abba Arsenius. Thinking that it was his attendant, the elder opened the door when he knocked—but fell on his face when he saw that it was somebody else. [The father] said to him: "Get up, abba, so I can greet you," but the elder said to him: "I am not getting up unless you leave." And, much though he was pleaded with, he did not get up until [the other] left.

Arsenius 38   They used to say of one brother who came to see Abba Arsenius at Scete that he came into church and besought the clergy [that he might] meet with Abba Arsenius. They said to him: "Take a little refreshment, brother and you shall see him," but he said: "I am not tasting anything until I meet with him." So they sent a brother to go with him because the elder's cell was far away. They knocked at the door and went in; when they had greeted the elder, they sat in silence. So the brother, the one from the church, said: "I am going [back]; pray for me." Since the brother from elsewhere was not having any communication with the elder, he said to the brother: "I am coming with you too," and out they went together. Then he begged

[15]cf. The Roman 1, 10.110, which may very well be about Arsenius.

him: "Take me to Abba Moses too, the one who was a brigand." They came to him and he received them joyfully. He treated them with honor and sent them on their way. Then the brother who was guiding him said: "Here I have taken you to the outsider and to the Egyptian; which of the two pleased you?" In reply he said: "The Egyptian pleased me so far." On hearing this, one of the fathers prayed to God: "Lord, show me this matter: one person avoids people in your name while another welcomes them with open arms in your name," and here there was shown to him two great boats on the river. In one of them he saw Abba Arsenius with the Holy Spirit sailing in *hesychia*, while in the other there sailed Abba Moses and the angels of God and they were feeding him honeycombs.

Arsenius 39 [10.10]   Abba Daniel used to say: "When Abba Arsenius was about to die, he instructed us: 'Do not bother arranging an *agapē* for me, for if I did a voluntary act of charity [*agapē*] I shall find it there.'"

Arsenius 40   When Abba Arsenius was about to die, his disciples were distraught and he said to them: "The hour is not yet come; I will tell you when it comes; but I will be judged together with you at the fearful judgment seat of Christ if you give my remains to anybody." They said to him: "What shall we do then, for we do not know how to bury?" and the elder said to them: "Do you not know how to fasten a rope to my foot and drag me to the mountain?" This is what the elder said: "Why did you abandon [the world] Arsenius? I often repented of having spoken, never of remaining silent." When he was about to give up the ghost, the brothers saw him weeping and they said to him: "Are you too truly afraid, father?" He said to them: "Truly, the fear that is with me in this hour has been with me ever since I became a monk," and so he fell asleep.

Arsenius 41 [3.3]   They used to say [of Abba Arsenius] that, all his life long, when he was sitting working with his hands, he had a rag on his lap on account of the tears falling from his eyes. When

Abba Poemen heard that Abba Arsenius had fallen asleep, he shed tears and said: "Blessed are you, Abba Arsenius, because you wept for yourself here in this present world; for he who does not weep for himself here will weep there eternally. Whether it be willingly here or there on account of the torments, it is impossible not to weep."

Arsenius 42 [15.11]   Abba Daniel recounted of [Abba Arsenius] that he never wanted to comment on any inquiry about Scripture, even though he was capable of commenting if he wanted to; nor would he readily write a letter. When he came to church from time to time he would place himself behind a pillar so nobody would see his face; nor would he look at another person. His appearance was angelic, like Jacob's, the hair completely white, the body noble but slender, the beard large, down to his belly. His eyelashes hung down from weeping. He was tall but bent over with age and he died at the age of ninety-five. He spent forty years in the palace of Theodosius the Great of godly memory where he became father to the most godly Arcadius and Honorius. He spent forty years at Scete, ten at Troe above Babylon, across from Memphis, three at Canopus, Alexandria, then for the other two years he came back to Troe again and fell asleep there, completing his course in peace and godly fear, "For he was a good man, full of the Holy Spirit and of faith" [Acts 11.24]. "He left me his leather tunic, his shirt of white wool, and his palm-leaf sandals and, unworthy though I be, I wore them to receive a blessing."

Arsenius 43   Abba Daniel also recounted this of Abba Arsenius: "He once summoned my fathers, Abba Alexander and [Abba] Zoïlos. He humbled himself and said to them: 'Since the demons are doing battle with me and I do not know whether they are making away with me when I am asleep, strive with me tonight and watch whether I fall asleep during the vigil.' In the evening they sat down in silence, one on his right, one on his left. My fathers said: 'We slept and awoke but we were not aware that he nodded off. Toward dawn (God only knows whether he did it of his own will so we would think he had nodded off or if he had really been asleep) he heaved a sigh three times and got up right away, saying: "I fell asleep, did I not?" and in reply we said: "We do not know." ""

Arsenius 44 [2.11]   Some elders once came to Arsenius and earnestly begged to have a conversation with him. He opened [the door] for them and they asked him to say something to them about those living in *hesychia* who encounter nobody. The elder said to them: "While a maiden is in her father's house, many want to be her fiancé, but once she takes a husband, she does not please everybody. Some look down on her, others praise her; she is not held in such esteem as formerly, when she was hidden. So it is with the business of the soul: once it begins to be common knowledge it cannot command the confidence of all."

Arsenius S 1 [N 15, Guy 20]   They used to say of Abba Arsenius that nobody could comprehend the manner of his way of life.

AGATHON

Agathon was at Scete when Poemen was there. He was younger than Poemen but so mature that he was known as Abba Agathon from an early age. He had several disciples, including Alexander and Zoïlos who subsequently lived with Arsenius. The sayings attributed to Agathon illustrate his detachment, his fine conscience, his fear of God, and his humility. Above all they show his exemplary charity, his spiritual discretion, and his extraordinary sense of true values. Especially revealing is Agathon 29, where his last words and death are recorded, surely to be counted among the finest and most faithful accounts of a saint's death that have come down to us in early monastic literature. It is both sober and circumstantial: two marks of authenticity.

Agathon 1 [10.11]   Abba Peter, [the disciple] of Abba Lot related: "I was once in the cell of Abba Agathon when a brother came to him saying: 'I want to live with brothers; tell me how I am to live with them.' The elder said: 'All the days of your life remain a stranger to them, just as you were the first day you came to them—so there be no familiar communication[16] with them.' Abba Macarius said to him: 'Why, what does familiarity do?' The elder said: 'Familiarity is like a great heat wave: when it happens everybody flees from the face of it and it destroys the fruit of the trees.' Abba Macarius said: 'Is familiarity as dangerous as that?' and Abba Agathon said: 'There is no other passion more dangerous than familiarity; it is the begetter of all the passions. The working monk should not indulge in familiar talking even when he is alone in his cell. I know that one brother spent a year living in his cell where he had a small side-bedroom. He said: "I could have moved away from the cell without being aware of that small side-bedroom if somebody else had not told me about it." Such a monk is a worker and a combatant.' "

Agathon 2   Abba Agathon said: "The monk must not allow his conscience to accuse him in any matter whatsoever."

Agathon 3   He also said: "A person does not advance even in a single virtue without keeping the sacred commandments."

Agathon 4 [Cf. Epiphanius 4]   He also said: "I never went to bed having anything against anybody, nor did I let anybody go to bed with anything against me, insofar as I was able."

Agathon 5 [10.12]   They used to say of Abba Agathon that, on hearing of his great discretion, some people went to him. Wanting to test him [to see] whether he would become angry, they said to him: "Are you Agathon? We hear that you are given to *porneia* and arrogant," but he said: "Yes, that is so." They also said to him: "Are you Agathon the tattler and slanderer?" and he said: "I am." Then again they said to him: "Are you Agathon the heretic?" and he replied: "I

---

[16]*parrēsia,* "outspokenness, frankness, freedom of speech"; also "loose talk." See Henry George Liddell et al., *A Greek-English Lexicon* (Oxford: Clarendon Press, 1996), s.v.

am not an heretic," and they begged him, saying: "Tell us why you accepted when we said so many things to you but you did not tolerate this description." He said to them: "I charge myself with the first [faults] because it is beneficial for my soul; but [to be] a heretic—that is separation from God, and I do not wish to be separated from my God." On hearing this they were amazed at his discretion and went their way enlightened.

Agathon 6 [6.4]   They recounted of Abba Agathon that he spent some considerable time building a cell with his disciples and that they eventually came to live there when they had completed the cell. The first week he saw something detrimental to him and he said to his disciples: "Get up; let us go away from here." Deeply troubled, they said to him: "If you were really of a mind to move, why did we endure so much toil, building the cell? People are going to be offended with us and say: 'Look, the unsettled ones moved on again!'" Seeing that they were fainthearted he said to them: "If some are offended, others will be edified, saying: 'Blessed are people like that; they moved for God and despised all.' So, let him come who wishes to come; for my part, I am going." They threw themselves to the ground, begging him until they were permitted to travel with him.

Agathon 7 [6.5]   They also said of him that he often moved on with only his own knife in his basket.

Agathon 8 [10.13]   Abba Agathon was asked: "Which is the greater: physical labor or interior vigilance?" and the elder said: "A person is like a tree; accordingly, physical labor is the leaves, interior vigilance the fruit. Given that which is written: 'Every tree not bearing good fruit is cut down and cast into the fire' [Mt 7.19], it is clear that our entire concern is with the fruit, meaning the vigilance of the mind; but there is also need of the protection and ornamentation the leaves provide: these are physical labor."

Agathon 9 [12.2]   The brothers also asked him: "Among [our] activities, father, which virtue demands most effort?" He said to them: "Forgive me; I reckon there is no other exertion like praying to God, for when a man wishes to pray, the enemies always want to interrupt him—for they know that they are not impeded in any other way except by prayer to God. One experiences some repose in every activity a person practices and perseveres in it; but to pray, that requires a struggle until the last breath."

Agathon 10 [10.14]   Abba Agathon was wise in thought, resolute in body and self-sufficient in all things: handiwork, food, and clothing.

Agathon 11 [4.8]   The same [elder] was once travelling with his disciples, one of whom found a little green plant by the wayside. "Do you bid me take it, father?" he said to the elder. The elder looked at him in wonder and said: "Did you put it there?" "No," the brother replied, and the elder said: "So how can you want to take what you did not put?"

Agathon 12   A brother came to Abba Agathon saying: "Let me live with you." Now the brother had found a little niter by the wayside on the way there and had brought it along. The elder said to him: "Where did you get the niter?" "I found it by the wayside as I was walking along and took it," the brother replied. Said the elder to him: "If you came to live with me, how have you taken up something you did not put down?" And he sent him to take it back to where he had taken it from.

Agathon 13 [7.2]   A brother asked the elder: "An order reached me and there is fighting in the place indicated by the order. I am willing to go there because of the order but I am afraid of the fighting." The elder said to him: "If it were Agathon he would carry out the order and win the battle."

Agathon 14 [10.15]   When a council was held at Scete concerning some matter and a decision was taken, the same Abba Agathon came later and said to them: "You have not made a good decision in this matter." They said to him: "And who are you to speak at all?" He said: "I am a son of man, for it is written: 'If you truly speak righteousness, then judge correctly, sons of men'"[Ps 57.2].

Agathon 15 [4.7]   They used to say of Abba Agathon that he kept a stone in his mouth for three years until he had learnt to keep silence.

Agathon 16   They also used to say of him and of Abba Amoun that when they were selling an item, they would state the price once, then take what was given to them in silence and calmly. And when they wanted to buy something too they paid the stated price in silence and took the item without breathing a word.

Agathon 17   The same Abba Agathon said: "I have never given charity, but giving and receiving were charity to me, for I reckon that the benefit of my brother is a fruitful undertaking."

Agathon 18   When the same [elder] saw something and his *logismos* wanted to find fault he would say to himself: "Agathon, do you not do it," and thus his *logismos* was in *hesychia*.

Agathon 19 [10.16]   The same [elder] said: "[Even] if someone given to anger were to raise a dead person he is not acceptable in the presence of God."

Agathon 20   Abba Agathon once had two disciples living in retreat, each alone. One day he asked one of them: "How are you living in your cell?" "I fast until evening," he said, "then I eat two dried loaves." [The elder] said: "That is a good regime; not too onerous." Then he said to the other one: "And how are you [living]?" "I fast every other day and then eat two dried loaves," he said. "Your labor is hard, fighting on two fronts," the elder said to him. "If one eats every day but does not eat his fill, he is laboring. Another person wants to fast every other day then to eat his fill, but you fast every second day and do not eat your fill."

Agathon 21 [2.26]   A brother asked Abba Agathon about *porneia*. He said to him: "Go, cast your frailty before God and you will experience repose."

Agathon 22   Abba Agathon was once sick and another of the elders too. As they lay in the cell, a brother was reading Genesis. When he came to the verse where Jacob says: "Joseph is not and Simeon is not and you will take Benjamin away [. . .] and you will bring my grey hairs down to Hades with sorrow" [Gen 42.36, 38], the elder replied saying: "Are the other ten not enough for you, Abba Jacob?" Abba Agathon said: "Whist, elder: if 'God justifies, who shall condemn?'" [Rom 8.33].

Agathon 23   Abba Agathon said: "Somebody who is dear to me, if he be excessively [dear] and I realize that he is dragging me into transgression, I cut him off from me."

Agathon 24   He also said: "A person must be consciously aware of the judgment of God all the time."

Agathon 25 [17.7]   When the brothers were speaking of love, Abba Joseph would say: "Do we know what love is?" and he told [this] about Abba Agathon: "He possessed a small knife; a brother came to him and spoke highly of it. [Abba Agathon] would not let him go out unless he took the knife."

Agathon 26   Abba Agathon used to say: "If it were possible for me to find a leper, to give him my body and take on his, I would do it gladly; for that is perfect love."

Agathon 27   They also used to say of him that, coming once into the city to sell [his] wares, he found a foreigner lying sick in the square with nobody to care for him. The elder stayed with him. He rented a cell, paying the rent with his handiwork, and disbursed the rest for the needs of the sick man. For four months he stayed—until the sick man was cured, then the elder returned to his cell in peace.

Agathon 28   Abba Daniel used to say: "Before Abba Arsenius came to my fathers they too stayed with Abba Agathon. Abba Agathon loved Abba Alexander for he was an ascetic and very meticulous. Now it came about that all his disciples were washing rushes in the river and Abba Alexander was washing them meticulously. The rest of the brothers said to the elder: "Brother Alexander is not doing anything." Wishing to teach them a lesson, he said to him: "Brother Alexander, wash them well, for they are flax," and he was sorrowful when he heard this. Afterwards the elder comforted him, saying: "But did I not know that you were doing [it] well? I said this to you on their account, to correct their *logismos* concerning your obedience, brother."

Agathon 29 [11.9]   They recounted of Abba Agathon that he would strive to keep every commandment. If he got into a boat, he would be the first to take an oar. When brothers visited him, immediately after the prayer his hand set the table; he was full of the love of God. When he was at the point of death he remained for three days with his eyes open but not moving. The brothers nudged him, saying: "Abba Agathon, where are you?" "I am standing before the judgment seat of God," he said. "Are you afraid, father?" they said. "I have done my best to keep the commandments of God," he said, "but I am a man; how do I know if my laboring was pleasing to God?" The brothers said to him: "Are you not convinced that your laboring was what God requires?" The elder said: "I cannot be sure unless I meet with God; the judgment of God is one thing, the [judgment] of men another." They wanted to ask him something else but he said: "Of your charity do not speak with me now for I am engaged"—and his life was forthwith terminated in joy. They saw him depart as one who takes leave of his own friends and loved ones. He had great watchfulness in everything and he used to say: "Without great watchfulness one does not make progress even in a single virtue."

Agathon 30   Abba Agathon once went into the city to sell a few wares and, on the way, he found a cripple. "Where are you going?"

the cripple said to him. Abba Agathon told him: "To the city to sell [my] wares." He said to him: "Of your charity, take me there." He brought him to the city, carrying him, and [the cripple] said to him: "Put me there where you sell the wares," and he did so. When he had sold some wares, the cripple said to him: "How much did you sell them for?" "For so much," he said. "Buy me a little cake," [the cripple] said to him and he bought him one. Then he sold some more wares and [the cripple] said: "How much for this?" and he said: "So much." "Buy me such and such," the other said and he bought it. When he had sold all his wares and wanted to come back, the cripple said to him: "Are you going?" "Yes," he said to him and he said: "Of your charity, take me to where you found me." He brought him to his place, carrying him. Then he said to him: "Agathon, you are blessed by the Lord in heaven and on earth." When [Agathon] raised his eyes he saw no one, for it was an angel of the Lord come to put him to the test.

AMMONAS

There are so many Egyptian monks with very similar names of this type that it is almost impossible to know which one is intended at any given time. It is possible that the Ammonas of the following eleven pieces is he who spent fourteen years at Scete before becoming associated with Antony then acceding to the episcopate[17] and eventually succeeding Antony as father of the monks at Pispir. The most one can say is that the spirituality of these pieces accords well with that of Antony.

Ammonas 1 [3.4]   A brother asked Abba Ammonas: "Tell me a saying." The elder said: "Go and frame your *logismos* the way the evil-doers who are in prison do, for they are always asking people: 'Where is the governor and when is he coming?'—weeping in expectation. So ought the monk always to pay heed and to be reproaching his

[17]See *HME* 15.

own soul, saying: 'Ah me! How can I stand before the judgment seat of Christ and how can I defend myself before him?' If you deliberate like this all the time, you can be saved."

Ammonas 2   They used to say of Abba Ammonas that he killed a basilisk. He went off into the desert to draw water from a lake. When he saw the basilisk he threw himself face down, saying: Lord, am I to die or is it?" and the basilisk promptly perished through the power of Christ.

Ammonas 3 [7.3]   Abba Ammonas said: "I spent fourteen years at Scete beseeching God night and day that he would grant me the favor of overcoming anger."

Ammonas 4 [10.20]   One of the fathers related how there was a hard-working elder at The Cells who only wore a mat.[18] When he went to visit Abba Ammonas, the elder, seeing him wearing the mat, said to him: "That does you no good." Then the [visiting] elder asked him: "Three *logismoi* perplex me: whether to wander around the desert, to go to a foreign land where nobody recognizes me, or to shut myself up in a cell, meeting nobody and eating every second day." Abba Ammonas said to him: "It will not do you any good to do any one of the three. Do you rather remain in your cell, eat a little each day, and always have in your heart what the Publican said[19]—then you can be saved."

Ammonas 5   Some brothers suffered affliction at their place [of residence]; wishing to abandon it, they came to Abba Ammonas. Now here the elder was sailing along and, when he saw them travelling along the bank of the river, he said to the sailors: "Put me ashore." He called to the brothers, saying: "I am Ammonas to whom you wish to come." He comforted their hearts and had them go back to where they had come from, for this was not a case of spiritual damage but of human affliction.

---

[18]*psiathion,* "a rush mat for sleeping on," Lampe ad loc.
[19]"God be merciful to me a sinner," Lk 18.13.

Ammonas 6   Abba Ammonas once came to cross the river and, finding the ferry ready to go, he sat himself down. Then here there came another boat to that place and took on the people who were there. They said to him: "You come too, abba; cross with us," but he said: "I only go on board the public ferry." He had a sheaf of palm-fronds [with him]; he sat there braiding a rope and undoing it again until they had made the crossing—that was how he crossed over. The brothers prostrated themselves, saying: "Why did you do that?" and the elder said to them: "So that I am not always going around with my *logismos* engaged." But this too is an indication of how we should travel the way of God in a calm state of mind.

Ammonas 7   Abba Ammonas once set out to visit Abba Antony but he lost his way. He sat down and slept a little. When he got up from sleeping, he prayed to God saying: "O Lord my God, I beseech you not to let your creature perish," and there appeared to him something like a human hand hanging from the sky, showing him the way until he came and stood before the cave of Abba Antony.

Ammonas 8   Abba Antony prophesied to this Abba Ammonas: "You can make progress in the fear of God." He led him out of the cell and showed him a stone, saying: "Insult that stone and hit it," and he did so. Then said Abba Antony to him: "Did the stone speak?" "No," he said, and Abba Antony said to him: "You too are going to attain that stature"—and that is what happened. Abba Ammonas made such progress that, of his great goodness, he was no longer mindful of evil. When he became a bishop (for instance), they brought a maiden to him who was pregnant. "So-and-so did this," they said to him, "give them a penalty." But he made the sign of the cross on the woman's belly and ordered her to be given six pairs of sheets, saying: "[This is] in case she or the infant should die when she comes to give birth and there be nothing to hand for the burial." Then those who were against her said to him: "Why did you do that? Give them a penalty," but he said to them: "She is near to death you see, brothers; what else can I do?" and he dismissed her. The elder did not dare to judge anybody.

Ammonas 9 [15.13]   They used to say of him that some folk came to be judged before him but the elder feigned insanity. Here there was a woman standing near to him and she was saying to her neighbor: "This elder is mad." The elder heard her; he called out to her and said: "How I labored away in the desert in order to acquire this madness and, because of you, I am going to lose it today!"

Ammonas 10   Abba Ammonas once came somewhere to eat and there was somebody there who had a bad reputation. A woman happened to come and go into the cell of the brother who had the bad reputation. They who were living in that place were troubled when they learned of it and they got together to drive him out of his cell. Knowing that Bishop Ammonas was at that place, they went and besought him to go along with them. When the brother became aware of this, he took the woman and concealed her in a large barrel. When the crowd arrived Abba Ammonas realized what had happened and covered the matter up for the love of God. He came in, sat down on the barrel and ordered the cell to be searched. When they had searched diligently and not found the woman, Abba Ammonas said to them: "What is this? God will forgive you," and offering a prayer, he obliged them all to withdraw. Then, taking the brother's hand, he said to him: "Pay attention to yourself, brother," and so saying, he went away.

Ammonas 11 [10.116, N 249]   An elder was asked: "What is 'the narrow and hard way'?" [Mt 7.14]. He answered: "'The narrow and hard way' is this: to constrain one's own *logismoi* and to cut back one's own desires in deference to God, for this is the meaning of 'Behold, we have abandoned all and followed you'" [Mt 19.27].

ACHILLES

According to an apophthegm known only in Armenian: "Abba Theodore of Phermē said that Abba Achilles was regarded as a

lion at Scete and considered to be formidable in his time," which
was before the end of the fourth century, when the great ascet-
ics rivaled each other in austerity and humility. He is reported
elsewhere to have counseled: "Make yourself like a beast so you
are totally unrecognizable." Not much else is known of this rugged
elder, but the depth of his generous love is evident in his sayings.

Achilles 1 [10.18]   Three elders, one of whom had a bad reputation, once visited Abba Achilles. One of the elders said to him: "Abba, make me one net," but he said: "I will not make [you one]." The other said to him: "Of your charity [make one] so we can have a souvenir of you at the monastery," but he said: "I haven't time." The other, the one with the bad reputation said to him: "Make me a net so I can have [something] from your hands, abba," and in answer he said without hesitation: "I will make one for you." The [other] two elders said to him in private: "How is it that when we asked you, you were unwilling to make [a net] for us yet you said to this one: 'I will make [one] for you?'" The elder said to them: "I said to you: 'I will not make [one],' and you were not dismayed, [thinking] I hadn't the time. But if I do not make one for this [brother], he will say: 'The elder refused to make me [one] because he had heard of my sin,' and straightaway we cut the connection. But I raised up his soul to prevent somebody like him from drowning in sorrow."

Achilles 2   Abba Bitimios said: "Once when I was going down to Scete some people gave me a few apples to give to the elders. I knocked at the cell of Abba Achilles so I could give him [some] but he said: 'Really brother, I did not want you knocking at my door just now, even if it were manna—and don't go to another cell.' So I withdrew to my cell and brought them to church."

Achilles 3 [4.10]   Abba Achilles once came to the cell of Abba Isaiah at Scete and found him eating; he was putting salt and water in a dish. Seeing that he had hidden it behind the rope, the elder said to him: "Tell me what you were eating," but he said: "Forgive me, Abba;

I was cutting palm-fronds, and, coming back in the heat of the day, I put a morsel [of bread] in my mouth with some salt, but my throat was dry from the heat and the morsel would not go down. For that reason I was obliged to put a little water with the salt so that, in this way, I might be able to swallow; please forgive me." But the elder said: "Come and see Isaiah eating soup at Scete! If you want to eat soup, go to Egypt."

Achilles 4 [4.9] One of the elders visiting Abba Achilles saw him spit blood from his mouth. "What is this, Father?" he asked him, and the elder said: "It is something a brother said that had distressed me, and I struggled not to make it known to him. I besought God for it to be taken away from me; then what he had said became like blood in my mouth. I spat it out, then I experienced repose, forgetting the distress."

Achilles 5 Abba Ammōes used to say: "Abba Bitimios and I visited Abba Achilles and we heard him meditating this verse: 'Fear not to go down into Egypt, Jacob' [Gen 46.3], and he went on meditating that verse for a long time. He opened when we knocked and asked: 'Where are you from?' Afraid to say: 'From The Cells,' we said: 'From the Mountain of Nitria,' and he said: 'What am I to do for you, for you have come from afar?' and he brought us in. We found that he worked in the night [producing] much rope. We asked him to tell us a saying but he said: 'From evening until now I have braided twenty fathoms and I don't really need them. But maybe God will be angry and accuse me, saying: 'Why did you not work when you were able to work?' That is why I toil and do it to the best of my ability.' We went away enlightened."

Achilles 6 Then again, another time, a great elder from the Thebaid visiting Abba Achilles said to him: "Abba, I am embattled on your account," but he said to him: "Come now, elder: you too are now embattled on my account?" Humbly, the elder said: "Yes, abba." There was an elder who was blind and crippled sitting there, by the door. The [visiting] elder said to him: "I wanted to stay a few days but I cannot stay because of this [handicapped] elder."[20] On hearing this, Abba Achilles was amazed at the humility of the elder; he said: "This is not *porneia* but jealousy of the wicked demons."

AMMŌES

Apart from the fact that he once visited Abba Achilles (Achilles 5, above) little is known of Ammōes other than what can be learnt from the five items that bear his name:

Ammōes 1 [11.11]   They used to say about Abba Ammōes that when he was on his way to church he would not allow his disciple to walk very close to him, but at a distance. And if he came to ask him about *logismoi*, no sooner did he speak to him than he would immediately chase him away, saying: "I do not let you be very close to me in case some alien discourse should raise its head while we are speaking of [spiritual] benefit."

Ammōes 2 [11.12]   In the beginning Abba Ammōes used to say to Abba Isaiah:[21] "How do you see me at present?" and he to him: "As an angel, Father." Later on, he would say to him: "How do you see me now?" but he would say: "As Satan; and even if you tell me a good saying I regard it as a sword."

Ammōes 3 [4.11]   They used to tell of Abba Ammōes that he was sick in bed for many years and yet he never let his *logismos* pay any attention to his inner cell to see what it contained, for they used to bring many things on account of his illness. When his disciple John was coming in and out, he would shut his eyes in order not to see what he was doing, for he knew that he was a trustworthy monk.

---

[20]This is an ambiguous and rather puzzling item. My impression is that the visitor has brought the handicapped elder with him and is caring for him. It is possible that some words have dropped out of the text. A critical edition might help.—Tr.

[21]or Aseōs.

Ammōes 4   Abba Poemen said: "A brother visited Abba Ammōes begging a saying from him. He stayed with him for seven days and the elder did not answer him. Then, sending him on his way, he said to him: 'Off you go; pay attention to yourself. As for me, my sins have become a wall of darkness between me and God.'"

Ammōes 5   They used to say of Abba Ammōes that he made fifty measures of grain for future need and set it out in the sun but, before it was well dried, he saw something in that place that was not beneficial for him and he said to his boys: "Let us go from here." They were very distressed and, when he saw that they were distressed, he said to them: "Are you distressed because of the loaves? Let me tell you, I have seen some refugees leaving dust-filled cupboards full of parchment books. They did not even close the doors but went off leaving them open."

AMOUN OF NITRIA

Amoun was the first monk to settle in the desert of Nitria, c. 320. Orphaned early, he was obliged by an uncle to marry a wife with whom he lived in chastity for eighteen years.[22] He was in contact with Antony who advised him on the creation of the new monastic settlement that came to be known as The Cells (see Antony 34, above). He predeceased Antony, who saw his soul being carried away.[23] The second of the following apophthegms relates to a different Amoun, somebody younger than Poemen.

Amoun 1 [17.3]   Abba Amoun of Nitria visited Abba Antony and said to him: "I observe that I labor harder than you do, so why is your name held in higher honor among folk than mine?" Abba Antony said to him: "It is because in my case I love God more than you do."

[22]*HL* 8; *HME* 22.
[23]*VA* 60.

Amoun 2 [11.56]   They used to say of Abba Amoun (he who lived two months on a measure of barley) that he visited Abba Poemen and said to him: "If I go to my neighbor's cell or he visits me for some need, we are afraid to speak with each other in case some alien discourse raises its head." "Well done," the elder said to him. "Youth needs vigilance." Abba Amoun said to him: "So what did the elders use to do?" and he said to him: "The elders who were advanced had nothing else in mind or any alien matter in their mouth that they might speak it." Abba Amoun said to him: "So if a necessity arises to speak with my neighbor, do you want me to speak of the Scriptures or of the sayings of the elders?" Said the elder: "If you cannot keep silent, it is better to speak of the sayings of the elders and not of the Scriptures, for *there* is no small danger."

Amoun 3 [N 422]   A brother came to Abba Amoun from Scete and said to him: "My father is sending me on an errand and I am afraid of *porneia*." The elder said to him: "Whenever temptation comes upon you, say: 'O God of might, deliver me by the prayers of my father.'" One day a maiden closed the door on him[24] and, when he called out in a loud voice: 'God of my father, deliver me,' he immediately found himself on the way to Scete.

ANOUB

Anoub was the older brother of Poemen, two of five brothers (the youngest being Paesios) who left their mother and sister to become monks at Scete. After the first raid of the Mazics in 407 they relocated at Terenouthis on a branch of the Nile, sixty kilometers northwest of Cairo.

Anoub 1 [15.12]   Abba John recounted how Abba Anoub, Abba Poemen, and the rest of their brothers from the one womb who had become monks at Scete, left there when the Mazics came the first

[24]i.e. she shut the two of them up together. N 422 names the abba Anophōr.

time and devastated it. They came to a place called Terenouthis until they should perceive where they ought to be staying. They stayed there a few days in an old temple. Abba Anoub said to Abba Poemen: "Of your charity, do you and each of your brothers remain apart in *hesychia*, and let us not meet with each other during this week." Abba Poemen said to him: "We will do as you wish," and so they did. Now there was a stone statue there in the temple itself; Abba Anoub would get up early in the morning and throw stones at the face of the statue; in the evening he would say to it: "Forgive me," and he spent the whole week behaving like that. On Saturday they met up with each other, and Abba Poemen said to Abba Anoub: "I saw you throwing stones at the face of the statue during this week, Abba, then making an apology to it too. Does a man of faith act like that?" "I did this deed on your account," the elder replied. "When you saw me stoning the face of the statue, was it angry, or did it speak?" "No," said Abba Poemen. "And then again, when I prostrated myself to it, was it troubled, and did it say: 'I do not forgive [you]'?" "No," said Abba Poemen. Abba Anoub said: "And here we are, seven brothers. If you want us to live with each other, let us become like this statue that is not troubled even if it is insulted. If you do not want to become like that, here there are four gates in this temple; let each one go where he will." But they threw themselves to the ground saying to Abba Anoub: "We will do as you wish, father, and attend to what you say to us." Abba Poemen said: "We stayed together all our time, working in accord with the instruction the elder spoke to us. He appointed one of us to be steward; we would eat whatever he set before us, and it was impossible for any one of us to say: 'Bring something else,' or to say: 'I don't want to eat this.' We passed our entire time in repose and peace."

Anoub 2 [11.7]   Abba Anoub[25] said: "Since the name of Christ was invoked over me, nothing false has come out of my mouth."

---

[25] Anouph in *HME* 11.5.

ABRAHAM

*This is probably not the Abraham who was disciple of Sisoes or of
Agathon or the companion of Isaac, the priest at The Cells.*

Abraham 1 [10.19]   They used to say of a certain elder that he went
fifty years without eating bread or readily drinking wine. He used to
say: "I have put to death *porneia,* avarice, and vainglory." There came
to him Abba Abraham who had heard that he said this, and he said
to him: "Did you say this?" and he said: "Yes." Abba Abraham said
to him: "Imagine you come into your cell and you find a woman on
your mat; can you not notice that it is a woman?" He said: "No, but I
fight against the *logismos* in order not to touch her." Abba Abraham
said to him: "So you see, you have not killed the passion; it lives but
it is in check. [Imagine] again you are walking along the way, and you
see stones and shards with a piece of gold among them; is your mind
capable of reckoning both of equal value?" "No," he said, "but I fight
against the *logismos* in order not to take [the gold]." The elder said:
"So you see, the passion lives, but it is in check." Abba Abraham also
said to him: "[Imagine] again that you are hearing of two brothers;
one loves you and the other hates you and speaks evil of you. If they
come to you, do you esteem them equally?" He said: "No, but I fight
against the *logismos* [and try] to do good to the one who hates me as
to the one who loves me." Said Abba Abraham to him: "So, therefore,
the passions are alive, only they are held in check by the holy ones."

Abraham 2   A brother asked Abba Abraham: "If I happen to eat
often, what is this?" In reply the elder said: "What are you saying,
brother? Do you eat that much? Or do you think you have come to
a threshing floor?"

Abraham 3   Abba Abraham used to say of one of the people at
Scete that he was a scribe and that did not eat bread. A brother
came begging him to write out a book for him. The elder's mind
was rapt in contemplation; he wrote in continuous lines without

punctuation. When the brother took it and wanted to punctuate [it] he found it lacked some verses and he said to the elder: "There are some lines missing, abba." Said the elder to him: "Go away, and first practice what is written; then come back and I will write the rest for you too."

ARES

Ares [14.3]   Abba Abraham visited Abba Ares, and as they were sitting a brother came to the elder and said to him: "Tell me what I am to do in order to be saved." The elder said to him: "Go and spend this year eating bread and salt in the evening, then come back again and I will speak to you." He went and did so. When the year was complete, the brother came back to Abba Ares; Abba Abraham happened to be there at that time too. Again the elder said to the brother: "Go and fast every second day of this year too." When the brother left, Abba Abraham said to Abba Ares: "Why do you speak to all the brothers with an easy yoke but lay heavy burdens on this brother?" The elder said to him: "The brothers go back having got what they came looking for; but this one comes in the name of God to hear a saying, for he is a worker and diligently performs whatever I tell to him to do. For that reason I too speak the Word of God to him."

ALONIUS

Alonius was well-known to Poemen, with whom he may have lived at Scete. He had a disciple named Joseph and was averse to teaching.

Alonius 1 [11.13]   Abba Alonius said: "Unless a person say in his heart: 'I alone and God are in the world' he will not experience repose."

Alonius 2   He also said: "Unless I had overturned everything I would not have been able to build myself up."

Alonius 3 [11.14]   He also said: "If a person wish it from dawn to dusk, he becomes of divine stature."

Alonius 4   Abba Agathon once asked Abba Alonius: "How shall I be willing to restrain my tongue so that it speaks no falsehood?" Abba Alonius said to him: "Even if you speak no falsehood you are going to commit many sins." "How is that?" he said, and the elder said to him: "Here are two men who have committed murder in your sight and one of them has taken refuge in your cell. Then here comes the magistrate, looking for him, and he asks you: 'Was the murder done in your sight?' Unless you speak falsely, you give the man over to death. Better to leave him unshackled in the presence of God, for he knows all."

Apphy

Oxyrynchos, now El-Bahnasa, 200 kilometers south of Cairo a little to the west of the Nile, was both an important monastic center—with more monks than worldlings (HME 5)—and the seat of a bishop, but very few apopthegms speak of it.[26]

Apphy [15.14]   They recounted of a bishop of Oxyrynchos named Abba Apphy that he endured much hardship when he was a monk and when he became bishop he wanted to practice the same hardship in the world but he lacked the strength. He cast himself down in the presence of God, saying: "Did your grace depart from me because of the bishopric?" It was revealed to him that it was not so: "But then it was the desert and, as there was nobody there, God took care of you. But now it is the world and folk are taking care of you."

[26]See N 214, N 282, N 132B.

APOLLO

Several monks appear to have been known as Apollo; the three apophthegms following are of three different fathers. On the third see HME, from which this is an extract (8.55–56).

Apollo 1 There was an elder at The Cells named Apollo and if anybody came asking him to undertake any task, he would go off joyfully saying: "Today I am going to work for my soul with Christ, for he is its reward."

Apollo 2 They used to say of an Abba Apollo at Scete that he used to be a rustic shepherd. Seeing a pregnant woman in the field, impelled by the devil, he said: "I want to see how the baby is lying in her womb." He cut her open and saw the baby; then straightaway his heart smote him. Conscience-stricken, he came to Scete and reported to the fathers what he had done. He heard them singing: "The days of our years for them are threescore years and ten; for the robust fourscore years but for the most part of them, labor and sorrow" [Ps 89.10]. He said to them: "I am forty years old and have never offered a prayer. If I now live another forty years, I will not cease praying God to forgive me my sins." He was not doing any handiwork either; just praying all the time, saying: "I have sinned as a man: do you forgive me as God" and that was his prayer, repeated by day and by night. There was a brother staying with him and he heard him saying: "I have entreated you, Lord: forgive me that I might experience a little repose," and assurance came to him that God had forgiven him all his sins, including the one of the woman; but he was not assured in the matter of the child. One of the elders said to him: "God has forgiven you for the child too but he is leaving you toiling because it is good for your soul."

Apollos 3 Concerning receiving the brothers as guests, the same [elder] said: "We must venerate the brothers who come [by]. It is not them we venerate but God; for when you saw your brother, you saw the Lord your God. We received this from Abraham," he said, "and when you receive [brothers] constrain them to take some refreshment. We have learnt this from Lot who constrained the angels [to enter and eat]" [Gen 19.3].

ANDREW

Andrew [11.120; otherwise unknown]   Abba Andrew said: "These three things are appropriate for the monk: voluntary exile, poverty, and silence with patience."

AIO

They used to say of an elder at the Thebaid, Abba Antianos, that he endured many disciplines in his youth but in old age he sickened and became blind. The brothers used to afford him plenty of relief because of his sickness, putting [food] into his mouth. They asked Abba Aio about this: "What about all this relief?" and he said to them: "I am telling you: if his heart desires it and he gladly consents, if he eats one date, God takes it from his labor. If he does not consent and receives it unwillingly, God retains his labor safe and sound because he was constrained against his will—and they have their reward."

AMMONATHAS

A magistrate once came to Pelusium wanting to levy a poll-tax on the monks, as he did on the worldlings. All the brothers gathered around Abba Ammonathas concerning this matter and elected some of the fathers to go to the emperor. But Abba Ammonathas said to them: "It is not necessary to go to that trouble. Do you rather keep *hesychia* in your cells and fast for two weeks. By the grace of Christ, I will deal with the matter alone." The brothers went off to their own cells and the elder maintained *hesychia* in his own cell. When the fourteen days were accomplished, the brothers were aggrieved at the elder (for they had never seen him move at all) and they said: "The elder has set our affair aside." On the fifteenth day the brothers gathered together as agreed and the elder came to them bearing the emperor's rescript duly sealed. The brothers were astounded when they saw it, saying: "When did you bring this, abba?" The elder said: "Believe me brothers, this very night I went to the emperor and he wrote this rescript; then I came to Alexandria and got it signed by the magistrates—and so I came to you." They were afraid on hearing this and prostrated themselves before him. Their affair was settled and the magistrate did not trouble them.

B—*Beta*

Basil the Great

One of the elders used to say that, while visiting a coenobion, after [giving] appropriate instruction, the holy Basil said to the higoumen: "Do you have a brother here who is obedient?" He said to him: "They are all your servants and are striving to be saved, master." Again [Basil] said to him: "Do you really have somebody who is obedient?" [The higoumen] brought one brother to him and the holy Basil engaged him to serve at mealtime. After they had eaten [the brother] made provision for him to wash and the holy Basil said to him: "Come now, I will make provision for *you* to wash," and the brother acquiesced in his pouring water [for him]. [Basil] said to him: "When I go into the sanctuary, do you step forward so I can make you a deacon." When that had happened, he made him a priest and took him with him to the episcopal residence on account of his obedience.[27]

Bessarion

Numbers 1–4 of the twelve apophthegms attributed to Abba Bessarion are personal reminisces of Doulas, his disciple (see also Elijah 2), showing his master as a powerful wonder-worker at Scete. The remaining items portray an experienced ascetic, humble and brave.

Bessarion 1 [19.1]   Abba Doulas the disciple of Abba Bessarion used to say: "Once, while we were travelling along the seashore, I

[27]cf. Cassian 5.

was thirsty and said to Abba Bessarion: 'Abba, I am very thirsty.' The elder offered a prayer and said to me: 'Drink from the sea.' The water was made sweet so I drank. But I poured some into the vessel in case I got thirsty further on. Seeing me, the elder said: "Why did you pour [some into the vessel]?" I said to him: "Forgive me; in case I get thirsty further on," and the elder said to me: 'God is here and God is everywhere.'"

Bessarion 2 [19.2]   Another time when he was in need he offered a prayer, crossed [the river] Chrysoroas on foot, and came to the other bank. Astonished, I prostrated myself before him saying: "How did your feet feel when you were walking on the water?" The elder said: "It felt like water up to the ankles; for the rest, it was dry land."

Bessarion 3 [19.3]   Again, another time, we were going to an elder when the sun went down. The elder prayed, saying: "I beg you, Lord, let the sun stand still until I arrive at your servant's," and so it happened.

Bessarion 4 [12.3 & 20.1]   Another time too I came to his cell and found him standing in prayer with his hands stretched out to heaven. He remained doing that for fourteen days. After that, he called me and said to me: "Follow me." We went out and travelled in the desert. I was thirsty and said: "Abba, I am thirsty." The elder took my sheepskin and went about a stone's throw away from me. After he had prayed, he brought it to me full of water. We walked around and came to some cave. In we went and found some brother sitting there, making rope—but not raising his eyes to us. He neither greeted us nor did he in the least want to talk with us. "Let us leave this place," the elder said to me, "perchance the elder is not confident to speak to us." Coming out of there we journeyed on toward Lyco until we came to Abba John.[28] Having embraced him, we offered a prayer. Then [the elders] sat down to speak of the vision that he had seen. Abba Bessarion said: "A decree came out that the temples be thrown

[28]The famous John of Lycopolis (Asyut); *HME* 1, *HL* 35.

down." That is what happened; they were thrown down. As we were returning we came again to the cave where we had seen the brother. The elder said to me: "Let us go in to him; perhaps God made him confident to speak to us," but when we went in we found that he had died. The elder said to me: "Come now, brother, let us wrap up his body; this is what God sent us here for," but as we were wrapping him up for burial we discovered that he was a woman. The elder was astounded; he said: "See how women too overthrow Satan while we in the cities[29] act shamefully. We glorified God, the sure protection of those who love him." Then we went away from there.

Bessarion 5 [19.4]   A person possessed of a demon once came to Scete; prayer was offered on his behalf in the church but the demon did not come out, for it was a difficult one. The clergy said: "What can we do about this demon? Nobody is able to cast him out other than Abba Bessarion; and if we appeal to him on this fellow's behalf, he will not even come into the church. Let us act like this: Here he comes to the church before everybody at dawn. Let us make the afflicted fellow sit in his place and, when he comes in let us stand in prayer and say to him: 'Wake the brother up too, abba'"—and that is what they did. When the elder came at dawn, they stood in prayer and said to him: "Wake the brother up too, abba." The elder said to him: "Get up and get out." The demon immediately went out of him and the fellow was healed from that moment.

Bessarion 6 [7.4]   Abba Bessarion said: "Forty nights and days I remained among thorns, standing without sleeping."

Bessarion 7 [9.2]   A brother who sinned was put out of the church by the priest. Abba Bessarion got up and went out with him, saying: "I too am a sinner."

Bessarion 8   The same Abba Bessarion said: "For forty years I never laid myself down but slept sitting or standing."

---

[29]This may mean "the monastic communities"; cf. *HL* 71.2.

Bessarion 9 The same [elder] said: "When you are at peace and not embattled, then humble yourself even more—lest some alien joy arising [in us] we boast and are delivered into battle. For, on account of our frailty, God often does not permit us to be embattled often—lest we be lost.

Bessarion 10 A brother living with brothers asked Abba Bessarion: "What am I to do?" Said the elder to him: "Maintain silence and do not measure yourself."

Bessarion 11 [11.15] When Abba Bessarion was dying, he would say: "A monk ought to be all eyes, like the cherubim and seraphim" [Rev 4.6, 8].

Bessarion 12 [see N 565, 15.116: Abba Serapion] Abba Bessarion's disciples recounted his life to have been like this: He lived out all the time of his life untroubled and carefree like one of the birds of the air, a fish or a land-animal. In his case he was not concerned with care about a house and it did not seem that his soul was in prey to longing for lands, a sufficiency of luxury, building dwellings, or the distraction of books. He seemed to be altogether free of bodily passions, nourished by the hope of things to come and secure in the fortress of faith. He endured like a prisoner [taken] here and there, existing in cold and nudity, burning in the heat of the sun, always in the open air. Advancing into the crags and precipices of the desert like one who has lost his way, he delighted in letting himself often to be swept along by the wide-open and uninhabited stretch of sand as if in a sea. If he chanced to come to milder regions where monks of a similar way of life were living in community, sitting outside the gates, he would weep and lament like someone thrown up by shipwreck. Then, when one of the brothers came out and found him sitting there begging like one of the world's indigents, he approached him and gently said to him: "Why are you weeping, fellow? If you are in need of some necessities, you will receive according to your strength, only do come inside and share our table, gaining some strength." But he would reply that he could not stay under a roof "Until I find the property of my house," for he said that he had lost much money in various ways, "For I fell among pirates and suffered shipwreck. I lost my status and, from being noble, became ignoble." Moved by this account, [the brother] went in, got some bread and gave it to him, saying: "Take this, father; as you say, God will restore you to your fatherland, your birthright, and the riches you mentioned." But he lamented even more, mightily gnashing his teeth and declaring: "I cannot say whether I will find the things I have lost and for which I am looking. But I would rather be pleased to be ever in danger, day by day until death, with no respite in my immense misfortunes, for I have to finish my course, continuously wandering."

BENJAMIN

This priest at The Cells is probably to be distinguished from the Benjamin of HL 12.

Benjamin 1   Abba Benjamin used to say: "When we came down to Scete from the harvest they brought us a gratuity[30] from Alexandria, for each one a *sextarius*[31]-jar of oil sealed with plaster. When harvest-time came round again, if there were any [oil] left over, the brothers brought it to church. In my case I had not opened my jar but had merely pierced [the seal] with a needle and taken a little. My heart would have it that I had done a great deed. When the brothers brought their own vessels, still sealed with plaster as they were [before] and there was my own, pierced, I felt as ashamed as if I had committed *porneia*."

Benjamin 2 [4.12]   Abba Benjamin, the priest at The Cells, said: "We visited an elder at Scete; we wanted to serve him some oil, and he said to us: 'Look, there lies the small vessel [of oil] that you

---

[30]*karpophorian.*
[31]Just over half a liter.

brought me three years ago; it stayed there where you put it.' We were astounded at the elder's way of life when we heard this."

Benjamin 3   The same [elder] said: "We visited another elder and he detained us to eat; he served us radish-oil and we said to him: "Father, rather do you serve us a little decent oil." When he heard this he signed himself and said: "If there is any other kind of oil beside this, I do not know of it."

Benjamin 4   When Abba Benjamin was dying he said to his sons: "Do these things and you will be able to be saved: 'Rejoice always; pray without ceasing; in everything give thanks'" [1 Thess 5.16–18].

Benjamin 5 [7.5]   The same [elder] said: "Travel the royal road [Num 20.17, 21.22], count the mile-posts and you will not be discouraged."

Biares

Somebody asked Abba Biares: "What shall I do so I may be saved?" He said to him: "Go, make your belly small and your handiwork little; be not troubled in your cell and you are being saved."

Γ—*Gamma*

Gregory the Theologian

Gregory 1 [1.3, N 3]   Abba Gregory said: "God requires these three things of every person who has received baptism: correct faith from his soul, truth from his tongue, self-control from his body."

Gregory 2   He also said: "The entire life of man is but a single day for those who labor with longing."

Gelasius

Gelasius became a monk early in life. In the mid-fifth century he founded a coenobion near Nicopolis in Palestine and became famous for his holiness and miracles. He was also a firm supporter of Chalcedonian Orthodoxy—one of the few Palestinian abbas who were. St Euthymius was another; they refused to acknowledge Theodosius, the usurping bishop of Jerusalem.

Gelasius 1 [16.2]   They used to say of Abba Gelasius that he had a book on parchment worth eighteen pieces of gold; it had the whole of the Old and the New Testaments written in it. It lay in the church so that any of the brothers who wished to do so might read it. A brother coming from abroad to visit the elder saw the book, and coveted it; he stole it and went away. But although the elder was aware of this he did not go after him to arrest him. [The thief] went into the city and was looking for a way to sell it. When he found the willing buyer he asked a price of sixteen pieces of gold but the willing buyer said to him: "First give it to me; I will value it then I will give you the price," so [the brother] gave him the book. He took it and brought it to Abba Gelasius to value it, telling him the price the seller stated. The elder said to him: "Buy it; for it is good and worth the price he stated." The fellow came and spoke differently to the one who was selling it and not as the elder had spoken, saying: "Look, I showed it to Abba Gelasius, and he told me that it was dear and not worth what you are asking for it." When he heard that, he said to him: "Did the elder not say anything else to you?" "No," he said. "I do not want to sell it any longer," the brother said, and, pricked in his conscience, he went to the elder, apologizing and begging him to accept [the book]—but [the elder] did not want to take it. Then the brother said to him: "If you do not take it, I shall have no repose." He said to him: "If you have no repose, here, I will take it then." That brother continued gaining spiritual benefit from the elder for the rest of his life.

Gelasius 2   At one time a cell and the adjacent land were left to this Abba Gelasius by an old man who was also a monk and had a dwelling in the region of Nicopolis. A certain [tenant-] farmer of Bakatos (who was then the governor of Nicopolis in Palestine), a relative of the dead old man, went to the same Bakatos demanding possession of the land in question on the pretext that, legally, it ought to come to him. He was very determined and attempted to take it from Abba Gelasius with his own hand. Abba Gelasius himself would not allow it; he did not wish to hand over a monastic cell to a worldling. Bakatos, having observed the beasts of Abba Gelasius transporting the olives from his inherited land, forcibly diverted them and took the olives to his house. He only just (and with ill-treatment) let the beasts and their handlers go. The blessed elder did not lay claim at all to the fruit but he did not renounce the ownership of the land for the reason given. Bakatos was exasperated; he set out for Constantinople where necessities and other matters summoned him (he was fond of lawsuits), making the journey on foot. He came to Antioch, where the holy Symeon[32] was then shining like a bright luminary. Hearing of him (who was indeed super-human) and being a Christian, he longed to see the saint. When holy Symeon saw him from his column suddenly coming into the monastery, he asked: "Where are you from, where are you going?" "I am from Palestine," he said, "and I am going to Constantinople." He said to him: "For what reason?" Bakatos said to him: "For many necessities and I hope, by the prayers of your holiness, to return and reverence your holy footsteps." The holy Symeon said to him: "Faithless of men, you are unwilling to admit that you are going up against a man of God. The journey will not be good for you and you will not see your house ever again. If you take my advice, you will leave this place now, go to him and prostrate yourself to him—if you arrive at that place among the living." [Bakatos] was immediately stricken with fever; he was put into a litter by those with him and made haste (according to the instruction of the holy Symeon) to reach the land and prostrate himself before Abba Gelasius. But he died when they came to Beirut—without seeing his house, as the holy one prophesied. This was recounted to many trustworthy men by his son (who was also called Bakatos) after the death of his father.

Gelasius 3 Many of his disciples narrated this too: A fish was once brought to them. The cook fried it and brought it to the cellarer. Impelled by some necessity, the cellarer went out of the cellar leaving the fish in a vessel on the ground and telling the little disciple of the blessed Gelasius to watch over it for a while until he returned. In his greed, the youth began eating the fish without restraint. When the cellarer came in and found him eating, he was angry with the youth who was sitting on the floor and, without thinking, kicked him. By the machination of some [demon] he was struck in a vital organ; he fainted away and then died. Terribly afraid, the cellarer laid him out on his own bed and covered him. Then he went and, falling at the feet of Abba Gelasius, told him what had happened. [The holy man]

[32]St Symeon Stylites, c. 390–459.

ordered him to say nothing to anybody else, telling him to bring [the youth] to the sacristy after everyone was settled down in the evening, to place him before the altar and then go his way. The elder came into the sacristy and stood there praying. When it was time for the nighttime psalm-singing and the brothers were assembled, out came the elder with the young man following him. Nobody, other than himself and the cellarer, knew what had happened until his death.

Gelasius 4 Not only the disciples of Abba Gelasius, but also many who frequently visited him, recounted how, at the time of the Ecumenical Council at Chalcedon, Theodosius, who provoked the schism against Dioscorus in Palestine, preceded the bishops who were about to return to their own churches (for he was in Constantinople himself, having been driven out of his own fatherland because he always rejoiced in disturbances). He approached Abba Gelasius at his monastery, speaking against the Synod as though it had reaffirmed the teaching of Nestorius. In this way he thought that he was subverting the holy man and co-opting him in his own fraud and his schism. But, from the man's disposition and his own God-given understanding, [Gelasius] perceived the corrupted nature of his opinion. He was not led astray by his apostasy—as almost everybody then was. Treating him with the dishonor he deserved, he sent him on his way—for he brought in among them the young disciple he had raised up from the dead and began saying in all seriousness to Theodosius: "If you want to discuss matters of faith, you have this one to listen to you and to discuss with you; I do not have the time to listen to you." Discomfited by this, [Theodosius] went off to the Holy City where he subverted the entire monastic community under the pretense of sacred zeal. He also subverted the Augousta[33] who was there at that time. Gaining support in this way, he took the throne of Jerusalem by force. He achieved this by murders and other lawless and uncanonical procedures, which many recall even now. When he was in possession and had reached his goal, he ordained very many

---

[33] Athenaïs-Eudocia?

bishops, seizing the thrones of bishops who had not yet returned. He summoned Abba Gelasius and invited him into the sanctuary, [thus] enticing and at the same time frightening him. When he came into the sanctuary, Theodosius began saying to him: "Pronounce Juvenal anathema!" But, not at all afraid, [Gelasius] said: "I know no other Bishop of Jerusalem but Juvenal." Taking care that others might imitate his pious zeal, Theodosius cleverly ordered that he be cast out of the church. Those of the same schism seized him and surrounded him with logs, threatening to burn him. But when they saw him not yielding an inch nor being in the least afraid, apprehensive of a rising of the people, for the man was famous (all this by celestial providence), they let the martyr go unharmed, a voluntary holocaust for Christ.

Gelasius 5   They used to say of him that he undertook a life of poverty and withdrawal in youth. There were very many others who, at that time, embraced the same way of life as he in the same parts. Among them there was an elder of supreme simplicity and poverty, living alone in one cell until he died, even though he had disciples in his old age. He disciplined himself until death to observe the [commandment] not to possess two tunics nor (together with his companions) to take thought for the morrow. When (at the instigation of God) Abba Gelasius came to set up the coenobion, much land was offered to him. He also acquired beasts of burden and oxen for the needs of the coenobion. He[34] who at first revealed to the godly Pachomius that he should set up a coenobion was working with this [father] too in all that concerned the setting up of the monastery. The above-mentioned elder, seeing him [immersed] in these things and maintaining a sincere affection for him, said to him: "Abba Gelasius, I am afraid that your *logismos* is attached to the lands and the rest of the property of the coenobion," to which he replied: "Your *logismos* is more attached to the needle with which you work than is the *logismos* of Gelasius to the property."

[34]i.e. an angel; see *HL* 32.

Gelasius 6 [7.13]   They used to say of Abba Gelasius that he was often harassed by his *logismoi* to go off into the desert. One day he said to his disciple: "Of your charity brother, whatever I do, put up with it and say nothing to me that week." He took a palm staff and began walking around in his courtyard. He sat a little when he was exhausted and then got up again and walked around. When evening fell, he said to his *logismos*: "He who walks around in the desert does not eat bread, only plants; but on account of your weakness, do you eat some green vegetables." That done, he also said to his *logismos*: "The person in the desert does not sleep under a roof but in the open air; so you too do that." He laid himself down and slept in his own courtyard. When he had spent three days walking around in his monastery, eating a little endive in the evening and sleeping in the open air at night, he was exhausted. He rebuked the *logismos* that was harassing him; he rebuked it, saying: "If you cannot perform the deeds of the desert, remain in your cell with patience, weeping for your sins and do not go astray. For the eye of God sees folk's deeds everywhere. Nothing is hid from him and he is aware of those who are doing good deeds."

Gerontius

The best known monk of this name was chaplain to Melania the Younger (d. 439) and subsequently her biographer. The following apophthegm is not his.

Gerontius [N 178, 5.2]   Abba Gerontius of Petra said: "Many are they who, tempted by the delights of the flesh, indulged in *porneia* in the mind without any physical contact. While maintaining the virginity of their bodies, they commit *porneia* in their soul. Therefore, beloved, it is good to do what is written: for each one to 'keep his own heart fully protected'" [Prov 4.23].

Δ—*Delta*

DANIEL

Daniel was the disciple of Alexander and Zoïlos at Pharan, then of Arsenius until that elder died, at Scete—which he must have left when it was devastated by the barbarians. His apophthegms tell us little of himself but much of Arsenius and other elders.

Daniel 1 [10.21] They used to say of Daniel that the fathers fled when the barbarians came to Scete, and the elder said: "If God does not take care of me, why should I even go on living?" He passed through the barbarians without them seeing him. Then he said to himself: "Here, God took care of me, and I did not die. So you too, do the human thing: flee like the fathers" [and he got up and fled].[35]

Daniel 2 A brother asked Abba Daniel: "Give me one commandment and I will observe it." He said to him: "Never put your hand in a dish with a woman to eat with her. In this way you will escape the demon of *porneia* somewhat."

Daniel 3 [15.15] Abba Daniel said that there was a daughter of a leading citizen in Babylon possessed of a demon. Her father had a monk whom he cherished, and that one said to him: "No one can cure your daughter except some anchorites I know. If you entreat them, they will not agree to do this out of humility. But let us do this: when they come to market, pretend you want to buy [their] wares; then when they come to get the price of them, we will tell them to offer a prayer, and I believe she will be healed." They went out into the marketplace and found a disciple of the elders sitting there to sell

[35]Some mss omit [. . .].

their wares. They took him and the baskets along to get the price of them. When the monk came into the house, the woman possessed of a demon came and gave him a slap, but he turned the other cheek, according to the Lord's commandment [Mt 5.39]. Tortured [by this], the demon cried out: "What violence! The commandment of Jesus is casting me out!" and the maiden was immediately purged. When the elders came, they told them what had happened; they glorified God and said: "It is usually the case that the arrogance of the devil falls as a result of the humility [required by] Christ's commandment."

Daniel 4 [10.22]   Abba Daniel also said: "Insofar as the body flour-ishes, so the soul declines; and insofar as the body declines, so the soul flourishes."

Daniel 5 [11.16]   Once when Abba Daniel and Abba Ammōes were travelling, Abba Ammōes said: "When are we too going to stay in a cell, father?" Abba Daniel said to him: "Who is taking God away from us now? God is in the cell, and God is outside too."

Daniel 6 [10.23]   Abba Daniel told how when Abba Arsenius was at Scete, there was a monk there who was stealing the elders' goods. Abba Arsenius took him into his cell, wishing to win him over and to give the elders some respite. He said to him: "I will provide you with whatever you desire, only just do not steal." He gave him gold, coins, clothes, and everything he needed, but he went off and stole again. So the elders expelled him when they realized that he had not stopped, saying: "If a brother is found at fault through some weakness, he should be tolerated; but if he steals and does not stop when he is warned, expel him, for he is both damaging his soul and disturbing everybody in the place."

Daniel 7 [18.4, N 761B; cf. 18.48]   Abba Daniel the Pharanite related that our father Abba Arsenius said of one of those at Scete that he was a great one in deeds but a simpleton in belief. He erred in his ignorance, saying that the bread that we receive in Commu-nion is not really the body of Christ but a representation. Two elders heard that he was making this statement; aware that he was a great one in the way he lived, they reckoned that he spoke without guile and in simplicity. They went to him and said: "Abba, we heard an unbelievable story about some fellow that he says the bread we share in Communion is not really the body of Christ but a representation." The elder said: "It is I who say that." They begged of him, saying: "Do not maintain that position, abba, but [the belief] that the catholic church has handed down. For we believe that the bread itself is the body of Christ and the chalice itself is truly the blood of Christ and no representation. Just as in the beginning [God] took clay from the earth and made the human being in his own image [Gen 2.7, 1.27], and nobody can say that it was not in the image of God, albeit incomprehensible, so too the bread that he said 'is my body' [Mt 26.26, etc.] we believe truly to be the body of Christ." The elder said: "Unless I am swayed by experience, I will not be convinced. They said to him: "Let us intercede with God about this mystery during this week, and we believe that God will reveal it to us." The elder accepted the proposition with joy; he interceded with God, saying: "Lord, you know that it is not in malice that I do not believe; reveal it to me, Lord Jesus Christ, so that I do not go astray in ignorance." The elders went off to their own cells and besought God themselves, saying: "Lord Jesus Christ, reveal this mystery to the elder so that he believes and does not lose his toil," and God heard them both. When the week was over, they came to the church on Sunday; the three individuals were standing together in a separate group with the elder in between them. Their inner eyes were opened, and when the bread was placed on the holy table, it appeared to the three individuals alone as a child. When the priest put forth [his hand] to break the bread, here there came down from heaven an angel of the Lord; he had a sword and he sacrificed the child, emptying its blood into the chalice. When the priest broke the bread into small pieces, the angel cut some small pieces from the child too. When they went to receive the holy mysteries, bleeding flesh was given to the elder only. He was terrified when he saw it and cried out, saying: "Lord, I believe that the bread is your body and the chalice is your blood." Immediately the meat in his hand became bread, as in the sacrament, and he partook of it, giving thanks to God. The elders said: "God knows that human nature is such that it cannot eat raw flesh, and for that reason he transformed his body into bread and his blood into wine for those who partake in faith." They gave thanks to God for not allowing the elder to lose his toil; the three [elders] went to their cells with joy.

Daniel 8 [18.8]   The same Abba Daniel related that another great elder living in lower Egypt used to say in his simplicity that it is Melchizedek who is Son of God. This was told of him to the blessed Cyril, archbishop of Alexandria, who sent for him. [Cyril] was aware that the elder was a wonder-worker, that whatever he asked of God was revealed to him, and that it was in simplicity that he made the statement [about Melchizedek]. [Cyril] shrewdly said to him: "Abba, I have a request: my *logismos* tells me that it is Melchizedek who is Son of God, while another *logismos* says he is not [that] but a man and a high priest of God. Since I am in two minds on this matter, I have sent for you so that you may pray to God so that he may reveal [the solution] to you and we may know the truth." Trusting in his own way of life, the elder confidently replied: "Allow me three days; I will personally ask God about this and report to you who he is." Off he went and interceded with God concerning this matter. Three days later he came and told the blessed Cyril: "Melchizedek is a man." The archbishop said to him: "How do you know, abba?" He said: "God showed me all the patriarchs passing before me, one by one, from Adam to Melchizedek. An angel said to me: 'This is Melchizedek; make no mistake that this is how he is.'" The elder went away and, of his own free will, announced that Melchizedek is a man. The blessed Cyril was very gratified.

DIOSCORUS

Dioscorus is not an uncommon name among the monks of Egypt (see HL 10–11, HME 20). It is unlikely that the following three sayings were uttered by a single person of that name.

Dioscorus 1 [4.13] They related of Abba Dioscorus of Nachiastis[36] that his bread was made from barley and lentils and that each year he would begin to observe one rule of life, saying: "I will not meet anybody this year," or "I will not speak," or "I will not eat anything cooked," or "I will not eat fruit or fresh vegetables"—and so he did with every activity. When he finished one, he undertook another and did so year by year.

Dioscorus 2 [3.23] A brother asked Abba Poemen: "My *logismoi* are troubling me; they are not allowing me to be concerned about my sins but are making me pay attention to the shortcomings of my brother." Abba Poemen told him how Abba Dioscorus was in his cell weeping over himself. His disciple was staying in another cell; when he visited the elder he found him weeping. He said to him: "Why are you weeping, father?" The elder said: "I am weeping for my sins." His disciple said to him: "You do not have sins, father." The elder replied: "Indeed, if I am permitted to see my sins, three or four others will not be enough to weep for them."

Dioscorus 3 Abba Dioscorus said: "If we wear our heavenly garment we shall not be found naked; but if we are not found wearing that garment, what shall we do, brothers? We too have to hear that voice which says: 'Cast him out into the outer darkness; there shall be weeping and gnashing of teeth' [Mt 22.13]. But now, brothers, great is our shame, after so much time wearing the habit, to be found lacking the wedding garment in the hour of necessity! What repentance is going to come upon us! What darkness is going to engulf us in the presence of the fathers and our brothers as they behold us being punished by the angels of punishment!"

[36]*de Namisias P&J*; Namiasis?

Doulas

A Doulas has already been mentioned as the disciple of Abba Bessarion; however, of the two sayings attributed to him here the second is certainly and the first probably the thought of Evagrius.

Doulas 1 [2.13]   Abba Doulas said: "If the enemy is coercing us to abandon *hesychia*, let us not listen to him, for there is nothing like it—and going without food. Together they constitute an alliance against him for they confer sharpness on the inward eyes."

Doulas 2 [2.14]   He also said: "Cut off your relationships with the multitude lest your battle for the mind become critical and disturb your habit of *hesychia*."

E—*Epsilon*

Epiphanius Bishop in Cyprus

Born in Palestine c. 315, Epiphanius first experienced monastic life with Hilarion in Egypt, then he returned to found and direct his own monastery at Eleutheropolis between Gaza and Jerusalem. In 367 he became Bishop of Salamis in Cyprus where he died in 403. A firm defender of Nicene Orthodoxy, in 382 he joined forces with Jerome to counter Origenism.

Epiphanius 1   The holy bishop Epiphanius recounted that in the time of the blessed Athansius the Great, crows flying around the Temple of Serapis were ceaselessly calling: "Cras, cras." Confronting the blessed Athanasius the pagans cried out: "Wicked elder, tell us what the crows are calling." In reply he said: "The crows are calling: 'Cras, cras' and *cras* in the Latin language is 'tomorrow'; and," he added, "tomorrow you shall see the glory of God." Then, the next day, the death of the emperor Julian was reported. When that happened, they congregated and cried out against Serapis, saying: "If you did not want him, why did you accept what was his?"[37]

Epiphanius 2   The same [elder] recounted that there was a charioteer in Alexandria who was the son of a mother [named] Mary. He fell while a chariot-race was in progress but he got up again, overtook the one who had overturned him, and won. The crowd yelled out: "The son of Mary fell, arose, and has triumphed." While this cry was still echoing, a rumor went round the crowd concerning the Temple of Serapis: that Theophilus the Great had gone up there, had overturned the statue of Serapis, and taken possession of the temple.

[37]See Sozomen, *HE* 4.10.

Epiphanius 3 [12.6]   It was reported to the blessed Epiphanius, bishop of Cyprus, by the abba of the monastery he had in Palestine: "Thanks to your prayers, we did not neglect the rule but are diligent in celebrating both the first hour, the third, the sixth, the ninth, and at lamp lighting," but he reprimanded them and declared: "You are clearly deficient in prayer, desisting from prayer at the other hours of the day, for the true monk must unceasingly have prayer and psalmody in his heart."

Epiphanius 4 [4.15]   Holy Epiphanius once sent to Abba Hilarion, inviting him: "Come, so we can see each other before we depart from the body." When he arrived they rejoiced in each other's company. While they were eating, a fowl was brought to them; the bishop took it and gave it to Abba Hilarion, but the elder said to him: "Forgive me, but I have not eaten flesh since I took the habit." Said the bishop to him: "Since I took the habit neither have I allowed anybody to go to sleep who had anything against me, nor did I go to sleep if I had anything against anybody." The elder said to him: "Forgive me; your way of life is greater than mine."

Epiphanius 5   The same [elder] used to say: "Melchizedek, the icon of Christ, blessed Abraham, the root of the Jews [Gen 14.19]. Much more so does Christ, who is truth itself, bless and sanctify all who believe in him."

Epiphanius 6   The same [elder] used to say: "The Canaanite woman cries out and is heard [Mt 15.22]; the woman with an issue of blood keeps silent and is blessed [Mt 9.20]. The Pharisee calls out and is condemned; the publican does not even open his mouth and he is heard" [Lk 18.10–14].

Epiphanius 7   The same [elder] used to say: "The Prophet David prayed late at night; he rose at midnight; he pleaded before dawn; at daybreak he stood [before the Lord]; he supplicated in the early morning; in the evening and at midday he interceded. That is why he used to say: 'Seven times a day I praised you'" [Ps 118.64].

Epiphanius 8   He also said: "The possession of Christian books is a necessity for those who have [the means], for the very sight of the books itself renders us more averse to sin and rather impels us to aspire to righteousness."

Epiphanius 9   He also said: "Reading the Scripture is a great assurance against sinning."

Epiphanius 10   He also said: "Ignorance of Scripture is a great precipice and a profound abyss."

Epiphanius 11   He also said: "It is a great betrayal of salvation to know none of the divine laws."

Epiphanius 12   The same [elder] used to say: "The transgressions of the righteous are related to their lips: those of the ungodly arise from the entire body, hence David sings: 'Set a watch, O Lord, before my mouth and a door that encloses about my lips' [Ps 140.3] and: 'I said I will keep a watch on my ways that I sin not in my tongue'" [Ps 38.2].

Epiphanius 13   The same [elder] was asked: "Why are there ten commandments of the law but nine beatitudes?" and he said: "The Decalogue is equal in number to the plagues of Egypt, whereas the number of the beatitudes is a triple icon of the Trinity."

Epiphanius 14   The same [elder] was asked whether one just person was sufficient to assuage God and he said: "Yes, for he himself said: 'Seek out one that does justice and righteousness and I will be gracious to all the people'" [Jer 5.1].

Epiphanius 15   The same [elder] said: "God forgives the debts of sinners who repent, as he did in the cases of the Woman who was a Sinner and of the Publican; but as for the righteous, he demands interest too. This is what he was saying to the apostles: 'Except your righteousness exceed that of the Scribes and Pharisees you shall in no wise enter into the Kingdom of Heaven'" [Mt 5.20].

Epiphanius 16   He used to say this too: "God sells righteousness very cheaply to those who want to buy, [but you pay] one penny for a little crust of bread, an old garment, [or] a cup of cold water."

Epiphanius 17   He added this too: "One person who borrows from another because he is poor or wants to be more affluent, expresses thanks when [the loan] is handed over, whereas he repays it secretly and with shame. But with the Lord God it is otherwise; he borrows in secret but repays before angels, archangels, and the righteous."

Ephraim

This is the great Ephraim Syrus c. 306–373, the deacon of Nisbis and Edessa whose many writings in Syriac were highly influential.

Ephraim 1 [18.6]   When Abba Ephraim was a child, he had a dream or a vision: a vine sprung up from his tongue, grew, and filled all the space under heaven, and it was very fruitful. All the birds of the air were coming to eat of the fruit of the vine, and while they were eating, its fruit was proliferating.

Ephraim 2 [18.7]   Another time one of the saints also saw a vision of a rank of angels coming out of heaven by the order of God with a scroll in their hands, meaning a book written both inside and out. They were saying to each other: "Who ought to be entrusted with this?" Some were saying this one, others that one, but in reply they said: "They are truly holy and righteous, but they cannot be entrusted with this." They mentioned many other names of holy ones and finally said: "Nobody can be entrusted with this other than Ephraim." The elder who had the vision saw that they gave the scroll to Ephraim. Rising early, he heard Ephraim teaching as though there were a spring flowing from his mouth; the elder who had the vision realized that what came out of the lips of Ephraim was coming from the Holy Spirit.

Ephraim 3 [10.26]   Once again when Abba Ephraim was passing by, there was a whore who approached him at somebody's instigation, and she fawned on him to move him to shameful intercourse, or at least to anger, for nobody had ever seen him being angry or contentious. But he said to her: "Follow me." Approaching a place that was much frequented, he said to her: "Here, in this place, come and do what you wanted to," but she, seeing the crowd, said to him: "How can we do it in the presence of such a crowd and not be ashamed?" He said to her: "If you are ashamed before folk, how much more ought we to be ashamed before God who reproves 'the hidden things of darkness'?" [cf. 1 Cor 4.5]. She went away ashamed, nothing accomplished.

EUCHARISTUS THE WORLDLING

Eucharistus [20.2]   Two of the fathers besought God to inform them what stature they had attained. A voice came to them, saying: "In such and such a village of Egypt there is a worldling, Eucharistus by name, and his wife is called Maria; you have not yet attained their stature." The two elders got up and came to the village. On inquiring, they found his cell and his wife. They said to her: "Where is your husband?" "He is a shepherd," she said, "and he is pasturing the sheep," and she brought them into her house. When evening fell, there came Eucharistus with the sheep. When he saw the elders, he prepared a table for them and brought water to wash their feet. The elders said to him: "We will not taste a thing unless you reveal your way of life to us," but Eucharistus, being humble-minded, said: "I am a shepherd and she is my wife." The elders persisted, begging him to speak, but he refused to speak. Then they said to him: "God has sent us to you." He was afraid when he heard this statement and he said to them: "Look, we got these sheep from our parents. Whatever profit the Lord grants us to gain from them we divide into three parts: one part for the poor, one for hospitality, the third part

for our own need. From when I took my wife neither I have been
defiled nor she. She is a virgin; each of us sleeps on his own. We
wear sackcloth by night, our clothes by day. None amongst humans
knew this until now." The elders were amazed when they heard this
and they went their way glorifying God.

EULOGIUS THE PRIEST

Eulogius [8.4]   A person named Eulogius was a disciple of the
holy John [Chrysostom] the archbishop. He was a priest and a great
ascetic who used to fast two days at a time and often went a whole
week eating nothing but bread and salt; he was held in high esteem
by the people. He visited Abba Joseph of Panepho expecting to see
some yet more severe austerity [while staying] with him. The elder
received him with joy and caused some refreshment to be served of
whatever he had to hand, but Eulogius' disciples said: "The priest
does not eat anything but bread and salt." For his part, Abba Joseph
just kept quiet and went on eating. [The guests] stayed three days
but did not hear [the hosts] singing psalms or praying, for their
activity[38] was in secret. So they went their way without reaping
any benefit. But, by divine providence, there came up a mist; they
wandered off track and came back to the elder['s monastery]. Before
they knocked at the gate, however, they heard [those inside] singing psalms. They waited a long time, then knocked, [whereupon
they within] silenced their psalm-singing and joyfully welcomed
them in. On account of the great heat, Eulogius' disciples put some
water in the bottle and gave it to him. It was a mixture of sea- and
river-water: he could not drink it. Coming to his senses, he fell
down before the elder. Wishing to learn his way of life [*diagōgē*],
he said: "How is this, abba?[39] At first you were not singing psalms;

[38]*ergasia*, "fulfilling of the commandments; total way of life, performance of
devotions, etc."; cf. *diagōgē*, a few lines further on.

[39]The text may be defective here. *Synag* 3.26.8.6 continues: "While we were with
you, you did not sing psalms, but after we went out from you, then there was a great

but now, after we went out, you are? And the bottle I just received, I found the water salty?" The elder answered him: "The brother is a fool, and in his wandering [mind] he mixed it with seawater," but Eulogius begged the elder, wishing to learn the truth and the elder said to him: "That little cup of wine was for the agapē; but this water is what the brothers drink all the time."[40] Then he taught him discretion regarding *logismoi*, and he detached all human concerns from him. [Eulogius] became accommodating and from then on would eat whatever was put before him. He too learned to perform his *activity* in secret; he said to the elder: "Your [pl.] *activity* is genuine indeed."

EUPREPIUS

Apart from Euprepius 7 (which is Evagrius'), the sayings of Euprepius all speak of poverty, privation, and detachment from material goods.

Euprepius 1   Said Abba Euprepius: "Since you have faith within you that God is faithful and powerful, trust in him and you shall partake of what is his. If you are discouraged, you are not believing. We all believe he is powerful and believe that all things are possible for him; but trust in him in your own affairs and believe that he works wonders in you too."

Euprepius 2   While he was being robbed, the same [elder] was giving a helping hand. After [the thieves] had carried of what lay within [the cell] leaving behind his own staff, Abba Euprepius saw it and was troubled. He picked it up and ran, wanting to hand it over—but they were unwilling to receive it for fear that something might happen to them. When he came across some people who were

deal of psalm-singing. Likewise then, you were drinking wine in our presence, but now I tasted your water and I found it saline and scarcely drinkable."

[40]*Synag.* 3.26.8.7 continues: "He also gave an explanation of the psalm-singing: that, κατ'οἰκονομίαν, they concealed their own activity, performing it in secret."

going the same way, he asked for the staff to be handed over [to the thieves] by them.[41]

Euprepius 3   Abba Euprepius said: "Bodily possessions are material. He who loves the world loves stumbling-stones. So if one ever chance to lose [something] he should accept [the loss] with joy and thanksgiving like persons set free from concerns."

Euprepius 4 [1.28]   A brother asked Abba Euprepius about life and the elder said: "Eat hay, wear hay, sleep on hay (meaning: despise everything), and acquire a heart of steel."

Euprepius 5   A brother asked the same elder: "How does fear of God come to the soul?" The elder said: "If a person have humility, is indifferent to goods, and does not pass judgment, the fear of God comes to him."

Euprepius 6 [1.30]   The same [elder] said: "Let fear, humility, a limited diet, and sorrow remain with you."

Euprepius 7 [10.24]   In his early days Abba Euprepius[42] visited some elder and said to him: "Abba, tell me a saying [showing] how I am to be saved," but he said to him: "If you wish to be saved, when you visit somebody, do not begin speaking until he questions you." Pricked in his conscience by the saying, he prostrated himself saying: "I have indeed read many books, but never knew such teaching." He went out having reaped great benefit.

HELLADIUS

Helladius 1 [4.16]   They used to say of Abba Helladius that he passed twenty years at The Cells and did not ever lift his eyes to see the roof of the church.

---

[41]For very similar stories, see Zosimas 12 [16.21, N337, *PS* 212] and Macarius the Egyptian 18 & 40.

[42]Evagrius in many other versions.

Helladius 2   They used to say of the same Abba Helladius that he used [only] to eat bread and salt. When Easter came round he would say: "The brothers are eating bread and salt. I ought to make a little effort for Easter. Since I eat sitting down on the other days, now that it is Easter I will make an effort and eat standing up."

Helladius S 1 [Guy 44]   On a Saturday that was a feast day the brothers were taking a meal in the church at The Cells. When the dish containing gruel was set out, Abba Helladius of Alexandria began to weep. In response Abba Jacob said to him: "Why are you weeping, abba?" and he said: "Because the joy of the soul has passed away (fasting, that is) and the comfort of the body has come in."

EVAGRIUS

Evagrius of Pontus (346–399), trained by the Cappadocian Fathers, was ordained by Gregory of Nazianzen and followed him to Constantinople. He left for Egypt in 381 to escape the wiles of the wife of a senior person in the imperial service. First at Nitria then at The Cells he lived the life of a humble monk and yet exercised his intellectual powers to become the first theoretician of monasticism. This "philosopher of the desert" had profound effect on Palladius, John Cassian, Dionysius the Pseudo-Areopagite, and Maximus the Confessor. Later charges of Origensim harmed his reputation and led to the loss of many of his writings. This also explains why some sayings known to be his appear under different names here. He was himself one of the first to commit monastic apophthegms to writing. The apophthegm known as "The Roman 1" [10.110] may refer to Evagrius.

Evagrius 1   Abba Evagrius said: "While you are staying in your cell, focus your *logismos* and call to mind the day of [your] death. Witness the necrosis of [your] body; envisage the calamity; feel the pain; condemn the vanity in the world so you may always remain firm in your purpose of *hesychia* and not weaken. Bear in mind too the present state of affairs in Hades; reckon what condition the souls there are in: what awful silence, what most bitter groaning; what fear and agony and apprehension; the unending distress, the unceasing tears of the soul. But recall too the day of resurrection and the appearance before God. Imagine that terrifying and fearful judgment. Add to that what lies in wait for the sinners: shame in the presence of God, angels and archangels, and all people, I mean: punishments, eternal fire, the worm that never sleeps, Tartarus, darkness, the gnashing of teeth, the fear, and the torture. Then add to that the good things that await the righteous: freedom of access to God the Father and to his Christ, to angels and archangels and the entire company of the saints; the kingdom of heaven, its gifts, the joy and its repose. Take the memory of both to yourself and weep over the condemnation of the sinners; lament for fear that you yourself be of their number. But rejoice and be glad at what awaits the righteous and strive to be at rest in [the expectation of] them, alienating yourself from those others. Whether you are in your cell or out of it somewhere, see that you never forget the memory of these [states] so that, by virtue of these, you may escape from filthy and damaging *logismoi*.

Evagrius 2   He also said: "Cut off relations with most people; let not your mind be swayed by circumstances and it interrupt your practice of *hesychia*."[43]

Evagrius 3 [11.17]   He also said: "It is a great thing to pray without distraction, but greater still to sing without distraction."

Evagrius 4 [11.18]   He also said: "Be ever mindful of your departure and do not forget the eternal judgment; then there will be no error in your soul."

Evagrius 5   An elder said: "Take away temptations and nobody is being saved."

[43]cf. Doulas 2.

Evagrius 6 [1.4, 17.35, 10.193]   He also said that one of the fathers used to say: "A dry and irregular diet coupled with love speedily bring the monk to the haven of *apatheia*."

Evagrius 7 [16.3]   Once there was a meeting at The Cells about some matter and Abba Evagrius spoke. The priest said to him: "Abba Evagrius, we know that if you were in your homeland you would probably have been a bishop and the head of many [clergy]; but now you are living here as an alien." He was pricked in his conscience but not disturbed. Nodding his head, he said to him: "It is true, father; nevertheless, 'I have spoken once; I will add nothing the second time'" [Job 40.5].

Evagrius S 1 [Guy 21]   He also said: "The beginning of salvation is to have a low opinion of oneself."

Evagrius S 2 [Guy 50]   He also said that another elder said: "I deny myself pleasures in order to exclude occasions of anger, for I am aware that [anger] is always on the attack concerning pleasures, troubling my mind and hunting down my awareness."

Evagrius S 3 [Guy 50]   He also said that one of the brothers inquired of one of the elders whether it was permitted for him to eat with his mother and sisters when visiting the house. "You are not to eat with a woman," he said.

EUDAEMON

Abba Eudaemon said of Abba Paphnutius, the father of Scete: "I went down there as a young man and he would not let me stay there, saying regarding me: 'I will not let a woman's face stay at Scete because of the battle with the enemy.'"

Z—Zeta

ZENO

Silvanus' most famous disciple was Zeno (from Zeus), a dry little man, all concentrated, full of divine warmth and eagerness, and with a great gift for sympathy, so that he was much sought after for spiritual counsel. He seems to have moved about considerably in Palestine (having followed Silvanus) and perhaps in Syria, but for some time toward the end of his life he was at Kefr She'arta, fourteen miles northeast of Gaza. A year before Chalcedon (450) he shut himself up near Gaza and would see no one; he seems to have died in the course of that year.[44]

Zeno 1 [8.5]   Abba Zeno, the disciple of the blessed Silvanus, said: "Do not dwell in a famous location or stay with a person of renown and do not ever lay a foundation so you can build yourself a cell."

Zeno 2   They used to say of Abba Zeno that at first he was unwilling to accept anything whatsoever from anybody, hence those who brought [anything] went away disappointed that he would not accept [it]. Others came to him wanting to receive [something] as from a great elder, but he had nothing to give them and they too went away disappointed. The elder said: "What am I to do, for both those who bring [things] and those who want to receive are disappointed. This however will be more appropriate: if somebody brings something, I will accept it, and if anybody asks, I will provide for him." So doing, he experienced repose and satisfied everybody.

Zeno 3   An Egyptian brother visited Abba Zeno in Syria and accused himself of his own *logismoi* before the elder. In his amazement

---

[44]Derwas Chitty, *The Desert a City* (Oxford: Basil Blackwell, 1966), 73.

[Zeno] said: "The Egyptians conceal the virtues they possess and are always accusing themselves of shortcomings which they do not have. But the Syrians and Greeks lay claim to virtues they do not possess while concealing the shortcomings that are theirs."

Zeno 4 [10.27]   Some brothers came to him and asked: "What is this that is written in Job: 'Heaven is not pure in his sight'?" [Job 15.15]. In answer the elder said to them: "The brothers have left their sins aside and are inquiring about the heavens![45] This however is the explanation of the phrase: Since only God himself is pure, on that account he said: 'Heaven is not pure.'"

Zeno 5 [18.8]   They used to say of Abba Zeno that when he was staying at Scete he came out of his cell by night meaning to go to the marsh but he lost his way; he spent three days and three nights walking around. Exhausted, he became faint and fell down to die. Then there stood before him a youth with bread and a bottle of water. "Get up and eat," he said to him. Up he got and prayed, under the impression that it was a vision but, in response, the other said to him: "Well done," so he prayed again a second time and likewise a third and he said to him: "Well done," so the elder got up, took, and ate. After that [the youth] said to him: "The more you walked around, the further you were from your cell, but get up and follow me." Immediately he found himself at his cell, so the elder said to him: "Come in and offer a prayer for us." When the elder went in the [youth] disappeared.

Zeno 6 [4.17]   Another time Abba Zeno was walking around in Palestine; he was fatigued and sat down to eat beside a cucumber bed. His *logismos* said to him: "Take one cucumber for yourself and eat it; for what is that?" but in reply he said to his *logismos*: "Those who steal go off to be punished; so test yourself here and now whether you can endure punishment." He got up and stood in the burning heat for five days and after frying himself he said: "You cannot endure punishment." He said to his *logismos*: "If you cannot, then do not steal and eat."

[45]or "into heavenly matters."

Zeno 7 Abba Zeno said: "He who wants God speedily to hear his prayer when he stands and stretches out his hands to God, before all else, even before for his own soul, let him pray for his enemies with all his soul and, thanks to this correct procedure, whatever he asks of God, [God] will hear him."

Zeno 8 They used to say that there was somebody in a village much given to fasting, to the extent that they used to call him "the faster." When Abba Zeno heard about him, he sent for him and off he went, gladly. When they had prayed, they sat down and the elder began working in silence. Finding no opportunity to talk with him, the faster began to be troubled by *accidie*; he said to the elder: "Pray for me, abba, for I want to go away." "Why?" the elder said to him and in reply he said: "Because my heart is as though it were on fire and I do not know what is the matter. For when I was in the village I used to fast until evening and it was never like this with me." The elder said to him: "In the village you were fed through your ears. Off you go and, from now on, eat at the ninth hour and whatever you do, do it in secret." When he began this practice, it was very hard for him to wait until the ninth hour. Those who knew him began to say: "The faster has been possessed by a demon." He came and reported it all to the elder but he said to him: "This is the godly way."

Zachariah

Zachariah was very young when he arrived at Scete with his father (see Carion 2). By the submission and patience with which he received his father's rugged training he surpassed him in virtue and was granted visions, of which Poemen recognized the origin.

Zachariah 1 [1.6] Abba Macarius said to Abba Zachariah: "Tell me, what is the task of the monk?" "You are asking me, father?" he said, and Abba Macarius said: "I have full confidence in you, Zachariah my son, for there is somebody inciting me to ask you." Abba

Zachariah said to him: "In my opinion, to constrain oneself in all things: that is being the monk."

Zachariah 2 [12.7]   Abba Moses once went to draw some water; he found Abba Zachariah praying by the well and the Spirit of God was resting over him.

Zachariah 3 [15.19]   Abba Moses once said to Brother Zachariah: "Tell me what I am to do." He threw himself on the ground at the other's feet when he heard this, saying: "You are asking me, father?" The elder said to him: "Believe me, Zachariah my son, I saw the Holy Spirit descending on you; therefore I am obliged to ask you." Then Zachariah took his own cowl from his head, put it beneath his feet and trod on it, saying: "Unless a person be crushed like that he cannot be a monk."

Zachariah 4 [15.18]   Once when Abba Zachariah was staying at Scete there came a vision to him; he got up and reported it to Carion, his abba. But, being a man of action, the elder was not exactly sure of such things. He got up and beat him, saying [the vision] was of the demons. But the *logismos* endured; so getting up and going to Abba Poemen by night he told *him* the matter and how it was burning within him. [This] elder, perceiving that [the vision] was from God, said to him: "Go to such and such an elder and do whatever he tells you." He went to [that] elder and, before questioning him, the elder anticipated him and told him all: "The vision is from God, but go and be subject to your father."

Zachariah 5 [15.20]   Abba Poemen said that Abba Moses asked Brother Zachariah when he was at the point of death: "What do you see?" and he said to him: "Is it not better to keep silent, father?" "It is, my son; be silent," [the elder] said to him. At the moment of his death, Abba Isidore (who was sitting there) looked up to heaven and said: "Rejoice Zachariah my son, for the gates of the Kingdom of Heaven have been opened for you."

H—*Eta*

ISAIAH

The name Isaiah occurs so often that it is extremely difficult to distinguish the persons with this name from each other.[46] Then there is the fifth-century Isaiah of Scete, author of the Spritual Discourses (from which numbers 9–11 are taken) and yet another Isaiah of Scete, the disciple of Achilles and Ammōes (see Achilles 3 and Ammōes 2, above) to whom Isaiah 4–6 (below) might be attributed.

Isaiah 1   Abba Isaiah said: "Nothing benefits a beginner as much as an insult. A beginner who is insulted like that and tolerates it is like a tree that is watered each day."

Isaiah 2   He also said to those who begin well and are subject to holy fathers: "The first dye does not fade, as with purple," and: "Like young branches that are easily bent and twisted, so are beginners who are in subjection."

Isaiah 3   He also said: "A beginner transferring from monastery to monastery is like a beast driven here and there on a halter."

Isaiah 4 [12.8]   He also said: "When there was an *agapē* in the church and the brothers were eating and talking to each other, the priest of Pelusium reproved them, saying: 'Be quiet, brothers; I personally saw a brother eating with you and drinking as many cups as you and his prayer is going up before God like fire.'"

---

[46]See *HME* 11 and *HL* 14.

Isaiah 5   They used to say of Abba Isaiah he once took a basket and went to the threshing floor and said to the landowner: "Give me some grain." "And have you harvested too, abba?" he said. "No," he said and the landowner said to him: "So how do you expect to get some grain if you have not harvested?" The elder said to him: "So you do not get a reward unless you harvest?" "No," said the landowner, and with that, the elder went his way. When the brothers saw what he had done they prostrated themselves before him, begging to learn why he had done that. The elder said to them: "I did it as an example that unless one work, he does not get a reward from God."

Isaiah 6   The same Abba Isaiah called one of the brothers and washed his feet, then he threw a handful of lentils in a pot and served them when it came to the boil. The brother said to him: "It is not yet cooked, abba," and he said to him: "Is it not enough for you that it saw the bright [flame] totally? That is great consolation."

Isaiah 7   He also said: "If God wishes to have mercy on a soul but it refuses and does not allow it but carries out its own will, [God] allows it to suffer what it does not want [to suffer] so that, by this means, it will set out in search of him."

Isaiah 8   He also said: "Whenever somebody wishes to render evil for evil he can wound his brother's conscience with no more than a nod."

Isaiah 9 [21.1]   The same Abba Isaiah was asked: "What is the love of money?" and he answered: "It is not believing in God that he is taking care of you, to despair of the promises of God, to love noxious delights, and to be arrogant."

Isaiah 10 [21.2]   He was also asked: "What is slandering?"[47] and he answered: "It is to be ignorant of God and of his glory; it is to be envious of one's neighbor."

---

[47] or "backbiting," *katalalia.*

Isaiah 11 [21.3]   He was also asked: "What is wrath," and he answered: "Strife,[48] falsehood, and ignorance."

Elijah

A number of monks named Elijah are known to have lived in Egypt in the fourth century, including one who was a steward (Elijah 3) and one at Scete who knew the great ones, especially Bessarion who, like Joshua, is said to have held back the sun (Elijah 2; cf. Bessarion 3).

Elijah 1 [3.6]   Abba Elijah said: "I am afraid of three things: the moment when my soul is going to exit the body; the moment when I am going to meet God, and the moment when sentence is going to be given against me."

Elijah 2 [19.5]   The elders were telling Abba Elijah in Egypt about Abba Agathon, that he was a good brother. The elder said to them: "He is good in his generation." They said to him: "And what about among those of old time?" and, in reply, he said: "I said to you that he was good in his generation. Among those of old time I saw a person at Scete who was able to stop the sun in the sky, like Joshua the son of Nun" [Josh 10:12–23]. They were astounded when they heard this and they glorified God.

Elijah 3   Abba Elijah, he of the stewardship,[49] said: "What strength has sin where there is repentance, and what benefit is love where there is arrogance?"

Elijah 4   Abba Elijah said: "I myself saw somebody carrying a wineskin on his arm and, to put the demons to shame (for it was a vision,) I said to the brother: 'Of your charity, take that off for it is

[48]Some mss have "heresy" here.
[49]*tēs diakonias,* "of the diaconate"—meaning that he was a steward, one who provided monks with the necessities of life; cf. John the Persian 2.

mine.' When he took his mantle off he was found to have nothing. I said this because even if you see something with your eyes or hear something, you do not assent to it. Much more so then, be on your guard against disputations, cogitations, and reflections, knowing that it is [the demons] who cast up such things to befoul the soul with inappropriate thoughts so that they can distract the mind from its sins and from God."

Elijah 5   He also said: "Folk have the mind focused either on their sins or on Jesus or on [other] folk."

Elijah 6   He also said: "If the mind does not sing along with the body, its labor is in vain. For if a person love affliction, it later becomes joy and repose for him."

Elijah 7   He also said: "Some elder was staying in a temple and the demons came saying to him: 'Get out of our place.' The elder said: 'You do not have a place,' and they began scattering his palm branches here and there—but the elder just went on gathering them up. Finally the demon seized his hand and began to pull him outside. As he came to the door the elder grasped it with his other hand, shouting: 'Jesus, help me,' and the demon immediately fled. The elder began to weep but the Lord said to him: 'Why are you weeping?' and the elder said: 'Because they dare to lay hold on a person and to behave like that,' but he said: 'It was you who was negligent. When you sought me, you saw how I stood by you.' I am telling you this because there is need for much toil and if there be no toil nobody can have God with him; for he was crucified on our behalf."

Elijah 8[50]   A brother visited Abba Elijah who was living in *hesychia* at the coenobion of the cave of Abba Zabba and he said to him: "Abba, tell me a saying." The elder said to the brother: "In the days of our fathers these three virtues were cherished: indifference to possessions, meekness, and continence. Now cupidity, gluttony, and arrogance hold monks in prey. Hold fast to which you will."

[50]Elijah 8 is a late addition taken from *PS* 52.

HERACLIUS

This father lived for a time at Scete with Abba Agathon (N 495).
The single apophthegm attributed to him is a good example of how
an old tale could be re-used to inculcate a new message.

Heraclius [14.30]   A brother tempted by the idea of living alone
announced it to Abba Heraclius. To fortify him, that [father] said to
him: "There was an elder who had an utterly obedient disciple for
many years; then, one day, tempted by the idea, he prostrated himself
before the elder saying: 'Make me become a monk,' and the elder
said to him: 'Look out a place; we will build a cell for you and you
shall become a monk,' so he went and found [a place] one mile away
and they went and made a cell. Then the elder said to the brother:
'Whatever I say to you, do it. Eat when you are hungry; drink and
sleep, only do not come out of your cell until Saturday and then come
to where I am,' and the elder returned to his own cell. The brother
passed two days according to the elder's instruction and on the third
day, falling into *accidie*, he said: 'Why did the elder treat me like
that?'—and he got up and sang several psalms. After sundown he
ate, then got up and went to get some sleep on his mat but he saw a
burnt-faced-one lying there, gnashing his teeth at him. In great fear
he came running to the elder and knocked at the door, saying: 'Take
pity on me, abba, and open the door quickly.' But being aware that
he had not obeyed his instruction, the elder did not open up to him
until dawn. When he did open [the door] at dawn he found [the
brother] outside pleading; taking pity on him, he brought him in.
Then he said to the elder: 'I beg of you, father: I saw a black burnt-
faced-one on my sleeping-mat when I went to get some sleep.' The
elder said to him: 'This happened to you because you did not obey
my instruction,' then, forming him according to his ability in the
pursuit of the solitary life, he dismissed him and, little by little, he
became an excellent monk.

Θ—*Theta*

THEODORE OF PHERMĒ

Theodore left Scete after the devastation of 407 for Phermē, "a mountain in Egypt on the way to the great desert of Scete. About five hundred men are living on that mountain, practicing spiritual discipline" (HL 20.1). Like Arsenius he was averse to all human distinction and, like him, would avoid visitors. He too had disciples but would not direct them.

Theodore of Phermē 1 [6.7]   Abba Theodore of Phermē possessed three fine books. Visiting Abba Macarius, he said to him: "I have three fine books and I benefit from them; the brothers borrow them and benefit too. Tell me what I ought to have done. Am I to keep them for my benefit and the brothers' or sell them and give [the proceeds] to the poor?" In answer the elder said: "Deeds are good, but indifference to possessions[51] is greater than all." On hearing this he went and sold them, donating [the proceeds] to the poor.

Theodore of Phermē 2 [7.9]   A brother living in solitude at The Cells was troubled; he went to Abba Theodore of Phermē and told him. The elder said to him: "Go and humble your *logismos*; be obedient and live with others." He came back to the elder and said to him: "I do not experience repose being with people either." The elder said to him: "If you do not experience repose either alone or with others, why did you come out to be a monk? Was it not to endure afflictions? Tell me now: how many years have you worn the habit?" "Eight years," he said and the elder replied: "Well now, I have worn the habit for seventy years without finding repose for one day—and

[51] *aktēmosynē*, often translated (inadequately) as "poverty."

you want to experience repose in eight years?" [The brother] went off reinforced on hearing this.

Theodore of Phermē 3 [8.9]   A brother once visited Abba Theodore of Phermē and spent three days imploring him to let him hear a saying, but [the elder] did not answer him, so he went out sorrowing. His disciple said to him: "Abba, why did you not tell him a saying? He has gone off sorrowing." The elder said to him: "Well now, I did not tell him a saying, for he is a trafficker and likes to be admired for others' sayings."

Theodore of Phermē 4 [10.32]   He also said: "If you are friends with somebody and it happens that he fall into temptation to [commit] *porneia*, give him a hand if you can and draw him up. But if he fall into heresy and be not persuaded by you to turn away [from it], quickly cut yourself off from him lest by delaying you be dragged down into the abyss with him [cf. Mt 15.14, Lk 6.9].

Theodore of Phermē 5 [1.12]   They used to say of Abba Theodore of Phermē that he exceeded many in these three points: indifference to possessions, spiritual discipline,[52] and avoiding people.

Theodore of Phermē 6 [15.32]   Abba Theodore was once passing some time with some brothers at Scete, and while they were eating, the brothers were discreetly taking cups [of wine] in silence; they were not saying: "Forgive." Abba Theodore commented: "The monks have lost their manners, not saying: 'Forgive.'"

Theodore of Phermē 7 [8.10]   A brother asked him: "Abba, do you want me not to eat bread for a few days?" The elder answered him: "You are doing well; I myself did that too." The brother said to him: "I want to get my chickpeas to the bakery and make them into flour," and the elder said to him: "If you are going to the bakery again, make your bread; then what is the need of this outing?"[53]

---

[52]*askēsis,* "asceticism."

[53]The meaning is unclear; maybe it is something like: "If you go to the bakery again you will make yourself some bread; so why go there twice?"

Theodore of Phermē 8 [10.34]   One of the fathers came to Abba Theodore and said to him: "Here such and such a brother has gone back to the world," and the elder said to him: "Are you surprised at that? Do not be surprised; but do be surprised if you hear that somebody has been able to escape from the jaws of the enemy."

Theodore of Phermē 9 [8.11]   A brother came to Abba Theodore and began to talk and inquire about things he was not yet putting into practice. The elder said to him: "You have not yet found the ship or loaded your goods and you have already gone away to that city before setting sail. When you have first put the action into practice, then you will come to that of which you are now speaking."[54]

Theodore of Phermē 10 [10.33]   The same [elder] once visited Abba John, a eunuch from birth, and as they were speaking, he said: "When I was at Scete, the works of the soul were our work; we regarded handiwork as secondary work. But now the work of the soul has become secondary work and the [former] secondary work the [main] work."[55]

Theodore of Phermē 11 [10.177]   A brother asked him: "Of what nature is the work of the soul (which we now regard as secondary work) and what is the nature of the [former] secondary work which we now regard as our [main] work?" The elder said to him: "All the things that come about by the commandment of God are the work of the soul; but to work and to gain for oneself, that we ought to regard as secondary work." The brother said to him: "Explain this proposition to me." The elder said to him: "Imagine you hear that I am ill and you ought to visit me. You say to yourself: 'Am I going to abandon my work and go right now? First I will complete it and then go.' Then another pretext occurs to you and you may not go at all. Or again a brother says to you: 'Give me a hand, brother,' and you say: 'Am I going to abandon my work to come and work with him?' If

[54]i.e. the brother either still had a hankering for life in the world or was not seriously trying to become a monk.

[55]cf. John the Eunuch 1.

you do not go, you deviate from the commandment of God (which is the work of the soul) to perform the secondary work—which is your handiwork."

Theodore of Phermē 12   Abba Theodore of Phermē said that a person who is grounded in penitence is not bound by precept.[56]

Theodore of Phermē 13   The same [elder] said: "There is no other virtue like not belittling."

Theodore of Phermē 14   He also said: "The person who learns the sweetness of the cell does not dishonor his neighbor in avoiding him."

Theodore of Phermē 15   He also said: "Unless I cut myself off from these feelings of pity they will not allow me to be a monk."

Theodore of Phermē 16 [10.35]   He also said: "Many are they who have chosen repose at this time before the Lord provides [it] for them."

Theodore of Phermē 17   He also said: "Do not sleep in a place where there is a woman."

Theodore of Phermē 18   A brother questioned Abba Theodore, saying: "I want to carry out the commandments." The elder told him about Abba Theonas: that he too once said: "I want to settle my account with God." He took flour to the bakery and made some loaves. When the poor asked of him, he gave them the loaves. Then when others also asked, he gave them the baskets and the mantle he was wearing. He went into his cell, his shawl about his loins and, like that, he reproached himself again, saying: "I have not carried out the commandment of God."

Theodore of Phermē 19   Once Abba Joseph was ill and he sent to Abba Theodore saying: "Come, so I can see you before I leave the body." It was midweek and he did not go. He sent, saying: "If you wait

[56]See the saying of John the Coenobite and the accompanying note, below.

until Saturday, I will come; but if you depart we shall see each other in that [other] world."

Theodore of Phermē 20   A brother said to Abba Theodore: "Tell me a saying for I am lost." With an effort he said: "I myself am in danger; what can I say to you?"

Theodore of Phermē 21   A brother came to Abba Theodore so he could teach him to sew and he brought some cord to him but the elder said to him: "Go away and come here at dawn." The elder got up, damped the cord for him and prepared what was needed, saying: "Do it like this and like this"—and left him. The elder went into his cell and sat down; then, when it was time, he made him something to eat and sent him off. He came back at dawn and the elder said to him: "Take your cord from here and go away. You came to put temptation and care in my way"—and he never let him in again.

Theodore of Phermē 22   The disciple of Abba Theodore said: "Somebody once came selling onions and he filled me a bowl. The elder said: 'Fill it with grain and give it to him.' There were two piles of grain, one cleaned, the other uncleaned, so I filled it from the uncleaned. The elder gave me a sharp and sorrowful look and I was so afraid I fell and broke the bowl. I prostrated myself before him and the elder said: 'Get up; it is not your fault but mine—for speaking to you.' The elder went in, filled the fold of his garment with cleaned grain and gave it to him together with the onions."

Theodore of Phermē 23   Abba Theodore once went with a brother to draw water. The brother arrived first at the lake and saw a serpent. The elder said to him: "Go tread on its head," but he was afraid and did not go. But the elder came and, when the beast saw him, it fled into the desert, put to shame.

Theodore of Phermē 24 [7.10]   Somebody asked Abba Theodore: "If a sudden catastrophe occurred, would you too be afraid, abba?" The elder said to him: "If the sky were to cleave to the earth,

Theodore would not be afraid." [The brother] had been praying God to take away timidity from him; that was why he asked him.

Theodore of Phermē 25 [15.33]   It was said of him that, when he became deacon at Scete, he was unwilling to acquiesce in serving as a deacon and ran off to several places. The elders brought him back again, saying: "Do not abandon your diaconate." Abba Theodore said to them: "Let me be and I will beseech God to convince me whether I should stay at the post of my function." As he besought God he said: "O God, if it be your will that I stay at the post of my function, convince me." There was shown to him a pillar of fire from earth to heaven; and there was a voice: "If you can be like this pillar, go and serve as a deacon." When he heard this, he resolved never to acquiesce. Thus when he came into church the brothers prostrated themselves before him, saying: "If you do not want to serve as deacon, at least hold the chalice," but he would not agree, saying: "If you do not excuse me I will move away from this place," and so they excused him.

Theodore of Phermē 26   They used to say of him that he came to stay at Phermē when Scete was devastated. He became ill when he grew old so they used to bring him some victuals. He gave what the first one brought to the second and so forth in order; what he received from the first he conferred on another; but when it was mealtime, he would eat what [the most recent] visitor was bringing.

Theodore of Phermē 27   They used to say of Abba Theodore that while he was staying at Scete there came to him a demon wanting to come in and he tied it up outside the cell. Then again another demon came [attempting] to enter and he tied that one up. There was added a third demon who came and, finding the two tied up, he said to them: "Why are you standing out here?" They said to him: "Because he is sitting inside, not letting us come in." Playing the tyrant [this demon] undertook to get in—but the elder tied that one up too. In their fear of the elder's prayers, they started begging him, saying: "Let us go!" and the elder said: "Begone!"—and at that, off they went, put to shame.

Theodore of Phermē 28   One of the fathers recounted of Abba Theodore of Phermē: "I went to him one afternoon and found him wearing a ragged *leviton*. His chest was bare and his cowl was hanging down in front. And—lo and behold—there came to see him a count. When he knocked, the elder went out to open [the gate]. He met him then sat down at the gate to speak with him. I took a piece of a shawl and covered his shoulders with it but the elder raised his hand and threw it off. When the count had gone away, I said to him: 'Abba, why did you do that? The man came to reap some benefit, not to be offended.' 'What are you telling me, abba?' the elder said to me; 'Are we now subservient to men? We did what was needed and then he went his way. He who wishes to reap benefit will benefit and he who wishes to be offended will take offense; but I present myself just as I am.' He instructed his disciple: 'If anybody comes wanting to see me, do not ever say anything suited to the person; if I am eating, say: 'He is eating,' and if I am sleeping, say: 'He is asleep.' "

Theodore of Phermē 29   Three brigands once came upon him. With two of them holding him the one began making off with his goods. When he had taken the books, he wanted to get the *leviton* too, then [the elder] said to them: "Leave that," but they would not. He put out his hands and tore it in two. They were afraid when they saw that [so] the elder said to them: "Have no fear; divide it into four pieces: take three and leave one"—and so they did. Because he got his piece, [this was] the *leviton* he wore for the *synaxis*.

THEODORE OF ENATON

Enaton indicates the ninth milepost to the west of Alexandria, a monastic center of some importance in the fifth century; see the sayings of Longinus and Lucius, below.

Theodore of Enaton 1   Abba Theodore of Enaton said: "I used to live in the desert when I was younger. I went to the bakery to make two batches and found a brother there who wanted to make some loaves, but he had nobody to give him a hand, so I left mine and gave him a hand. When I was free, another brother came and I gave him a hand too and made buns. There also came a third one and I did likewise—and so I did for each one who came; I made six batches. When at last nobody else was coming, I made my own two batches.

Theodore of Enaton 2 [7.11]   They used to say of Abba Theodore and Abba Lucius of Enaton that they spent fifty years mocking their *logismoi*, saying: "After this winter we are moving on." When summer came round again they would say: "After this summer we are going somewhere else"—and the ever-memorable fathers went on like that all the time.

Theodore of Enaton 3 [11.35]   Abba Theodore of Enaton said: "If God were to lay to our account our lack of attention in prayers and our distractions in psalm-singing, we could not be saved."

THEODORE OF SCETE

[A brother questioned] Abba Theodore of Scete [on the subject of *porneia* and the elder][57] and said: "The *logismos* comes along; it terrifies me and grabs my attention but it cannot make me perform the deed. It just hinders me from being virtuous. The man who is watchful shakes it off and gets up to pray."

---

[57]The words in [...] are not found in the Greek text, but appear in several versions.

Theodore of Eleutheropolis

There is no mention elsewhere of either of the fathers named here;
Eleutheropolis is the hometown of Epiphanius (q.v.).

Abba Abraham the Iberian asked Abba Theodore of Eleutheropolis: "Father, which is better: to acquire distinction for myself
or disgrace?" The elder said: "For my own part, I want to acquire
distinction rather than disgrace. For if I do a good deed and reap
distinction, I can denounce my *logismos* on the grounds that I am
not worthy of that distinction. But disgrace results from disgusting
deeds, so how can I console my heart when folk have been offended
with me? Therefore it is better to do good and receive distinction."
"You have spoken well, father," Abba Abraham said.

Theodotus

Theodotus 1 [4.19]   Abba Theodotus said: "Shortage of bread
depletes the body of the monk," but another of the elders[58] used to
say that the all-night vigil depletes the body more.

Theodotus S 1 [N 11, Guy 22]   He also said: "Do not judge the one
guilty of *porneia* if you are chaste yourself, for in so doing you transgress the commandment: He who says 'indulge not in *porneia*' also
says: 'Do not judge' [Jas 2.11]."

Theonas

Theonas 1 [11.36]   Abba Theonas said: "We are taken prisoner by
the passions of the flesh because of our lack of mental attention in
our contemplation of God."

[58]Named Abba Daniel elsewhere.

THEOPHILUS OF ALEXANDRIA

In spite of his determined opposition to John Chrysostom, Theoph-
ilus (Archbishop of Alexandria 385–412) probably gained his place
here and the title of abba on account of his condemnation of
Origenism, as did Epiphanius. Yet his relations with monks were
by no means cordial.

Theophilus 1 [15.31]   The blessed archbishop Theophilus once
visited the Mount of Nitria and the abba of the Mount came to him.
The archbishop said to him: "What did you find in this way [of life]
that is extra, father?" The elder said to him: "Always to accuse and
blame oneself." Abba Theophilus said to him: "There is indeed no
other way but this one."

Theophilus 2 [15.59]   The same Abba Theophilus the archbishop
once visited Scete. When the brothers were assembled they said to
Abba Pambo: "Tell the pope one saying so he might reap benefit in
this place." Said the elder to them: "If he reaps no benefit from my
silence, nor can he benefit from my speaking."

Theophilus 3 [N 162, 4.76]   Some fathers once went into Alexandria at the invitation of Theophilus the archbishop to offer prayer
and tear down the [pagan] temples. As they were eating with him,
veal was set on the table and they began eating indiscriminately.
Taking a slice, the bishop gave it to the elder nearest to him saying:
"Here, this is a good slice; eat, abba." They however replied: "We were
eating vegetables until now; if it is flesh, we are not biting on it," and
not one of them went on tasting it.

Theophilus 4   The same Abba Theophilus would say: "What fear,
trembling, and anguish we are going to see when the soul is separated from the body! A host and a force of adversaries, the rulers of
darkness, will come upon us; world rulers of wickedness, powers
and authorities, the spirits of wickedness, and in some manner of
trial they will detain the soul and get the better of it, bringing forth

all the sins it has committed, knowingly or in ignorance, from youth until the age at which it was taken. They will stand up accusing [it] of everything done by it. Then what trembling do you think the soul will experience at that time until the sentence is given and its freedom comes about? That is its moment of anguish, until it sees what the outcome will be. But then again the divine forces are standing in the face of the enemies and they are bringing forth [the soul's] good [deeds]. Then the soul, standing in the middle, understands in what sort of fear and trembling it is standing until its case receives a sentence from the just judge. If [the soul] is worthy, [the adverse forces] receive a rebuke and [the soul] is seized away from them. Then you are without concern, or rather you are dwelling (as it is written): 'As the dwelling place of all who delight is in you' [Ps 86.7]. Then will be fulfilled that which is written: 'Woe, sorrow, and mourning are fled away' [Is 35.10]. Then [the soul], set free, will proceed to that unspeakable joy and glory in which it is to be established. But if it be found to have lived in neglect, it will hear the most terrible voice: 'Let the impious one be taken away, that it not see the Lord's glory' [Is 26.10]. Then will the day of wrath overtake it, a day of affliction, a day of darkness and gloom. Handed over to the outer darkness and condemned to the eternal fire, it will be punished for unbounded ages. Where then is the boasting of the world? Where the vainglory? Where the luxury, where the relaxation, where the pomp, where the repose, where the vaunting, where the riches, the nobility, father, mother, brother? And who of these will be able to draw out [the soul] that is being burned with fire or subject to sharp tortures? These things being so, in what holy and devout activities must we exist? What love ought we to possess, what struggle, what way of life, what race [to run], what scrupulosity, what prayer, what assurance? 'Seeing that we are expecting such things,' he says, 'let us be eager to be found unspotted and unblemished by him in peace' [2 Pet 3.14] so we may be made worthy to hear him saying: 'Come you blessed of my father, inherit the kingdom prepared for you from the foundation of the world' [Mt 25.34] for ever and ever, amen."

Theophilus 5 [3.15]   When the same Abba Theophilus, the arch-bishop, was at the point of death, he said: "Blessed are you, Abba Arsenius, for you were ever mindful of this hour."

THEODORA

Nothing is known of Amma Theodora other than what can be learnt from these sayings attributed to her.

Theodora 1   Amma Theodora asked Pope Theophilus what is the meaning of the Apostle's expression: "Redeeming the time" [Col 4.5], and he said to her: "The term indicates the profit [to be gained]. For instance: an occasion for being maltreated comes upon you. Purchase the time of maltreatment with humility and long-suffering and gain a reward for yourself. Does an occasion of dishonor occur? Purchase the time with forbearance and get rewarded. And every adverse situation produces a reward for us if we are willing."

Theodora 2   Amma Theodora said: "Strive to enter by the narrow gate [Lk 13.24, Mt 7.13]. As trees cannot bear fruit if they do not undergo winter storms and rains, so for us this age is a winter. We will be not able to inherit the Kingdom of Heaven other than through many afflictions and temptations."

Theodora 3   She also said: "It is good to be in *hesychia*. A wise man practices *hesychia* and it is truly a great thing for a virgin or a monk to be in *hesychia*, especially for the young ones. But be aware that if one proposes to take up *hesychia*, the evil one comes right away and weighs down the soul by attacks of *accidie* and discouragement and with *logismoi*. He weighs down the body too with illnesses, debility, by enfeebling the knees and all the members; draining the energy of soul and body so that I am sick and cannot offer the *synaxis*. But if we are vigilant all these things are dissolved. There was a monk who, as soon as he began to offer the *synaxis*, started being hot and cold with a severe headache. In this state he said to himself: 'Here, I am sick and I shall die any time. Let me get up and offer the *synaxis* before I die,' and he coerced himself against this *logismos* and offered the *synaxis*. And as he was finishing the *synaxis* his fever finished too. And again the brother resisted this *logismos*, offered the *synaxis*, and conquered the evil *logismos*."

Theodora 4   The same Amma Theodora also said: "A devout person was once reviled by somebody and he said to him: 'I too could have said the same to you but the law of God closes my mouth.'" She used to say this too: "A Christian having a discussion with a Manichaean about the body spoke thus: 'Impose the law on the body and you shall see that the body [belongs] to the Creator.'"

Theodora 5   The same [amma] also said that the teacher ought to be a stranger to the lust for power,[59] alien to vainglory, distant from pride, not taken in by flattery, not blinded by gifts, not conquered by his belly, not prey to anger; but long-suffering, gentle, and as humble-minded as possible.[60] He should be approved and patient; caring and a lover of souls."

Theodora 6   The same [amma] also said: "It is neither spiritual discipline nor vigil nor diverse toil that saves us if there be not genuine humble-mindedness. For there was a solitary driving off demons and he used to examine them: 'What makes you come out? Is it fasting?' They would say: 'We neither eat nor drink.' 'Vigil?' he would say—and they: 'We do not sleep.' 'Withdrawal [from the world]?' and they would say: 'We exist in the deserts.' 'What then makes you come out?' and they would say: 'Nothing conquers us other than humble-mindedness.' Do you see that humble-mindedness is victorious against demons?"

Theodora 7   Amma Theodora also said: "There was a monk who had so many temptations that he said: 'I am going away from here.'

[59] or "the love of money."
[60] or "and above all, humble-minded."

When he put on his own sandals he saw another man putting his sandals on too, saying to him: 'You are not leaving because of me? Here, I am going ahead of you wherever you go.'"

Theodora S 1 [Guy 22–23] The same [amma] was asked about what one hears: "How can a person at one and the same time listen to worldly talking yet nevertheless be with God alone, as you say?" She said: "When you are sitting at table and there are plenty of provisions, you partake but not with pleasure. So too, if worldly discourse comes to your ears, keep your heart fixed on God and in this way you will hear without pleasure and not be harmed at all."

Theodora S 2 [Guy 23] Another monk had an itching of the body and a multitude of lice (and he was from a wealthy background). The demons would say to him: "You are content to live like this, sprouting worms?"—and that one conquered by long-suffering endurance.

Theodora S 3 [Guy 23] One of the elders asked Amma Theodora: "At the resurrection of the dead how do we arise?" She said: "We have Christ our God who died for us and arose as a pledge, an example, and a first-fruit."

I—*Iota*

JOHN COLOBOS (THE DWARF)

"Who is John who has the whole of Scete hanging on his little finger on account of his humility?" one father asked (John Colobos 36). He was "one of the glories of Scete in the fourth century . . . remarkable not only for his virtues and the spiritual gifts with which God favored him, but also for his natural qualities of gentleness and goodness, which drew souls to him. In spite of his devotion to solitude he did not hesitate to help others, even to go into the city to save a prostitute . . ."[61]

John Colobos 1 [14.4] They used to say of Abba John Colobos that, having withdrawn from the world to be with an elder from Thebes at Scete, he was living in the desert. His abba took some dry wood, planted it and said to him: "Irrigate it every day with a bottle of water until it bears fruit." Water was a long way from them, so one had to go in the evening and return at dawn. After three years [the dry wood] became alive and bore fruit. The elder took its fruit and brought it to the church, saying to the brothers: "Take and eat some fruit of obedience."[62]

John Colobos 2 [10.36] They used to say of Abba John Colobos that he once said to his elder brother: "I wanted to be free of concern just as the angels are free of concern, not working at all, but unceasingly worshipping God" [cf. Mt 6.25–29, Lk 12.22–28]. He took off his garment and went out into the desert. After he had spent a week

[61]Regnault, *Les Sentences*, 123.

[62]A much longer version of this tale in which the stick does *not* take root is told by John Cassian of Abba John of Lycopolis; *Inst.* 4.24.

there, he came back to his brother. When he knocked at the gate, before opening up, [his brother] gave heed to him, saying: "Who are you?" "I am your brother John," he said, and in reply [the other] said to him: "John has become an angel and is no longer among humans." But he begged him saying: "It is I"—but he did not open up for him; he left him to be afflicted until dawn. When he finally did open, he said to him: "You are human, so you have got to get back to work again in order to be fed." He prostrated himself saying: "Forgive me."

John Colobos 3 [4.20]   Abba John Colobos said: "If a king wishes to capture a city of the enemy, he first takes control of the water supply and the supply of food: thus the enemy submits to him, reduced by famine. So it is with the passions of the flesh too: if a person exists with fasting and hunger, the enemy wastes away from his soul."

John Colobos 4 [5.3]   He also said: "He who stuffs himself and speaks with a child has already indulged in *porneia* with him in the *logismos*."

John Colobos 5 [4.21]   He also said: "Travelling up the road from Scete with some rope one day I saw the camel-driver talking and inciting me to get angry. I abandoned my wares and fled."

John Colobos 6   On another occasion too, at harvest time, he heard a brother speaking angrily to his neighbor, saying: "Ah, you too . . . ?" He quit the harvesting and fled.

John Colobos 7 [10.37]   Some elders happened to be eating together at Scete and Abba John Colobos was with them too. A great priest got up to offer the bottle of water but nobody accepted any of it from him, except only John Colobos. They were astonished and said to him: "How did you who are the most junior of all dare to be served by the priest?" But he said to them: "For my part, when I get up to offer the bottle, I am delighted if everybody accepts—so that I get a reward. So for this reason I too accepted—in order to get a reward for him and so he would not be distressed since nobody had accepted from him." They were astonished when he said this and they much benefitted from his discretion.

John Colobos 8 [16.4]   One day he was sitting before the church surrounded by the brothers who were questioning him about their *logismoi*. One of the elders, one who was embattled by jealousy, saw him and said to him: "Your bottle is full of poison, John." Abba John said to him: "So it is, abba; and you said that seeing only the outside. What could you say if you were to see the inside?"

John Colobos 9 [3.16]   The fathers used to say that once when the brothers were eating at an *agapē*, one of the brothers laughed at table and Abba John wept when he saw him, saying: "What on earth can that brother have in his heart that he laughed when he should rather have wept, since he is eating an *agapē*?"

John Colobos 10 [11.37]   Some of the brothers once came to test him whether he neither let his own *logismos* be distracted nor spoke of a matter pertaining to this world. They said to him: "We thank God that it rained heavily this year; the palm-trees were watered and they are putting out shoots, so the brothers are finding [materials for] their handiwork." Abba John said to them: "So it is with the Holy Spirit; when he descends into the hearts of the holy ones they are renewed and put out shoots in the fear of God."

John Colobos 11 [11.38]   They also used to say of him that he once braided cord for two baskets and stitched it together as one basket but didn't realize it until he approached the wall, for his *logismos* was occupied in contemplation.

John Colobos 12 [11.40]   Abba John said: "I am like somebody sitting beneath a large tree who sees many wild beasts and serpents coming at him. Seeing that he cannot withstand them, he runs up into the tree and is saved. So it is with me: I stay in my cell and I see the evil *logismoi* before me. And when I do not have the strength [to oppose] them, I flee to God in prayer and am saved from the enemy."

John Colobos 13 [7.12]   Abba Poemen said about Abba John Colobos that he besought God and the passions were taken away from him; he then became without a care. He went and said to an elder: "I see myself experiencing repose with no battle on my hands." The elder said to him: "Go and beseech God for the battle to come upon you, likewise the affliction and the humility you had before, because it is by means of battles that the soul makes progress." So he besought [God] and, when the battle came, he no longer prayed for it to be taken away but would say: "Lord, give me endurance in the battles."

John Colobos 14 [18.10]   Abba John said: "One of the elders had a vision when he was in a trance: here there were three monks standing on the other shore of the sea. A voice came to them from this shore saying: 'Take wings of fire and come to me.' Two of them took [wings] and flew to the other shore but the other remained [there], weeping greatly and crying out. Wings were later given to him, not of fire, but feeble and weak. He got across with much affliction, being dipped into the sea and toiling to rise from it. So it is with this generation: if it receives wings at all, they are not of fire but only just of the feeble and weak variety."

John Colobos 15 [9.12]   A brother asked Abba John Colobos: "How is it that my soul, wounded though it be, is not ashamed to slander[63] my neighbor?" The elder told him a parable about slandering: "There was a man who was poor and he had a wife. Seeing another [woman] who could be persuaded, he took her too; both women were naked. Now there was a fair somewhere and they begged him, saying: 'Take us with you.' He took them both, put them into a barrel, got into a boat and came to the fairground. When it became hot and people were resting, one of the women peeped out and, seeing nobody, ran to the rubbish dump, gathered together some old rags

---

[63]*katalalein*, "to backbite, to recriminate."

and made herself a skirt; then she boldly paraded around. But the other woman, staying naked inside [the barrel] said: 'Just look at that whore! She has no shame to walk around naked!' Her husband was annoyed; he said: 'How amazing! At least she covers her unseemliness; are you, totally naked, not ashamed, speaking like that?' That is how it is with slandering."

John Colobos 16   Concerning the soul that is willing to repent, the elder used to say to the brother: "There was a beautiful prostitute in a certain city who had many friends. One of the governors came to her and said to her: 'Promise me to be chaste and I will take you for my wife,' and she so promised him. He took her and brought her to his house. But her lovers were looking for her and saying: 'So-and-so the governor has taken her to his house; if we go to his house and he learns of it he will punish us. But come on behind the house; we will whistle for her. When she recognizes the sound of the whistling she will come down to us and we will not be reproachable.' But when she heard the whistle she blocked her ears, hastened to the inner room and closed the doors." He used to say the prostitute is the soul; her lovers are the passions and people; the governor is Christ; the interior dwelling is the eternal mansion; they who whistle to her are the evil demons. [The soul] always takes refuge in the Lord.

John Colobos 17 [17.10]   Once when Abba John was going up from Scete with other brothers their guide lost his way and it was night. The brothers said to Abba John: "What shall we do, abba, for the brother has lost the way; maybe we will wander off and die?" The elder said to them: "If we tell him he will be grieved and ashamed. But look here: I will pretend to be sick and will say: 'I cannot travel [further] so I am staying here until dawn,'" and so he did. The rest of them said: "Neither are we going on; we are staying with you." They stayed [there] until dawn and did not offend the brother.

John Colobos 18 [11.41]   There was an elder at Scete who was hardworking so far as his body was concerned but not too sharp in his *logismoi*. So he went to Abba John Colobos to ask him about forget-fulness. Having heard a saying from him he returned to his cell—and forgot what Abba John said to him; so he went back again to ask him. Having heard the same saying from him again, he returned; but when he reached his own cell, he forgot again. He went on com-ing many times and being overcome by forgetfulness on returning. Later on he met the elder and said to him: "Do you know, abba, I forgot what you said to me again, but I did not come [back] so as not to trouble you." Abba John said to him: "Go and light a lamp," and he lit one. He spoke to him again: "Get some other lamps and light them from it," and he did so. And Abba John said to the elder: "The lamp was not damaged in any way when you lit the other lamps from it, was it?" "No," he said. So the elder said: "Neither is John; if the whole of Scete were to come to me it would not impede me from the grace of Christ, so come whenever you wish, without questioning." And thus, by the patient endurance of them both, God removed the forgetfulness from the elder. This was the practice of the [monks] at Scete: to give eagerness to the combatants and to coerce themselves to win each other over for the good.

John Colobos 19 [11.44]   A brother asked Abba John: "What am I to do? There is a brother who often comes to take me to work, but I am ailing and weak; I am exhausted by that sort of thing. So what shall I do [to keep] the commandment?" In answer the elder said to him: "Caleb said to Joshua the son of Nun: 'I was forty years old when Moses, the servant of the Lord, sent me and you to this land and now I am eighty-five. I am as strong now as I was then to go to and to come back from war' [Josh 7.10–11]. So do you too go [to work] if you are capable of coming out as you enter in. If you are not capable of doing that, remain in your cell weeping for your sins; for, if they find you sorrowing, they will not oblige you to go out."

John Colobos 20   Abba John said: "Who sold Joseph?" and some brother replied: "It was his brothers [Gen 37.36]. The elder said to him: "No; it was his humility that sold him. He could have said: 'I am their brother' and contradicted them, but he kept quiet—and sold himself by humility. And humility made him as a commander in Egypt" [Gen 41.41].

John Colobos 21 Abba John said: "We have left aside the light burden [Mt 11.30] (that is: to blame ourselves) and borne the heavy one (meaning: to justify ourselves)."

John Colobos 22 [15.35] The same [elder] said: "Humble-mindedness and the fear of God are superior to all the virtues."

John Colobos 23 [cf. Tithoes 6] The same [elder] was once sitting in the church when he heaved a sigh, unaware that there was somebody behind him. When he realized it, he prostrated himself saying: "Forgive me, abba; I have not yet been trained."

John Colobos 24 [11.42] The same [elder] used to say to his disciple: "Let us honor *the One* and all will honor us. If we despise *the One* (who is God) everybody will despise us and we will be on the road to ruin."

John Colobos 25 They used to say of Abba John that, coming into the church at Scete, he heard the disputation of some brothers. He returned to his cell, walked around it three times then went in. Some brothers who saw him were at a loss as to why he did this. They came to ask him and he said to them: "My ears were full of disputation so I walked around to cleanse them and so entered my cell in *hesychia* of mind."

John Colobos 26 A brother once came to the cell of Abba John in the evening, anxious to get away. While they were speaking about virtues, dawn broke and they were not aware of it. [The elder] came out to see him on his way and they went on talking until the sixth hour. He brought him in and when [the brother] had eaten, he went away.

John Colobos 27 [11.43] Abba John used to say: "Prison means staying soberly in one's cell, ever mindful of God, for that is [the meaning of]: 'I was in prison and you came to me' [Mt 25.36]."

John Colobos 28 [4.61]   He also said: "Who is strong as the lion? Yet it falls into a snare because of its belly and all its strength is brought low."

John Colobos 29   He also said: "While the fathers of Scete were eating only bread and salt they would say: 'Let us not oblige ourselves [to eat] bread and salt,' and thus were they strong for the work of God.'"

John Colobos 30   A brother came to get some baskets from Abba John's; he came out and said to him: "What do you want, brother?" "Some baskets, abba," he said. He went in to get them—and forgot. He sat there sewing. [The brother] knocked again; when [the elder] came out he said to him: "Bring the basket, abba." He went in again and sat down again to sew. The other knocked again; he came out and said: "What do you want, brother?" "The basket, abba," he said and, taking him by the hand, [the elder] led him inside saying: "If it is baskets you want, take [some] and go your way; I do not have the time."

John Colobos 31 [11.39]   The camel-driver came one day to take his wares and go off to another place but [Abba John], going in to fetch him the cord, forgot, having his thoughts fixed on God. So the camel-driver alerted him again by knocking at the door and, again, Abba John went in and forgot. When the camel-driver knocked a third time, he went in saying: "Cord, camel. Cord, camel." He was saying this so he would not forget.

John Colobos 32   The same [elder] was "fervent in spirit" [Rom 12.11]. Somebody visiting him praised his work (he was making cord) but he kept silent. That person spoke to him again, and again he kept silent. The third time he said to the visitor: "Ever since you came in here you have been taking God from me."

John Colobos 33   An elder came to Abba John's cell and found him sleeping, with an angel standing by, fanning him. Having seen, he went away. When [Abba John] got up he said to his disciple: "Did somebody come here when I was sleeping?" "Yes," he said; "elder so-and-so," and Abba John perceived that the elder was of his [own] stature and that he saw the angel.

John Colobos 34 [1.13]   Abba John said: "Personally, I would like a person to participate a little in all the virtues. So when you arise at dawn each day, make a fresh start in every virtue and commandment of God with greatest patience, with fear and long-suffering, in the love of God, with all spiritual and physical zeal and much humiliation; enduring affliction and constriction of the heart, with much prayer and intercession, with groans, in purity of the tongue and restriction of the eyes, being reviled and not getting angry, living peaceably and not giving back evil for evil; not noticing the faults of others; not measuring oneself (being beneath the whole of creation), having renounced material goods and the things that pertain to the flesh; on a cross, in combat, in poverty of spirit, in determination and spiritual asceticism; in fasting, in repentance, in weeping, in the strife of battle, in discretion, in purity of the soul, in generous sharing, [doing] your handiwork in *hesychia*, in nightly vigils, in hunger and thirst, in cold and nakedness, in toils, closing your tomb as though you were already dead, so that all the time you are thinking your death is at hand."

John Colobos 35   They used to say of the same Abba John that when he came from the harvest or from visiting elders, he would devote himself to prayer, meditation, and psalm-singing until his *logismos* was restored to its former state.

John Colobos 36   One of the fathers said of him: "Who is John who has the whole of Scete hanging on his little finger on account of his humility?"

John Colobos 37   One of the fathers asked Abba John Colobos: "What is a monk?" and he said: "Toil, for the monk toils at every task. The monk is like that."

John Colobos 38   Abba John Colobos said: "A spiritual elder sequestered himself; he was distinguished in the city and had a great reputation. It was revealed to him: 'One of the holy ones is about to depart; come and greet him before he dies.' He thought to himself: 'If I come out in the daytime, folk will come running. My reputation will be greatly enhanced and I will experience no repose from that. I will leave in the evening when it is dark, unknown to all,' so he came out of the cell in the evening, wishing to be unknown. But here two angels with torches were sent by God to light his way—and then the whole city came running, ogling his reputation. The more he attempted to escape it, the more it was augmented. In this was fulfilled that which is written: "Whosoever humbles himself shall be exalted" [Lk 14.11].

John Colobos 39   Abba John Colobos said: "It is not possible to build the house from top to bottom, but [only] from the foundation up." They said to him: "What is this saying?" The elder replied: "The foundation is one's neighbor to be won over and he ought to come first; for on him hang all the commandments of Christ" [Mt 22.40].

John Colobos 40 [13.17; cf. N 43]   They used to recount of Abba John Colobos that a certain young woman's parents died, leaving her an orphan; her name was Paēsia. She chose to make her house a hostel for the use of the fathers of Scete. So it came about that she stayed there for some time offering hospitality and caring for the fathers. After a while, as her resources were eroded away, she began to be in need. Some perverted people attached themselves to her and turned her aside from her excellent intention; she began leading a disorderly life, going even so far as to prostitute herself. The fathers heard of this and were deeply saddened. Appealing to Abba John Colobos, they said: "We have heard concerning that sister that she is leading a disorderly life. She displayed her charity to us when she was able to do so; let us too now display charity to her and help her. Take the trouble of going to her and dealing with her situation according to the wisdom that God has given you." So Abba John went to her place and said to the old doorkeeper: "Announce me to your mistress," but she sent him off saying: "You [people] consumed her substance at first and now, look, she is poor." Abba John said to her: "Tell her I can be very beneficial to her," but, grinning, her servants said to him: "So what can you give her, since you wish to meet her?" But he answered saying: "How do you know what I intend to provide for her?" The old woman went up however and told her about him and the younger woman said to her: "Those monks are always going up and down the Red Sea and they find pearls." She decked herself out and said to her: "Kindly bring him to me." When he came she had installed herself on the couch in anticipation. When Abba John came he sat down beside her; looking into her face, he said to her: "What have you got against Jesus that you are come to this?" She froze up on hearing this and, bowing his head, Abba John began to weep bitterly, so she said to him: "Abba, why are you weeping?" Raising his head, he bent over again weeping and said to her: "I see that Satan is laughing in your face; am I not to weep?" On hearing this she said to him: "Is there repentance, abba?" "Yes, there is," he said to her, and she said to him: "Take me wherever you like." "Let us go," he said to her; she got up to follow him. Abba John noted that she gave no instructions or said anything about her house and he was amazed. It was late when they arrived at the desert. Making something like a small pillow of sand for her, he made the sign of the cross and said to her: "Sleep here." He made one for himself a little distance away, offered his customary prayers and lay down. Waking around midnight, he saw something like a path of light fixed from heaven to her and he beheld the angels of God taking up her soul. Getting up, he went and nudged her with his foot. Seeing that she had died, he flung himself face down, beseeching God, and he heard that her one hour of repentance had been accepted ahead of the repentance of many who take their time and do not demonstrate the ardor of such repentance.

John Colobos S 1 [Guy 23]   The elder also said: "There were three philosophers who were friends, and when one of them died he bequeathed his son to one of his friends. But when [the son] became a young man he made overtures to the wife of the one who had raised him. When he learnt of it, that person threw him out and, even though he was very repentant, he would not have him back, saying: 'Go and do three years as a river worker and in that way I will forgive you.' He came three years later and [the other] said to him: 'You have not yet repented; go and do another three years, giving away your earnings and enduring insult.' So he did; and after that [the other] said to him: 'So now go to the city of the Athenians and learn philosophy.' Now there was an old man sitting at the Philosophers' Gate insulting those who came in by it. When the young man was insulted, he laughed. The old man said to him: 'What is this? I insulted you and you laughed!' He said: 'Do you not want me to laugh? For three years I have been giving away my earnings to get insulted—and here today you insult me *gratis*! That is why I laughed.'" Abba John said: "This is the gate of God, and our fathers joyfully entered the city of God through many insults."

John Colobos S 2 [Guy 23]   The same [elder] said to his brother: "Even though we are sadly impoverished in the sight of folk, let us rejoice in the way we are honored in the presence of God."

John Colobos S 3 [Guy 24]   Abba Poemen used to say that Abba John said: "The holy ones are like a garden of trees bearing different fruits but irrigated by the same water. The activity of one holy one is different from that of another, but there is one spirit at work in them all."

John Colobos S 4 [Guy 24]   The same [elder] said: "If a person has something of God in his soul he can remain in his cell even though he have nothing of this world. And if a person has something of this world and nothing of God he too can remain in his cell, having something of this world. But he who has nothing either of God or of this world cannot remain in his cell at all."

John Colobos S 5 [Guy 24] The elder also said: "Notice that the first blow the devil struck at Job began by being directed at his riches and he saw that [Job] was neither distressed nor withdrew from God. He struck the second blow at [Job's] body and neither did the noble warrior sin in the words of his mouth at this [Job 16–2.10], for within him he had the riches of God and he was always drawing on these."

John Colobos S 6 [Guy 24] Once he was sitting at Scete with the brothers around him asking about their *logismoi*. One of the elders said to him: "John, you are like a prostitute who makes herself beautiful, increasing the number of her lovers." Abba John put his arm about him saying: "What you say is true, father." Afterwards one of his disciples said: "Were you not troubled within, abba?" "No," he said, "for as I am outside, so I am within."

John Colobos S 7 [Guy 24] They also used to say of him that [the wages of] all the labor he expended on the harvest he would take and bring to Scete saying: "My widows and orphans are at Scete."

JOHN THE COENOBITE

A sixth-century Latin version of this item[64] does not say that this John lived in a coenobion, which makes more sense. It also ends with the twelfth saying attributed to Theodore of Phermē (above).

There was a brother living in a coenobion much given to *askēsis*. When some brothers at Scete heard about him they came to see him. They came into the place where he was working; he greeted them then turned back to his work. When the brothers saw what he did they said to him: "John, who gave you the monastic habit or who made you a monk? Did he not teach you to relieve the brothers of their sheepskin; to say to them: 'Offer a prayer' or 'Sit down'?" He said to them: "John the sinner has no time for that."

[64]*PL* 74.381–394, No. 44, at 388D.

ISIDORE THE PRIEST AT SCETE

John Cassian calls this Isidore "the Great."[65] He pertained to the first generation of monks at Scete and was renowned for his ability to counsel difficult cases.

Isidore of Scete 1 [16.6]   They used to say of Abba Isidore the priest of Scete that if anybody had a brother who was contradictory, contemptuous, or insolent and he wanted to throw him out, he used to say: "Bring him here to me." He would take the brother [in] and save him through his long-suffering patience.

Isidore of Scete 2 [4.24]   A brother asked him: "Why do the demons fear you so very much?" The elder said to him: "Since I became a monk I have disciplined myself not to allow anger to rise up in my throat."

Isidore of Scete 3 [4.25]   He also used to say that for forty years he was aware of sin in his mind and he had never given in either to lust or to anger.

Isidore of Scete 4 [11.46]   He also said: "For my part, when I was younger and staying in my cell, I had no time limit to *synaxis*; night and day were *synaxis* for me."

Isidore of Scete 5   Abba Poemen said of Abba Isidore that he used to braid a sheaf of palm-fronds by night and the brothers would beg him, saying: "Repose yourself a little, for now you are old,' and he would say to them: "If they were to burn Isidore and scatter his ashes to the wind, then there would not be any more grace for me because the Son of God came here on our account."

Isidore of Scete 6   The same [elder] said of Abba Isidore that his *logismoi* used to say to him: "You are a great man," and he would say to them: "Am I like Abba Antony then, or have I become altogether like Abba Pambo or the rest of the fathers who have been

[65]Conf. 18.15.

well pleasing to God?" When he had produced these [examples] he experienced repose. But when the enemy used to discourage him [saying] he would be cast into chastisement after all this, he would say to them: "Even if I am cast into chastisement, I will find you beneath me."

Isidore of Scete 7   Abba Isidore said: "I once went into the marketplace to sell a few wares and, seeing anger approaching me, I left the goods and fled."

Isidore of Scete 8   Abba Isidore once went to [visit] Abba Theodore, the archbishop of Alexandria. When he returned to Scete, the brothers asked him: "How was the city?" and he said: "To tell you the truth, brothers, I did not see anybody's face other than the archbishop's." They were troubled when they heard this and they said: "Were they utterly destroyed, abba?" "Not so," he said, "but my *logismos* did not overcome me to look at anybody." They were astounded when they heard this and strengthened in their resolve to keep their eyes from wandering.

Isidore of Scete 9   The same Abba Isidore said: "The sagacity of the holy ones is this: to recognize the will of God, for a person overcomes everything 'in obedience to the truth' [1 Pet 1.22], for he is the image and likeness of God. It is more terrible than all the spirits to follow one's own heart (meaning one's own *logismos*) and not the law of God. Afterwards, one is plunged into sorrow for sin for having neither known the mystery nor found the way of the holy ones, to work in it. Now is the time to act for the Lord, for salvation [comes] in time of affliction, as it is written: 'You shall procure your souls in your patient endurance' [Lk 21.19]."

Isidore of Scete S 1   The same [elder] said of Abba Isidore that when he spoke to the brothers in church, this was the only thing he said: "Brothers, it is written: 'Forgive your neighbor that you may receive forgiveness' [Mt 6.14]."

ISIDORE OF PELUSIUM

Although he hailed from Alexandria, this Isidore (d. c. 435) is said to be "of Pelusium" (a city to the west of the Nile Delta) because that is where he was monk and priest. He does not appear to have been in contact with the fathers of Scete. The sayings attributed to him here are all taken from his voluminous writings and were added to the corpus rather late in the day.

Isidore of Pelusium 1   Abba Isidore of Pelusium used to say: "A life without a word is more advantageous than a word without life; for the first, even in silence, is advantageous, while the second is a trouble-maker when it cries out, whereas if life and word run together they constitute the portrait of all philosophy."

Isidore of Pelusium 2   The same [elder] said: "Honor the virtues, do not cultivate the things that pass away; for the former are something immortal while the latter are readily extinguished."

Isidore of Pelusium 3   He also said: "Many folk reach out for virtue but shrink from traveling the road that leads to it; others think there is no such thing as virtue. Those must be persuaded to set aside their shrinking, these be taught that virtue really is virtue."

Isidore of Pelusium 4   He also said: "Evil distances folk from God and separates them from each other. One must fly headlong from it and pursue virtue—which draws us to God and joins us with each other. The definition of virtue and philosophy is: unaffectedness with prudence."

Isidore of Pelusium 5   He also said: "Since great is the stature of humble-mindedness and [great] the calamity of boastfulness, I counsel you to embrace the former and not to fall into the latter."

Isidore of Pelusium 6   He also said: "The terrible and shameless love of riches, which is never satisfied, drives the captured soul to the ultimate of evils. Let us therefore drive it off, especially in the first stages, for if we hold on to it, it will become unmanageable."

ISAAC, PRIEST AT THE CELLS

Isaac was a disciple of Cronios, then of Theodore of Phermē. He may have been one of the Origenist monks exiled by Archbishop Theophilus in 400; he was still alive after the first devastation of Scete in 407. His sayings reveal a certain nostalgia for standards no longer maintained.

Isaac of The Cells 1   Once they came to make Abba Isaac a priest. When he heard, he fled into Egypt, went into a field, and hid amidst the crop. The fathers went after him and, when they got to that same field, sat down to rest a little there, for it was night. They set the ass free to pasture, but the ass went and stood by the elder. When they sought the ass at dawn, they found Abba Isaac too. They were amazed and wanted to bind him but he would not let them. "I am not running away any more," he said, "for it is the will of God and no matter where I run away to, I will come to it."

Isaac of The Cells 2   Abba Isaac said: "As a young man I was staying with Abba Cronios and he never told me to do a task even though he was aged and tremulous. Of his own accord he would get up and offer the water bottle to me and likewise to all. After that I stayed with Abba Theodore of Phermē and neither did he ever tell me to do anything. He would lay the table himself and then say: 'Brother, come and eat if you like.' I would say to him: 'Abba, I came to you to reap some benefit; why do you never tell me to do anything?' but the elder kept completely quiet. I went and told this to the elders. The elders came to him and said to him: 'Abba, the brother came to your holiness to reap some benefit; why do you never tell him to do anything?' The elder said to them: 'Am I the superior of a coenobion to order him around?' For the time being I don't tell him [to do] anything. He will do what he sees me doing if he wants to.' So from then on I began anticipating, doing whatever the elder was about to do. For his part, if he was doing anything, he used to do it in silence; this taught me to act in silence."

Isaac of The Cells 3   Abba Isaac and Abba Abraham were living together. Abba Abraham went in and found Abba Isaac weeping. "Why are your weeping?" he said to him, and the elder said to him: "Why should we not weep? For where can we go? Our fathers have died and our handiwork is insufficient for us [to pay] the price of the boats we take to go visiting the elders. So now we are orphaned—and that is why I too am weeping."

Isaac of The Cells 4 [4.22]   Abba Isaac said: "I know a brother who was harvesting in a field and he wanted to eat an ear of grain. He said to the owner of the field: 'Will you let me eat one ear of grain?' He was astounded on hearing this and said to him: 'The field is yours, father, and you ask me?' That was the extent to which the brother was scrupulous."

Isaac of The Cells 5 [10.44]   He also said to the brothers: "Do not bring children here; four churches at Scete have become deserted because of children."

Isaac of The Cells 6   They used to say of Abba Isaac that he used to eat ashes from the thurible [used at] the Eucharist with his bread.

Isaac of The Cells 7 [6.10]   Abba Isaac used to say to the brothers: "Our fathers and Abba Pambo wore old, patched up clothes made of palm-fiber; now you are wearing expensive clothing. Go away from here, for you have turned this location into a desert." When he was about to go harvesting, he said to them: "I am not giving you any more instructions for you do not keep them."

Isaac of The Cells 8 [6.9]   One of the fathers recounted how one of the brothers once came into the church at The Cells in the time of Abba Isaac wearing a little cloak[66] and, looking at him, the elder chased him out, saying: "This is a place for monks; you who are a worldling, you cannot stay here."

---

[66]or maybe "a garment of superior quality."

Isaac of The Cells 9   Abba Isaac said: "I never brought into my cell a grudge [*logismos*] against a brother who had offended me and I endeavored not to let a brother go to his cell who had a grudge against me."

Isaac of The Cells 10   Abba Isaac was ill with a grave illness and it was long-lasting. The brother made him a little compote and put some prunes in it—but the elder would not taste it. The brother begged him, saying: "Take a little, abba, for your sickness," and the elder said to him: "The fact is that I really wanted to spend thirty years with this sickness, brother."

Isaac of The Cells 11   They used to recount of Abba Isaac that, when he was about to die, the elders gathered around him, asking: "What shall we do after you [are gone] father?" He said: "You see the way I conducted myself in your presence? If you too are willing to follow [in that way] and keep the commandments of God he will send his grace and protect this place. If you do not keep [them] you will not remain in this place. We too grieved when our fathers were about to die but, keeping the commandments of the Lord and their instructions, we survived as though they were with us. Do you do likewise and you will be saved."

Isaac of The Cells 12 [6.11]   Abba Isaac said that Abba Pambo used to say: "The monk ought to wear the sort of clothing that, if he threw it out of the cell for three days, nobody would take it."

JOSEPH OF PANEPHO

Panepho (Panephysis) is on the eastern side of the Nile delta. John Cassian visited it and encountered a Joseph there who may be the Joseph of these sayings, in which case he was originally from Thmuis, born of an illustrious family, and it is he whose teaching is recorded in Conf. 16 and 17.[67]

[67]Conf 11.3; 16.1.

Joseph of Panepho 1 [13.1]   Some of the fathers once went up to Abba Joseph at Panepho to ask him about encountering brothers who were receiving hospitality from them: whether they should fraternize and converse freely with them. Before he was asked, the elder said to his disciple: "Take note of what I am going to do this day and bear with me." Then, placing two cushions, one on the right, the other on his left, the elder said: "Sit down," and entering his cell, he put on some old clothes, came out, and passed through the midst of them. Then in he went again, put on his [own] clothes, came out, and sat down between them. They were amazed at the elder's behavior. "Did you take note of what I did?" he said to them. "Yes," they said, and he said to them: "I was not changed by that wretched clothing, was I?" "No," they said; the elder also said: {"And I was not changed by the fine clothing?" "No," they said. He said}[68] to them: "If then I am the same person in both, just as the first [clothing] did not change me nor the second one do me any harm, so ought we to act when we encounter brothers who are guests, as it says in the holy Gospel: 'Render unto Caesar that which is Caesar's and unto God that which is God's' [Mt 22.21, Lk 20.25]. So when there are brothers present, let us receive them with joy; but when we are alone, then we need grief to remain with us." Those who heard this were amazed that he told them what was in their hearts before they asked him, and they glorified God.

Joseph of Panepho 2 [9.8]   Abba Poemen said to Abba Joseph: "Tell me how I may become a monk." Said the elder to him: "If you want to find repose both here and there, say in every situation: 'I, who am I?' and do not pass judgment on anybody."

Joseph of Panepho 3 [10.38]   The same [elder] also asked Abba Joseph: "What am I to do when the passions approach: resist them or let them come in?" The elder said to him: "Let them come in and do battle with them." He went back to Scete and stayed there. One

[68]The passage { . . . } is missing in some versions, but clearly necessary to the narrative.

of the Thebans came to Scete and said to the brothers: "I asked Abba Joseph: 'If a passion approaches me, do I resist it or do I allow it to come in?' and he said to me: 'On no account allow the passions to come in but cut them off immediately.'" So, on hearing that Abba Joseph had spoken thus to the Theban, Abba Poemen rose up and went to Panepho and said to him: "I entrusted my *logismoi* to you and here you spoke in one way to me and otherwise to the Theban." The elder said to him: "Do you not know that I love you?" "Yes," he said. "And were you not telling me to speak to you as though to myself?" "It is so," he said. "{Did I not then speak well?"}[69] the elder said to him; "For if passions come in and you give and receive [blows] to and from them, they make you more experienced. So for my part I spoke to you as though to myself. But there are others for whom it is not advantageous for the passions to approach; these need to cut them off immediately."

Joseph of Panepho 4 [10.40]   A brother asked Abba Joseph: "What am I to do, for I can neither endure hardship nor work to provide charity?" The elder said to him: "If you cannot do even one of these things, keep your conscience clear from thinking any evil of your neighbor or belittling him and you will be saved."[70]

Joseph of Panepho 5 [10.39]   One of the brothers used to say: "I once visited Abba Joseph at Lower Heracleon; there was a very beautiful mulberry tree in the monastery and, early in the day, he said to me: "Go and eat." But it was a Friday, so I did not go because of the fast. I begged him saying: "For the Lord's sake, explain this *logismos* to me. Here you said to me: 'Go and eat,' but for my part I did not go because of the fast. Then I was ashamed, thinking of your command: 'In what *logismos* was the elder speaking to me?' What then should I have done since you told me to go?" He said: "The fathers do not speak directly to the brothers at first, but perversely; and if

[69]{. . .} appears to have been omitted; the phrase is found in *Synagōgē*, 4.6.1.21.

[70]There is some confusion about the final sentence; we have given what appears to be the most likely version. Some versions add: "for God is looking for the sinless soul."

they see that they are carrying out the perverse [commands] they no longer speak to them perversely, but the truth, knowing that they are obedient in all things."

Joseph of Panepho 6 [11.45]   Abba Joseph said to Abba Lot: "You cannot become a monk unless you become altogether like a flaming fire" [cf. Heb 1.7, Ps 103.4].

Joseph of Panepho 7 [12.9]   Abba Lot visited Abba Joseph and said to him: "Abba, to the best of my ability I do my little *synaxis*, my little fasting; praying, meditating, and maintaining *hesychia*; and I purge my *logismoi* to the best of my ability. What else then can I do?" The elder stood up and stretched out his hands to heaven; his fingers became like ten lamps of fire. He said to him: "If you are willing, become altogether like fire."

Joseph of Panepho 8   A brother asked Abba Joseph: "I want to come out of the coenobion and live alone." The elder said to him: "Stay wherever you see your soul experiencing repose and not being damaged." The brother said to him: "I experience repose both in the coenobion and living alone; what do you want me to do?" The elder said to him: "If you experience repose both in the coenobion and living alone, put your two *logismoi* as though in a balance and do that which is the more likely to be to your benefit and [to which] your *logismos* prompts you."

Joseph of Panepho 9   One of the elders visited his colleague so they could go off and visit Abba Joseph and he said: "Tell your disciple to saddle the ass for us." [The other] said: "You call him: he will do what you want." [The first one] said: "What is he called?" and the other said: "I don't know." The [first one] said: "How long has he been with you and you don't know his name?" "It has been two years," [the other] said. "If you don't know your disciple's name after two years, why do I have to learn it in one day?" [the first one] said.

Joseph of Panepho 10   Some brothers were once gathered around Abba Joseph and he rejoiced as they sat there, asking him questions.

He was fervently saying to them: "Today I am a ruler for I have over-ruled the passions."

Joseph of Panepho 11   They used to say that when Abba Joseph of Panepho was about to die; while the elders were sitting [there] he looked at the door and saw the devil sitting by the door. Calling his disciple he said: "Bring [my] staff, for that fellow thinks I have grown old and can no longer deal with him." When he got the staff, the elders saw [the devil] let himself out through the door like a dog and disappear.

JAMES

James 1   Abba James said: "It is better to be a guest than a host."[71]

James 2 [15.108]   He also said: "One who is praised ought to take his own sins into account and bear in mind that he is not worthy of the things that are being said [about him]."

James 3 [3.17]   He also said: "Just as a lamp in a darkened chamber illuminates [it], so the fear of God, when it comes into a person's heart, illuminates him, teaching him all the virtues and the commandments of God."

James 4 [10.111]   He also said: "There is need not only of sayings, for there are many sayings amongst folk nowadays. But there is need for action; that is what is sought, not sayings—which bear no fruit."

James S 1 [Guy 25, N 440 bis]   He also said that one of the elders said: "When I was staying in the desert there was a youngster living on his own near me. Paying him a fatherly visit I saw him at prayer, beseeching God that he might be at peace with the wild animals. Following the prayer a hyena that was suckling her young came by. The youngster got under her and began suckling with them."

[71]Lit. "to be entertained than to entertain," or "to be in voluntary exile . . ."

James S 2 [Guy 25, N 440 bis]   "Another time I saw him at prayer beseeching the Lord: 'Give me the spiritual gift of being the friend of fire.' He made a fire then knelt down in it, praying to the Lord-and-master."

HIERAX

Three elders of this name are known: one at Nitria (HL 22) one in the Thebaid (N 33), and from a Coptic text, one at Scete. The first saying attributed to Hierax (below) is found in various forms under different names; Hierax S1 may be the original version.

Hierax 1   A brother asked Abba Hierax: "Tell me a saying: how may I be saved?" The elder said to him: "Remain in your cell. Eat if you are hungry, drink if you are thirsty; speak ill of nobody and you will be saved."

Hierax 2   The same [elder] said: "I never spoke or wanted to hear a worldly discourse."

Hierax S 1 [Guy p. 25]   A brother asked Abba Hierax: "Tell me how I may be saved." The elder said to him: "Remain in your cell; speak ill of nobody and you will be saved."

JOHN THE EUNUCH

The first of the following sayings is a variant of Theodore 10; the rest are taken from PS 115 where they are attributed to John of Cilicia.

John the Eunuch 1   When Abba John the Eunuch was younger he asked an elder: "How is it that you could perform the work of God in repose? We are unable to perform it even with effort." The elder said: "We were able because we put the greatest importance on the work of

God, the least on physical need. But you put the greatest importance on physical need and do not hold the work of God to be more pressing. That is why you are laboring and that is why the Savior said to the disciples: 'Oh you of little faith, first seek the Kingdom of God and all these things will be added unto you'"[72] [Mt 6.30, 33].

John the Eunuch 2   Abba John said that our father Abba Antony said: "I never preferred my own advantage over my brother's benefit."

John the Eunuch 3   Abba John the Cilician, higoumen of Rhaïthou, used to say to the brothers: "As we fled from the world my sons, so let us flee from the desires of the flesh."

John the Eunuch 4   He also said: "Let us be imitators of our fathers who lived here in such hardship and *hesychia*."

John the Eunuch 5   He also said: "My sons, let us not defile this place that our fathers cleansed of demons."

John the Eunuch 6   He also said: "This is a place for ascetics, not of merchants."

JOHN OF THE CELLS

John of The Cells 1   Abba John of The Cells recounted: "There was an exceedingly beautiful prostitute in Egypt and she was very rich; men of the ruling class used to come to her. Finding herself by the church one day she wished to go in, but the subdeacon who stood by the doors would not let her. 'You are not worthy to come into the house of God for you are unclean,' he said. As they were arguing the bishop heard the disturbance. He came out and the prostitute said to him: 'He is not allowing me to come into the church.' Said the bishop to her: 'It is not possible for you to come in because you

[72]cf. Theodore of Phermē 10.

are unclean.' Conscience-stricken, she said to him: 'I will play the prostitute no longer,' and the bishop said to her: 'If you bring your money here I will know that you are playing the prostitute no longer.' He took it when she brought it and burned it with fire. She went into the church weeping and saying: 'If it was like this for me here, what am I going to suffer there?' She both repented and became a choice vessel" [Acts 19.15].

John of The Cells 2 [15.36]   John of the Thebaid said: "Before all else, the monk ought to attain humble-mindedness for this is the first commandment of the Savior, saying: "Blessed are the poor in spirit for theirs is the Kingdom of Heaven" [Mt 5.3].

ISIDORE THE PRIEST

Isidore ("the gift of Isis") is such a common name in Egypt that it is impossible to say with certainty that this is the priest at Scete.

Isidore the Priest 1 [4.23]   They used to say of Abba Isidore the priest that a brother once came to invite him for a meal but the elder refused to go, saying: "It was because he was led astray by food that Adam was lodged outside Paradise." Said the brother to him: "Are you altogether afraid to come out of your cell?" but he spoke again: "I am afraid my son, because 'The devil, like a roaring lion, is seeking whom he may devour'" [1 Pet 5.8]. And he often used to say that if a person gave himself to wine-drinking, he would not escape the onslaught of the *logismoi*; for, obliged by his daughters, Lot became drunk with wine and, on account of his drunkenness, the devil made easy work of contriving for him to commit lawless *porneia*[73] [cf. Gen 19.31–35].

Isidore the Priest 2 [6.12, N 390a]   Abba Isidore said: "If you long for the Kingdom, despise money and strive for the divine reward."

[73]Changed to "a lawless act" in 4.23, presumably to avoid the suggestion that *porneia* could ever be lawful.

Isidore the Priest 3 [5.12, N 390b]   He also said: "It is impossible for you [sg.] to live a godly life if you are in love with pleasure and money."

Isidore the Priest 4 [10.41]   Abba Isidore said: "If you [pl.] are practicing *askēsis* according to the rules, do not be conceited when you fast. For if you become arrogant on this account, it is better to eat meat; because it is better for a person to eat meat than to become puffed up and boastful."

Isidore the Priest 5 [10.42]   He also said: "Persons under instruction must love those who are their instructors like fathers and fear them like rulers, neither diminishing fear through love nor obscuring love through fear."

Isidore the Priest 6 [10.43]   He also said: "If you [sg.] really long for salvation, practice all the things that lead you to it."

Isidore the Priest 7 [2.18]   They said of Abba Isidore that he used to withdraw yet further into his cell when a brother came to him. The brothers said to him: "What is this you are doing, abba?" and he said: "The wild animals who withdraw into their dens, they are saved too." He said this for the benefit of the brothers.

JOHN THE PERSIAN

PS *151 speaks of a John the Persian who lived in the time of Gregory the Great (d. 604), but he cannot be the originator of the second of the sayings attributed to him because this appears already in the sixth century* P&J. *The first item below is attributed to Macarius elsewhere, but which Macarius?*

John the Persian 1   A youth once came to be cured of a demon and some brothers from a coenobion in Egypt were visiting too. The elder came out and saw a brother committing sin with the youth and he did not reprove him. "If the God who made them sees and does not burn them, who am I to reprove them?" he said.

John the Persian 2 [6.8]   One of the fathers recounted of John the Persian that he attained a most profound innocence by his abundant grace. He lived in Egyptian Arabia. One day he borrowed a piece of gold from a brother and bought some linen thread so he could work. A brother came to him begging, saying: "Grant me a little linen thread abba, so I can make myself a *leviton*" and he joyfully gave him [some]. Then another one came begging in the same way, saying: "Give me a little linen thread so I can make a towel"; he gave him [some] too. When others asked in the same way, he simply and gladly gave. Later on the owner of the piece of gold came, wanting it. The elder said to him: "I will go myself and get it for you," but not having the wherewithal to repay him, he got up and went to Abba James the steward to ask him to give him the piece of gold so he could repay the brother. As he was going along, he found a coin lying on the ground, but he did not touch it; he offered a prayer and returned to his cell. Again the brother came importuning him for his coin and the elder said to him: "I am certainly looking into it." Off he went again and found the coin lying on the ground where it was [before]. Again he offered a prayer and returned to his own cell and here there came the brother, importuning him as before. The elder said to him: "Forgive me; I will certainly bring it for you this time." Getting up he came to that place again and found it lying there. Offering a prayer, he took it and came to Abba James, saying: "Abba, I found this coin on the road as I was coming to you. Do me the kindness of making it known in the district in case somebody lost it; and if the owner of it be found, give [him] it." So the elder went and for three days made it known, but nobody was found who had lost the coin. Then the elder said to Abba James: "If nobody has lost that coin, give it to such and such a brother, for I owe it to him and it was while I was coming to you to get it from you as alms to pay back the loan that I found it." The elder was amazed that, being in debt then finding [the wherewithal] he did not immediately take it and give it back. And this was the amazing thing about him: if anybody came to borrow something from him, he did not provide it himself, but said to the brother: "Go and help yourself to what you need." And if one brought something back he would say to the brother: "Put it back where it belongs." And if one who was taking something brought nothing back, he would not say anything to him.

John the Persian 3   They used to say of Abba John the Persian that when evildoers set upon him he brought a bowl and would ask to wash their feet. For their part they were ashamed and began to apologize.[74]

John the Persian 4   Somebody said to Abba John the Persian: "We have toiled so hard for the Kingdom of Heaven, but are we going to inherit it?" The elder said: "As for me, I believe [that I] shall inherit Jerusalem that is on high, inscribed in the heavens, for he is faithful who promised [Heb 10.23]. Why should I not believe? I have become hospitable like Abraham, gentle like Moses, holy like Aaron, patient like Job, humble like David, a hermit like John, a mourner like Jeremiah, a teacher like Paul, faithful like Peter, wise like Solomon. As did the thief, I believe that he who granted me these things will also, of his own goodness, accord me the Kingdom" [cf. Lk 23.43].

JOHN THE THEBAN

This John has already been mentioned in Ammōes 3, above. In the Ethiopian Collection [13.61] there is this:

John the Theban 1   I have heard it said of Abba Ammōes of Tameryas that some brothers came to him asking for a saying. He called his disciple John and said to him: "Show the brothers how to become a monk." "Are you making fun of me, father?" John said; "Not

---

[74]or "to repent," or "to prostrate themselves."

at all," said Abba Ammōes. John said to his father Abba Ammōes: "Do you want it to be I who speak and you who remain silent?" "That is correct," Ammōes told him. Then John took his clothes off and made himself naked. Abba Ammōes said to him: "What are you doing, John?" John told him: "Unless a man strip himself of honor and praise like this he absolutely cannot become a monk."[75]

John the Theban 2 [16.5]   They used to say of little John of Thebes, the disciple of Abba Ammōes, that he spent twelve years waiting on the elder when he was sick, sitting on a mat with him. The elder did not think much of him and, although he labored mightily in his service, he never said to him: "May you be saved." But when he was about to die and the elders were sitting there, he took [Abba John's] hand and said: "May you be saved, may you be saved, may you be saved"—and he bequeathed him to the elders, saying: "This is an angel, not a man."

John the Disciple of Paul

John the disciple of Paul [14.5]   They used to say of Abba John the disciple of Abba Paul that he was extremely obedient. Somewhere there were some tombs and a vicious hyena was living there. The elder saw that there were turds around that place; he told John to go and bring them, but he said to him: "And what am I to do about the hyena, abba?" Teasing him, the elder said: "If it comes at you, tie it up and bring it here." So the brother went there in the evening and here the hyena came at him. Following the elder's instruction, he lunged to grab it, but the hyena ran away. Giving chase, he said: "Hold on, my abba told me to tie you up," and grabbing it, he tied it up. But the elder was troubled; he sat there waiting for him. [Eventually] here he came—with the hyena tied up. The elder was amazed at the sight. Intending to humble him, he struck him saying: "Idiot, have

[75]Regnault, *Les Sentences*, 303.

you brought me an idiot dog here?" The elder immediately loosed it and let it go.

ISAAC OF THEBES

Isaac of Thebes 1 [9.5]   Isaac of Thebes was once visiting a coenobion; seeing a brother committing a fault he passed judgment on him. When he went out into the desert, an angel of the Lord came and stood before the door of his cell saying: "I am not letting you in." He began to entreat him, saying: "What is the matter?" In answer the angel said to him: "God sent me saying: 'Tell him: "Where do you bid me put the brother who was at fault, the one you judged?"'" Abba Isaac immediately prostrated himself, saying: "I have sinned; forgive me!" "Get up," said the angel; "God has forgiven you; but take care in future not to pass judgment on anybody before God passes judgment on him."

Isaac of Thebes 2 [11.47]   Concerning Abba Apollo,[76] they used to say that he had a disciple named Isaac, trained to perfection in every good work, and that he had acquired the *hesychia* of the holy Eucharist. When he was going to church he would not allow anybody to come into contact with him. His explanation was to the effect that everything is good in its own time, "For there is a time for every matter" [cf. Eccl 3.1]. And when the *synaxis* was terminated he would seek to regain his cell like somebody chased by fire. An allowance of a single dried loaf and a cup of wine was often given to the brothers after the *synaxis* but he would not take it, not to reject the blessing of the brothers, but to maintain the *hesychia* of the *synaxis*. He happened to fall sick and the brothers came to visit him when they heard of it. As they sat, they asked him saying: "Abba Isaac, why do you run away from the brothers after the *synaxis*?" and he told them: "I am not running away from the brothers but from the

[76] cf. *HME* 8.

evil craftiness of the demons. For if a person has a lighted lamp and hangs around, standing out in the wind, it is extinguished by it. So we who are enlightened by {the Holy Spirit in the}[77] holy Eucharist, if we hang around outside the cell, our mind is darkened." Such was the way of life of holy Isaac.

JOSEPH OF THEBES

Joseph of Thebes [1.14]   Abba Joseph of Thebes said there are three things that are precious in the sight of the Lord: When a person is sick and temptations come upon him, he accepts them gratefully. The second is when someone renders all his deeds pure in the sight of God, with no human element in them. The third is when someone is living in submission to a spiritual father and renounces all his own desires. This person has an extraordinary crown; but I preferred sickness.

HILARION

According to Jerome, Hilarion was born c. 291 in Palestine and was an early convert to monasticism, inspired by the example of Antony (with whom he stayed for a brief period).

Hilarion [17.4]   Abba Hilarion from Palestine visited Abba Antony at the mountain and Abba Antony said to him: "Welcome, star of the morning, rising at dawn." "Peace be with you, pillar of light supporting the world," said Abba Hilarion to him.

[77]The words { . . . } are not found in all the mss.

Ischyrion

Ischyrion [18.9] The holy fathers of Scete predicted concerning the last generation, saying: "What have we accomplished?" In reply one of them, great in life and name, Abba Ischyrion, said: "We have carried out the commandments of God." In reply the elders said: "But those who come after us, what will they accomplish?" He said: "They are going to attain the half of what we have done." They said: "And what of those after them?" and he said: "Those of that generation will do no work at all. Temptation is going to come upon them and those who are found to be tried and tested in that age will be found greater both than us and than our fathers."

K—*Kappa*

[JOHN] CASSIAN

Six of the following apophthegms are from the Institutes *of John Cassian (c. 360–435) 5.24–31 and 7.19. Cassian 2 is from an unknown source; Cassian 8 is very similar to Arsenius 29.*

Cassian 1 [13.2]   Abba Cassian related: "Coming from Palestine to Egypt, I and the holy Germanus visited an elder [there]. Having received us as [his] guests he was asked by us: 'How is it that, when you are entertaining brothers from elsewhere, you do not observe our rule of fasting as we received it in Palestine?' 'Fasting is forever with me,' he said in reply, 'but I cannot keep you with myself forever. Fasting is a useful and necessary practice, but we do it by our own choice; whereas the law of God enjoins the practice of charity as obligatory. When I receive Christ in [the person of] you, I am obliged to care of [him] with full attention. When I send you on your way, I can resume the rule of fasting, for 'the companions of the bridegroom cannot fast[78] while the bridegroom is with them; but when he is taken away from them, then will they fast' [Mt 9.15] legitimately.'"

Cassian 2   The same [elder] said: "There was an elder who was waited upon by a holy virgin. Folk were saying: 'They are not pure,' and the elder heard it. So when he was at the point of death he said to the fathers: 'When I die, plant my staff on [my] grave and, if it blossoms and bears fruit, you will learn that I am pure regarding her. If it does not blossom, you will know that I fell with her.' The staff

---

[78][sic]; Cassian *Inst.* 5.24—but *mourn* in NT.

was planted; it blossomed on the third day and bore fruit; everybody glorified God."

Cassian 3 [13.3, *Inst.* 5.25]   He also said: "We visited another elder and he had us eat. He urged us to partake of more food when we were already replete. When I said it was no longer possible, he answered: 'For my part I have now set the table six times for different brothers coming this way; inviting each one [to eat]. I ate with them and I am still hungry. Yet you, who have eaten but once, are so full that you are no longer able to eat?'"

Cassian 4 [4.26, *Inst.* 5.27]   The same [elder] also recounted: "Abba John, who was the higoumen of a large coenobion, visited Abba Paesios who had been living in the remotest desert for forty years. As he had great love for him and, consequently, freedom of speech, he said to him: "In retreat like this for such a long time and not easily disturbed by anyone, what good have you accomplished?" He said: "The sun never saw me eating since I started living alone." Said Abba John: "Nor did it ever see me being angry."

Cassian 5 [1.15, *Inst.* 5.28]   "When this Abba John was about to die and was migrating to God joyfully and eagerly, the brothers gathered around him, asking him to leave them some concise and salvific saying as a legacy by which they would be able to advance toward perfection in Christ. But he sighed and said: 'I have never done my own will, nor did I teach anyone to do that which I did not first practice myself.'"

Cassian 6 [11.48, *Inst.* 5.29, 31]   He also recounted of another elder dwelling in the desert that he called upon God to grant him never to nod off when a spiritual discourse was in progress but immediately to fall asleep if somebody tried to introduce vain or malicious topics, so that his ears would not taste such poison. He used to say the devil was a devotee of vain talking, but the opponent of all spiritual teaching, using this example: "I was once talking to some brothers about what is beneficial," he said, "when they were overcome by such a deep sleep that they could not even raise their eyelids. But I, wishing to demonstrate the operation of the demon, introduced some vain talk, at which they immediately and cheerfully awoke. Then I said with a sigh: 'Until now we were discussing heavenly matters and the eyes of you all were in the grip of sleep; but when a vain subject was introduced, you all awoke with eagerness.' So I beg of you, brothers, that being aware of the operation of the evil demon, you pay attention to yourselves and be vigilant against nodding off when you are doing something of a spiritual nature or listening to it."

Cassian 7 [6.14, *Inst.* 7.19]   He also said that a senator renounced the world and gave his own goods to the poor, retaining a little for his own comfort, for he was unwilling to embrace the humble-mindedness of utter poverty and the genuine submission of the coenobitic rule. It was against him that Basil (now among the saints) spoke a saying like this: "You have lost out as a senator and have not made a monk."

Cassian 8   He also said: "There was a monk living in a cave in the desert. It was communicated to him by his relatives in the flesh: 'Your father is gravely ill and is going to die: come so you can inherit from him,' but he answered them: 'I died to the world before him; a dead man does not inherit from one who is alive.'"

CRONIOS

Cronios, the priest at Nitria who knew Antony and lived to a great age (HL 21, 20.13) may be the originator of these sayings, but Palladius mentions another Cronios, also a priest (HL 47), and yet a third person of that name is encountered in the versions. The following apophthegms are distinguished by their application of Scripture to the monastic endeavor.

Cronios 1   A brother said to Abba Cronios: "Tell me a saying," and he said to him: "When Elisha came to the Shunamite woman he found her having nothing to do with anybody; yet she conceived and gave birth through the presence of Elisha" [2/4 Kg 4.14–17]. Said the brother to him: "What is this saying?" The elder said to him: "If the soul be vigilant and withhold itself from distraction and abandon its own desires, then the Spirit of God comes upon it and it ends up able to engender, even though it be sterile."

Cronios 2   A brother asked Abba Cronios: "What am I to do about the forgetting that holds my mind captive and prevents me from being aware until it brings me up against the sin itself?" The elder said: "When the foreigners took the Ark (on account of the evil behavior of the children of Israel[79]), they dragged it until they brought it into the house of Dagon their god—and then [Dagon] fell on his face" [1 Sam 5.1–4]. The brother said: "What is this?" The elder said: "If [the enemy] succeed in taking a man's mind captive by his own means, in the same way will they drag him until they bring him to the invisible passion. But if the mind turn about in that place, seek after God, and be mindful of the eternal judgment, the passion immediately falls and becomes invisible, for it is written: 'When you turn and lament, then will you be saved and know where you were'" [Is 35:15].

Cronios 3 [15.37]   A brother asked Abba Cronios: "In what way does one arrive at humble-mindedness?" The elder said: "Through fear of God." The brother said to him: "And through what action does one arrive at fear of God?" The elder said: "In my opinion, let him withdraw himself from every affair and dedicate himself to physical toil, to the best of his ability bearing in mind his departure from the body and the judgment of God."

Cronios 4   Abba Cronios said: "If Moses had not led the sheep under Mount Sinaï he would not have seen the fire in the bush" [Ex 3.1–17]. The brother asked the elder: "What is the bush taken to mean?" and he said to him: "The bush is taken to mean physical

---

[79]"of Eli" in some mss.

activity, for it is written: 'The Kingdom of Heaven is like treasure hidden in a field'" [Mt 13.44]. The brother said to the elder: "Does a person then not advance to any distinction without physical toil?" The elder told him: "Well, it is written: 'Looking unto Jesus, the author and finisher of our faith who, for the joy that was set before him, endured the cross' [Heb 12.2]. And again David says: 'If I give sleep to my eyes or slumber to my eyelids, etc.'" [Ps 131.4].

Cronios 5   Abba Cronios said that Abba Joseph of Pelusium told us: "When I was staying at Sinaï there was there an excellent and ascetic brother, but he was also handsome in body. He used to come into church for the *synaxis* wearing a patched up little old shawl. Then one time, seeing him coming to the *synaxis* like that, I said to him: 'Brother, do you not see the brothers, how they are like angels when in church for the *synaxis*? Why do you always come here wearing old rags, like that?' But he said: 'Forgive me abba: I have nothing else,' so I took him to my cell and gave him a *leviton* plus anything else he needed. From then he wore what the rest of the brothers [wore] and he was like an angel to behold. Once it was necessary for the fathers to send ten brothers to the emperor for some necessity and they chose him too among the delegates. On hearing this, he prostrated himself before the fathers, saying: 'Forgive me for the Lord's sake; I am a slave of one of the grandees who are there and if he recognizes me he will defrock me and bring me back to serving him.' After the fathers were convinced and had excused him, later on they learnt from somebody who had accurate knowledge of him that, when he was in the world, he was the commander of the Praetorian Guard. He excused himself to avoid recognition and being harassed by people. Such was the determination of the fathers to flee from the glory and repose of this world."

CARION

An Abba Carion is mentioned in Zachariah 4 as the father of Zachariah. Another case of an abba being both the natural and the spiritual father occurs in Phocas 1 (below). This must have been a very rare occurrence, given the fathers' antipathy to cohabiting with youths—see Carion S 1.

Carion 1 [15.17]   Abba Carion said: "I have performed many physical tasks, more than my son Zachariah, but I have not achieved his stature in his humility and silence."

Carion 2   There was a monk at Scete called Abba Carion. When he had acquired two children he left them with his own wife and retired [from the world]. Some time later there was a famine in Egypt and his wife, being in tight straits, came to Scete bringing the two children with her; one was a boy named Zachariah, one a girl. She [the wife] remained at a distance from the elder, at the marsh. (There is a marsh beside Scete, there where the churches were built and where the sources of water are located.) The custom at Scete when a woman came to speak to her brother or somebody else not related to her, was for them to speak with each other while remaining at a distance. On that occasion the wife said to Abba Carion: "Here you have become a monk and there is a famine; who is to feed your children?" Abba Carion said to her: "Send them here to me." The wife said to the children: "Go to your father." As they were coming to their father, the girl turned back to her mother but the boy came to his own father. Then he said to her: "See, it is well; do you take the girl and go back and I [will keep] the boy." So he raised [his son] at Scete and everybody knew that it was his child; but when he became of age a grumbling arose in the brotherhood about him. When Abba Carion heard, he said to his child: "Get up, Zachariah; let us go away from here for the fathers are grumbling." The little one said to him: "Abba, here they are all aware that I am your son; but if we go elsewhere, they will not be saying that I am your son." The elder said to him: "Get up; let us go away from here," and they came to the Thebaid. They took a cell and stayed there a few days then the same grumbling arose there too because of the child. Then his father said to him: "Get up Zachariah; let us go to Scete." To Scete they came; a few days went by, then there was grumbling about him again. Then the child Zachariah came to the marsh of niter, took off his clothes and went in up to his nostrils, immersing himself. He stayed there a long time (for as long as he could), making his body unsightly—for he became like a leper. He got out, put his clothes on, and went to his own father—who scarcely knew him. When he went to Holy Communion as usual he revealed what he had done to holy Isidore, the priest of Scete. Amazed on seeing him, he said: "The child Zachariah came and made his Communion last Sunday as a man; now he has become like an angel."

Carion S 1 [Guy 26]   Abba Carion said: "A man who stays with a youth comes to grief if he be not strong. If he be strong he does not come to grief; however, he does not progress."

Coprès

This is Coprès of Scete, not the Coprès of the Thebaid (HL 10).
His sayings are characterized by great simplicity and humility.
In Syriac we have this: "Abba Coprès said: 'Whoever prefers the
satisfaction of his own will rather than of the will of God does not
fear God.' "[80]

Coprès 1   Abba Poemen used to say of Abba Coprès: "He achieved such stature that, when he was sick and confined to bed, he would give thanks and inhibit his own will."

Coprès 2   Abba Coprès said: "Blessed is he who endures toil with thanksgiving."

[80]Regnault, *Les Sentences*, 240.

Coprès 3 [15.38]   Those of Scete were once assembled to inquire into the question of Melchizedek [Dan 8] but they had forgotten to call Abba Coprès. Later on when they did call him, they began asking him about [Melchizedek.] He struck his mouth[81] three times saying: "Woe to you, Coprès, for you have been leaving aside the things God commanded you to do and are inquiring into what he does not require of you." The brothers ran off into their cells on hearing this.

CYRUS

Cyrus [5.5]   When he was questioned regarding the *logismos* of *porneia*, Abba Cyrus of Alexandria answered thus: "If you do not have a *logismos*, you do not have hope. If you do not have *logismoi*, you have the act. This means that he who does not battle sin in his mind nor contradict it, physically indulges in it. For he who does the deeds is not troubled by *logismoi*." The elder asked the brother: "You are not in the habit of talking with a woman?" and the brother said: "No; old and young images are my *logismoi*; it is memories that trouble me and statues of women." The elder [said] to him: "Have no fear of the dead but flee from the living and persevere more in prayer."

[81]"his face" in some mss.

Λ—*Lamda*

Lucius

See Theodore of Enaton 2.

Lucius [12.10]   Some monks called Euchites once visited Abba Lucius at Enaton and the elder asked them: "What is your handiwork?" "We do not have anything to do with handiwork, they said, "but we 'pray without ceasing' [1 Thess 5.17] as the Apostle said." "Do you not eat?" said the elder. "Yes," they said, and the elder said: "Who prays for you when you are eating?" Again he said to them: "Do you not sleep?" "Yes," they said, and the elder said: "Who prays for you when you are asleep?" and at this they did not find him an answer. And he said to them: "Forgive me but, look: you do not do as you say. I will show you that I pray without ceasing while toiling at my handiwork. I soak a few rushes for myself then, sitting down with God, I braid them into a rope, saying: 'Have mercy upon me O God according to your great goodness: according to the multitude of your mercies blot out mine offences'" [Ps 50.1], and he said to them: "Is that not prayer?" "Yes," they said, and the elder said: "When I remain working and praying all day long, I make sixteen coins more or less. I put two of them at the door and eat with the rest. He who takes the two coins prays for me while I am eating and when I am sleeping and, by the grace of God, to 'pray without ceasing is fulfilled for me.'"

LOT

An Ethiopic text reads: "A brother said to me: 'Abba Joseph, the disciple of Abba Lot, said to me: "We, brothers of these times, eat and drink for the delight of the flesh; that is why we do not make progress the way our fathers did. For our fathers loved all the austerities for the Lord's sake and that is why they came close to the living God.'"[82] *See also Joseph of Panepho 6 and 7.*

Lot 1   One of the elders came to Abba Lot at the small marsh of Arsinoe and begged him for a cell—which he accorded him. But the elder was sick and Abba Lot tended him; then if visitors came to visit Abba Lot, he would have them visit the sick elder too. [The elder] however began speaking sayings of Origen to them. Abba Lot was disturbed, saying: "Perhaps the fathers will think that we are like that too?"—but, because of the commandment [cf. Mt 25.35] he was afraid to throw him out of the place. Abba Lot got up and went to Abba Arsenius and told him about the elder. Said Abba Arsenius to him: "Do not chase him away but say to him: 'Here, eat the gifts of God and drink what you like; only do not say that thing any more,' and if he is willing, he will reform. If he is unwilling to reform himself, of his own free will he is going to ask to withdraw from the place and the initiative will not have come from you." Abba Lot went off and did so. The elder was not willing to reform himself when he heard this; he uttered an entreaty, saying: "For the Lord's sake, send me away from here for I can no longer tolerate the desert." And thus he got up and went out, speeded on his way with love.

Lot 2 [cf. N 190]   Somebody recounted this of a brother who had fallen into sin: "He visited Abba Lot but was disturbed; he kept going in and coming out and could not keep still. Abba Lot said to him: 'What is the matter with you, brother?' 'I have committed a grave sin,' he said, 'and cannot declare it to the fathers.' 'Confess it to me,' said the elder, 'and I will bear it.' Then he said to him: 'I fell into *por-*

[82]Regnault, *Les Sentences*, 300.

neia and I sacrificed [to idols] to achieve my end.' The elder said to him: 'Be of good cheer: there is repentance. Go stay in the cave and fast every other day and, together with you, I will bear half the sin.' When the three weeks [*sic*] were accomplished, the elder was assured that God had accepted the brother's repentance and he remained in obedience to the elder until his death."

LONGINUS

Other sayings attributed to an Abba Longinus are found in APanon *(558–564, 708–710) and in* APsys *(15.113, 19.7, 9), but it cannot be assumed that it is the same Longinus in each case. Of the following apophthegms only the first is found in* P&J, *hence is known to have been extant prior to AD 600.*

Longinus 1 [10.45]   Abba Longinus once asked Abba Lucius about three *logismoi*: "I want to live in voluntary exile."[83] The elder said to him: "Unless you master your tongue you are not in exile wherever you go. So master your tongue here and you are in exile." He also said: "I want to fast." The elder replied: "The prophet Isaiah said: 'If you bend your neck like a collar and a ring, not even so will he call it an acceptable fast' [Is 58.5]. Do you rather master the evil *logismoi*." A third time he spoke to him: "I want to escape from people." The elder replied: "Unless you first live a good life with people, you will not be able to live a good life alone either."

Longinus 2 [4.28]   Abba Longinus said: "Once you become distressed, say: 'Be distressed then and die; but if you ask me for something to eat other than at mealtime, I will not even provide you with the daily ration.'"

Longinus 3 [19.6]   There was a woman with the condition known as cancer in her breast who sought to meet with Abba Longinus when

[83] i.e. to be a stranger in a foreign land.

she heard of him. He was staying at the ninth [Enaton] milepost to the west of Alexandria. When the woman came looking for him that blessed one happened to be gathering wood by the sea. When she found him, unaware that it was he, she said to him: "Abba, where is the servant of God Longinus staying?" "What do you want with that imposter?" he said. "Do not go to him for he is an imposter. What is the matter with you?" The woman showed him her condition: the elder made the sign [of the cross] over the place and dismissed her, saying: "Off you go. God is healing you; Longinus cannot be of any benefit to you." The woman went her way believing what was said and was immediately healed. After she had told the matter to some people and said what the characteristics of the elder were she learned that it was Abba Longinus.

Longinus 4 [19.8]   Another time too some people brought a person possessed of a demon to him but he said to them: "I can do nothing for you; go rather to Abba Zeno." Subsequently Abba Zeno began to put pressure on the demon, chasing it out. The demon began shouting out: "Now you think I am coming out because of you, Abba Zeno, but see: Abba Longinus is in prayer over there, pleading against me. It is in fear of *his* prayers that I am coming out; otherwise I would have given you no response."

Longinus 5   Abba Longinus said to Abba Acacius: "The woman knows she has conceived when her [flow of] blood is stanched. So too does the soul know it has conceived the Holy Spirit when its flow of base passions is stanched. As long as it is immersed in those, how can it vainly boast of being unfeeling?[84] Give blood and receive Spirit."

---

[84]ἀπαθής.

M—*Mu*

Macarius the Egyptian / the Great

Palladius gives a brief biography and some anecdotes of Macarius in HL 17; we learn more about him from the following apophthegms. He appears to have been born c. 300 and to have withdrawn to Scete when he was about thirty years old. Already as a young man he was held in high esteem and attracted many disciples. He visited Antony at least twice. His death occurred c. 390. Some of the apophthegms below may really apply to Macarius of Alexandria ("the city-dweller"); numbers 28 and 37 almost certainly do; probably also 8, 9, and 10, and the doublets 11/35 and 18/40.

Macarius the Egyptian 1 [15.39]   Abba Macarius recounted this about himself: "As a young man I was living in a cell in Egypt; they laid hands on me and made me a cleric at the village church. I fled elsewhere, not willing to accede [to the office]. A devout worldling came to me; he began taking my handiwork and looking after me. Now it happened that, through devilish temptation, a maiden at the village fell. When she conceived in her womb she was asked who it might be that had done this. 'The anchorite,' she said. Out came the villagers and took me to the village. They hung soot-blackened pots and the handles of jars around my neck then paraded me around the village street by street, hitting me and saying: 'This monk has defiled our maiden; get him, get him!' and they beat me almost to death. But one of the elders came and said to them: 'How much longer are you beating the foreign monk?' He who was looking after me was following, chagrined, for they were insulting him a great deal and saying: 'Here is the anchorite for whom you gave guarantees and—what has he done?' Her parents said: 'We are not letting him go until he bind himself to maintain her.' I spoke with my attendant and he bound himself over for me. I went to my cell and gave him as many baskets as I had, saying: 'Sell them and give [the proceeds] to my wife so she can eat,' and I said to my *logismos*: 'Here, you have found yourself a wife Macarius; you are going to have to work a little harder in order to feed her.' I started working night and day and sending [money] to her. When the time came for the wretch to give birth, she was in pain for many days without giving birth and they said to her: 'What is going on?' 'I know,' she said, 'I slandered the anchorite accusing him falsely, but he is not responsible: it was young so-and-so.' My care-giver came to me joyfully, saying: 'That maiden could not give birth until she confessed and said: 'The anchorite is not responsible; I lied about him.' Here all the village wants to come this way in pomp, apologizing to you.' When I heard that, I got up and fled here, to Scete, so folk would not harass me. That is the beginning of the reason why I came hither."

Macarius the Egyptian 2 [20.4]   Abba Macarius the Egyptian once came from Scete to the Mount of Nitria for the Eucharist of Abba Pambo. "Tell the brothers a saying, father," the elder said to him, but he said: "I have not yet become a monk. I have however seen monks. Once when I was staying in my cell at Scete my *logismoi* troubled me, saying: 'Go off into the desert and see what you will behold there.' I went on combating that *logismos* for five years, saying: 'Maybe it is from demons?' but, as my *logismos* persisted, I went off into the desert. I found a lake of water there with an island in the middle of it. The creatures of the desert came to drink from [the lake] and, among them, I saw two naked men. My body trembled with fear for I thought they were spirits, but when they saw me trembling, they spoke to me: 'Do not be afraid; we too are men.' I said to them: 'Where are you from and how did you come into this desert?' 'We are from a coenobion,' they said, 'and, having made an agreement, we came out here forty years ago.' One of them was Egyptian, the other Libyan. They questioned me, saying: 'How is it with the world? Does the water [of the Nile] rise at its appointed time? Is the world enjoying prosperity?' 'Yes,' I told them; then I too asked them: 'How can I become a monk?' They told me: 'A person cannot become a monk unless he renounce all that has to do with the world.' 'I am a weakling and cannot be like you,' I told them; and they too said to me: 'If you cannot be like us, remain in your cell and weep for your sins.' I asked them: 'Are you not cold when it is winter and do your bodies not burn when [searing] heat comes?' but they said: 'God has so arranged things for us that we neither feel cold in winter nor does the heat harm us in summer.' That is why I told you that I have not yet become a monk but that I have seen monks; forgive me, brothers."

Macarius the Egyptian 3 [18.13]   Abba Macarius was living in the remote desert (having retreated there all alone), but there was another desert further down there, [the dwelling] of several brothers. The elder looked carefully at the trail and saw Satan coming to pass him by, disguised as a human. He seemed to be wearing a linen garment with holes, and a little flask was hanging out of each hole. The great elder said to him: "Where are you going?" and he said: "I am going to jog the memories of the brothers." The elder said: "And what are these little flasks of yours?" He said: "I am bringing victuals for the brothers." The elder said: "All of these?" "Yes," he replied, "and if one does not please somebody, I offer another; if not that one either, I give another. There certainly is one of them that will please him," and having said that, off he went. The elder stayed there keeping watch on the trails until that one came back again. When the elder saw him he said to him: "I hope you are well," but he replied: "How could I be well?" The elder said to him: "Why is that?" and he said: "They were all savage with me and no one received me." The elder said: "You have not one friend there?" "Oh yes," he said, "I have one friendly monk there and he obeys me and spins around like a weather-cock when he sees me." The elder said to him: "What is the brother called?" "Theopemptos," he said, and so saying, off he went. Abba Macarius went along to the desert down there. When the brothers who were collecting palm branches heard, they came out to meet him. Each one made preparations thinking that the elder would stay with him; but he began to inquire who might be the one on the mountain called Theopemptos. When he found him, he went into his cell [where] Theopemptos gladly welcomed him. When he began to have him to himself, the elder said: "How are things with you, brother?" "Well, thanks to your prayer," he said. "Do your *logismoi* not battle against you?" the elder said; but the brother said: "So far, so good," for he was embarrassed to speak out. The elder said: "Here I have been in the ascetic life all these years, revered by all and, elder though I be, the spirit of *porneia* disturbs me," and in reply Theopemptos replied: "Believe me abba, me too!" The elder pretended that other *logismoi* did battle him—until he made him confess. Then he said to him: "How do you fast?" "Until the ninth [hour]," he said. The elder told him: "Fast until evening; discipline yourself and recite by heart the Gospel and the other Scriptures. If a *logismos* comes upon you, do not ever look down, but always look up and the Lord will immediately help you." When he had instructed the brother, the elder went out to his own desert and, as he looked out, he saw that demon again and he said to him: "Where are you off to again?" "Going to jog the brethren," he said and off he went. When he came back again the holy one said to him: "So: how are the brothers doing?" but he said: "Badly." "Why is that?" the elder said, and he said: "They are all savage. The worst of it is that the one friend I used to have and who would listen to me, I don't know how, but he too has been turned around and not even he obeys me; he has also become the most savage of them all. I swore I would never set foot there again in many a year." That said, he went his way and left the elder; the holy one went into his cell.

Macarius the Egyptian 4 [7.14]   Abba Macarius the Great visited Abba Antony at the mountain. When he knocked at the door [Antony] came out to him and said to him: "Who are you?" "I am

Macarius," he said, whereupon [Antony] closed the door, went in, and left him. But when he saw his patience he opened up to him and, taking delight in him, said: "I have been wanting to see you for a long time for I have heard tell of you." He received him as his guest and gave him refreshment, for he was extremely exhausted. When evening fell, Abba Antony steeped some palm-fronds for himself; Abba Macarius said to him: "Let me steep some for myself too," and [Antony] said: "Steep [some]." He made a great bundle and steeped it. From evening on they sat braiding [fronds], speaking about salvation of souls. The cord went out of the window down into the cave. When the blessed Antony came in at dawn and saw the extent of the cord of Abba Macarius he said: "Great power is coming out of these hands."

Macarius the Egyptian 5 [18.16]   Concerning the desolation of Scete, Abba Macarius would say to the brothers: "When you see a cell built near to the marsh, learn that its desolation is near. When you see trees, it is at the door. When you see children, take your sheepskins and get away."

Macarius the Egyptian 6 [18.15]   Wishing to encourage the brothers he would also say: "A child possessed of a demon came here with his mother and he was saying to his mother: 'Get up, let us be gone!' 'I am unable to walk,' she said and the child said to her: 'I shall carry you.' I was amazed at the knavery of the demon: at how he wanted to put them to flight."

Macarius the Egyptian 7 [19.12]   Abba Sisoes used to say: "When I was at Scete with Abba Macarius we went harvesting with him, seven persons in all, and here there was a widow gleaning behind us who never stopped crying. The elder called the landowner over and said to him: "What is the matter with that old woman that she is crying all the time?" He said to him: "Her husband had a loan from somebody and he died suddenly without telling where he had put it. The lender wants to take her and her children for slaves." The elder said to him: "Tell her to come to us when we take a rest from the heat." When the woman came, the elder said to her: "Why are you always crying like this?" She said: "My husband died having taken a loan from somebody and when he lay dying he did not say where he had put it." "Come and show me where you buried him," the elder said to her and, taking the brothers with himself, he went out with her. When they came to the place, the elder said to her: "Go back to your house," and when they had prayed at the place, the elder invoked the dead man, saying: "Ah, so-and-so, where did you put the loan you had from another?" And he replied, saying: "It is hidden in my house, at the foot of the bed." The elder said to him: "Go back to sleep again until the day of resurrection." The brothers fell at his feet for fear when they saw this and the elder said to them: "This did not happen on my account, for I am nothing. God achieved this thing on account of the widow and the orphans. The great thing is that God desires the soul without sin and whatever it asks it receives." He came and informed the widow where the loan was lying; she retrieved it, gave it to her master, and set her children free. All those who heard glorified God.

Macarius the Egyptian 8   Abba Peter used to say of the holy Macarius that one day he came across an anchorite and found him distressed. He asked him what he would like to eat, for there was nothing in the cell. When he said: "A cookie," the courageous man did not hesitate to get himself to the city of Alexandria and give [it] to the patient. The wonder became known to nobody.

Macarius the Egyptian 9   He also said that, since Abba Macarius was benevolent in his relations with all the brothers, some folk said to him: "Why do you conduct yourself like this?" He said: "I served my Lord for twelve years so he would grant me this spiritual gift; are you all advising me to set it aside?"

Macarius the Egyptian 10 [4.29]   They used to say of Abba Macarius that, if he was enjoying the company of some brothers, he would impose a rule on himself: "If there is wine, drink for the brothers' sake and in place of one cup of wine don't drink water for one day." The brothers would give him wine by way of refreshment and the elder would take it with pleasure in order to torture himself. But his disciple, aware of [his] practice, said to the brothers: "For the Lord's sake, do not give it to him for otherwise he is going to afflict himself in his cell." When the brothers learnt [this] they did not give him [wine] any more.

Macarius the Egyptian 11 [15.40]   Abba Macarius was once coming from the marsh to his own cell carrying reeds when here the devil met him on the way, carrying a scythe; he wanted to strike him but could not. He said to him: "There is a great force about you Macarius, for I cannot get at you. See, whatever you do, I do it too. You fast, I do not eat at all; you keep watch, I do not ever sleep. There is only one thing in which you have the better of me." "What is that?" Abba Macarius said to him, and he said: "Your humility; because of that I cannot get at you."

Macarius the Egyptian 12 [3.18]   Some of the fathers asked Abba Macarius the Egyptian: "How is it that your body is emaciated both when you are eating and when you are fasting?" The elder said to them: "The stick used to poke the burning twigs is wholly eaten up by the fire. Likewise, if a person cleanses his own mind in the fear of God, the fear of God itself eats up his body."

Macarius the Egyptian 13 [7.15]   Abba Macarius once went up from Scete to Terenouthis and he went into a sepulcher to sleep. There were some old mummies of pagans there; he took [one] and put it under his own head as a pillow. The demons resented his audacity when they saw it; wishing to scare him they called as though addressing a woman: "Hey, so-and-so, come to the baths with us." Another [demon] underneath him replied as though from the dead: "I have a stranger on top of me and I cannot come." But the elder was not scared; he confidently struck the mummy saying: "Get up and go into the darkness if you are able." The demons cried out with a loud voice when they heard this, saying: "You have conquered us," and away they ran, covered in shame.

Macarius the Egyptian 14 [19.10]   They used to say of Abba Macarius the Egyptian that, [once] when he was coming up from Scete carrying [a load of] baskets, he was exhausted and sat down. He prayed, saying: "O God, you know that I have no more strength," and he immediately found himself at the river.

Macarius the Egyptian 15 [19.11]   There was a person in Egypt who had a paralyzed son. He brought him to Abba Macarius' cell and, leaving him weeping at the door, went some distance away. The elder peeped out and saw the child weeping. "Who brought you here?" he said to the child. The child said: "My father abandoned me here and went away." "Get up and go after him," the elder said to him." He was instantly made whole; he got up and went after his father and in this way they departed to their house.

Macarius the Egyptian 16 [4.30]   Abba Macarius the Great used to say to the brothers at Scete when he was dismissing the congregation: "Flee, brothers!" One of the elders said to him: "Where can we flee to that is more remote than this desert?" and he placed his finger on his mouth, saying: "Flee from this," and he went into his own cell, shut the door, and stayed there.

Macarius the Egyptian 17 [4.31]   The same Abba Macarius said: "If you are moved to anger in reproving somebody, you [merely] satisfy your own passion. Do not go lose your own self in order to save others."

Macarius the Egyptian 18 [16.8]   When the same Abba Macarius was in Egypt he found somebody who had a beast of burden carrying off his things. Standing beside the robber as though he were a stranger, he helped him load up the beast then sent him on his way in great *hesychia*, saying: "'We brought nothing into this world and it is clear that neither can we carry anything out' [1 Tim 6.7]. 'The Lord has given and it has transpired as he willed it to; blessed be the Lord in all things' [see Job 1.21]."

Macarius the Egyptian 19 [12.11]   Some people asked Macarius: "How ought we to pray?" The elder said to them: "There is no need to make 'vain repetitions' [Mt 6.7], but frequently to stretch out your hands and say: 'Lord, as you wish and know how to, have mercy on me,' and if a battle comes: 'Lord, help me.' He knows what is appropriate and he deals mercifully with us."

Macarius the Egyptian 20   Abba Macarius said: "If being despised were the same as being praised for you, poverty as riches, indigence as affluence, you would not die. It is impossible for one whose faith is sound and who toils devoutly to fall into the impurity of passions or the deceit of demons."

Macarius the Egyptian 21   They used to say that two brothers erred at Scete and Abba Macarius the city-dweller expelled them. When some folk came and told Abba Macarius the Great, the Egyptian, he said: "It is not the brothers who have been expelled but Macarius who has been expelled," for he loved him. Abba Macarius [the city-dweller] heard that he had been expelled by the elder and he fled to the marsh. Abba Macarius the Great went out and, finding him devoured by mosquitoes, he said to him: "You expelled the brothers and here they had to go back to the village. I expelled you and like a good virgin you fled here, to the inner chamber. I summoned the brothers and inquired of them; they said that none of those things happened. So do you brother look out against being led astray by demons when you have not seen anything—and prostrate yourself for your error." Said he: "If it please you, give me a penance." Perceiving his humility, the elder said: "Go and fast for three weeks, eating once a week"—for that was his constant practice, to fast a week at a time.

Macarius the Egyptian 22   Abba Moses said to Abba Macarius at Scete: "I wish to live in *hesychia* but the brothers will not let me."

Abba Macarius said to him: "I see that yours is a tender nature and you cannot turn a brother away. But if you wish to live in *hesychia*, get off to the inner desert, to Petra, and live in *hesychia* there." This he did—and experienced repose.

Macarius the Egyptian 23 [cf. 10.47]   A brother visited Abba Macarius the Egyptian and said to him: "Abba, tell me a saying [indicating] how I can be saved." The elder said: "Go to the tomb and insult the dead," so the brother went. He insulted and stoned [them] then he came and told the elder. "And they said nothing to you?" he said to him. "No," said [the brother]. The elder said to him: "Go again tomorrow and praise them." The brother went and praised them, saying: "Apostles, holy and righteous ones," then he came to the elder and told him: "I praised [them]." "And they made no response?" he said to him. "No," said the brother, and the elder said to him: "You know how much you insulted them and they gave no answer; and how much you praised them but they said nothing to you. So too must you become dead if you want to be saved. Pay no attention (like the dead) either to the injustice of folk or to their praise—then you can be saved."

Macarius the Egyptian 24   Once when Abba Macarius was passing through Egypt with some brothers he heard a young woman saying to her mother: "Mama, a rich man loves me and I hate him while a poor man hates me and I love him." Abba Macarius was amazed on hearing this. The brothers said to him: "Father, what is this saying that you were amazed [at it]?" The elder said to them: "Truly our Lord is rich and he loves us—and we do not want to hear him. Our enemy the devil is poor and hates us—and we love his impurity."

Macarius the Egyptian 25   Abba Poemen besought him with many tears: "Tell me a saying [indicating] how I can be saved." In reply the elder said to him: "The thing you are inquiring about has now departed from the monks."

Macarius the Egyptian 26   Abba Macarius once visited Abba Antony then came back to Scete when he had spoken with him. The fathers came to meet him and, as they were speaking, the elder said to them: "I told Abba Antony that we do not have the Eucharist in our place." The fathers began speaking of other things and did not inquire any further to learn the reply from the elder, nor did the elder tell them. So one of the fathers used to say this: "If the fathers notice that it has slipped the brothers' mind to inquire about some matter beneficial to them, they are obliged to speak of it first themselves. But if they are not obliged by the brothers to do so, they pursue the discourse no further, so that they do not seem to speak without being asked nor their discourse sound like idle chatter."

Macarius the Egyptian 27   Abba Isaiah asked Abba Macarius: "Tell me a saying," and the elder said to him: "Flee from folk." Abba Isaiah said to him: "What is it to 'flee from folk?'" Said the elder to him: "It is to remain in your cell and to weep for your sins."

Macarius the Egyptian 28   Abba Paphnutius the disciple of Abba Macarius [the city-dweller] used to say: "I besought my father, saying: 'Tell me a saying' but he said: 'Do no evil to anybody and do not condemn anybody. Keep these [commandments] and you are being saved.'"

Macarius the Egyptian 29   Abba Macarius said: "Do not sleep in the cell of a brother who has a bad reputation."

Macarius the Egyptian 30   Some brothers once visited Abba Macarius at Scete and they found nothing in his cell but some stale water. They said to him: "Come up to the village, abba, and we will refresh you." The elder said to them: "You know the bakery of so-and-so in the village, brothers?" "Yes," they said, and the elder said to them: "I know it too. Do you know the property of so-and-so, there where the river flows?" "Yes," they said to him and the elder said to them: "I know it too. So when I want [to go there] I will not need you: I will go up myself."

Macarius the Egyptian 31   The used to say of Abba Macarius that, if a brother approached him timidly as a great and holy elder, he would not say anything to him. But if one of the brothers spoke to him as though he were putting him down: "Abba, when you were a camel-driver and you used to steal niter to sell it, did the guards not beat you?"—if somebody spoke to him like that, he would happily converse with him if he asked him anything.

Macarius the Egyptian 32   They used to say of Abba Macarius the Great that he became "a god on earth" (as it is written)[85] for just as God overshadows the earth, so was Abba Macarius overshadowing shortcomings, as though not seeing what he saw and not hearing what he heard.

Macarius the Egyptian 33 [20.3]   Abba Betimos recounted that Abba Macarius used to say: "Once when I was living at Scete, two young strangers came down there. One of them had a beard, the other was beginning to have a beard. They came to me saying: 'Where is Abba Macarius' cell?' and I said to them: 'Why do you want him?' 'We heard about him and about Scete,' they said, 'and we have come to see him.' 'I am he,' I said to them and they prostrated themselves, saying: 'We want to stay here.' But, seeing they were delicate and as though from affluent [circumstances], I told them: 'You cannot live here.' The older one said: 'If we cannot live here we will go somewhere else.' I said to myself: 'Why am I sending them off and offending them? The toil will make them run away of their own accord.' I said to them: 'Come, make yourselves a cell if you can.' 'Show us a place and we will make it,' they said."

The elder gave them an axe and a basket full of bread and salt. The elder showed them some hard rock, saying: "'Get some stones here and bring yourselves wood from the marsh; set up a roof and live here,' for I thought (he said) they were going to run away because of the toil. But they asked me: 'What work do they do here?' 'Rope-making,' I told them. Taking some palm-fronds from the marsh, I

[85] *Apostolic Constitutions* 2.26.4.

showed them the elements of rope-making and how one has to sew [it]. 'Make some baskets; deliver them to the guardians and they will bring you loaves,' I told them; and so I went my way. But for their part, they patiently performed everything I had said to them, and for three years they did not visit me. I went on doing battle with my *logismoi*, saying: 'What on earth is their activity that they have not come to inquire of me about a *logismos*?' There are those from far away who come to me, but these who are near have not come, nor were they going anywhere else—other than to church in silence to receive the sacrament. For a week I fasted and prayed to God to show me their activity. After a week I got up and went to them to see how they were living. When I knocked they opened [the gate] and greeted me—in silence. I offered a prayer and sat down. The older one gave a sign to the younger one to go out then he sat there braiding rope, not saying a word. At the ninth hour he knocked; the younger one came and prepared a little gruel, setting a table at the older one's prompting. He placed three dried loaves on it then stood in silence. 'Get up, let us eat,' I said; we got up and ate. He brought the bottle and we drank. When evening fell, they said to me: 'Are you going?' 'No,' I said; 'I am sleeping here.' They put out a mat for me in one place and [one for] themselves in the other corner. Removing their girdles and their scapulars, they lay down together on the mat in front of me. When they had lain down I prayed to God to reveal their activity to me and here the roof was opened and it was light as in the day, but they were not seeing the light. When they thought I was sleeping, the older one nudged the younger in the ribs; they got up, put their girdles on and stretched out their hands to heaven. I was observing them but they were not observing me. I saw the demons coming at the younger one like flies; some came and settled on his mouth, some on his eyes. I also saw an angel of the Lord who had a fiery sword; he was defending him and chasing the demons away from him; but they were unable to approach the older one. Toward dawn they lay down; I made as though I had just woken up and they did likewise. The older one merely said this to me: 'Do you want us to offer the twelve psalms?' 'Yes,' I said and the younger one sang five psalms, six verses at a time with an *allelujah*. With each verse a lamp of fire came out of his mouth and went up into the heavens. Likewise the older one too, when he opened his mouth to sing, something like a rope of fire came out, stretching up to heaven; I said a little too from memory. As I was leaving I said: 'Pray for me,' but they prostrated themselves in silence; I discovered that the older one was perfect while the enemy was still in combat with the younger one. A few days later the older brother died: the younger one the third day after."

When some of the fathers visited Abba Macarius, he would bring them to their cell saying: "Come and see the martyrs' shrine of the young strangers."

Macarius the Egyptian 34 [3.20]   The elders at the Mountain[86] once sent to Abba Macarius at Scete with a request. They said to him: "To spare all our company the toil of coming to you, we beg you to grace us with your presence so we can see you before you migrate to the Lord." When he presented himself at the mountain the entire company congregated about him. The elders were asking him to tell the brothers a saying, but when he heard he said: "Let us weep, brothers, and let our eyes pour forth tears before we go where our tears will burn our bodies." They all wept and they fell on their faces saying: "Pray for us, father."

Macarius the Egyptian 35   Another time too a demon attacked Abba Macarius with a sword wishing to cut off his foot, but it was unable to do so, on account of his humble-mindedness. It said to him: "We have whatever you have; it is only your humble-mindedness that distinguishes you from us—and you prevail."

Macarius the Egyptian 36 [10.48]   Abba Macarius said: "If we keep in remembrance the bad things done to us by people, we are destroying the power of the remembrance of God; but if we keep the bad things of the demons in remembrance, we will be unharmed."

[86]of Nitria

Macarius the Egyptian 37   Abba Paphnutius, the disciple of Abba Macarius [the city-dweller], said that the elder used to say: "When I was a child, I and the other children used to pasture cattle and they went off to steal some figs. One [fig] fell as they were running along: I took it and ate it and, when I recall that, I sit weeping."

Macarius the Egyptian 38 [3.19]   Abba Macarius said: "Once when I was walking around in the desert I found the skull of a dead person lying on the ground. When I prodded it with my palm-staff the skull spoke to me. I said to it : "Who are you then?" The skull answered me: "I was the high priest of the idols and of the pagans who inhabited this place; but you are the spirit-bearing Abba Macarius. Whenever you feel compassion for those in chastisement and pray for them they are a little relieved." The elder said to him: "What is the relief and what the chastisement?" [The skull] said to him: "There is as much fire beneath us as the sky is distant from the earth [Is 55.9] and we are located in the midst of the fire, head to feet. Nobody can see another face-to-face because the face of each one is glued to the back of another. So when you pray for us, one has a partial glimpse of the face of another; that is the relief." Weeping, the elder said: "Sad was the day in which a person was born if this is relief from chastisement!" The elder said to him again: "Is there another punishment worse than this one?" The skull said to him: "There is a greater punishment beneath us." The elder said to him: "And who are in it?" The skull said to him: "We who did not know God are at least a little pitied; but they who knew God but denied him and did not do his will, they are down below us." The elder took the skull and buried it.

Macarius the Egyptian 39   They used to say of Abba Macarius the Egyptian that he was once going up from Scete to the Mountain of Nitria and when he drew near to the place he said to his disciple: "Go on ahead a little." As he went ahead he encountered a priest of the pagans. The brother called out to him shouting: "Hey, hey demon, where are you running to? [The other] turned round and dealt him a few blows, leaving him half dead, then took his club and ran on. A little further on Abba Macarius encountered him running and said to him: "I hope you are well, I hope you are well, you who toil." Amazed, [the pagan] came to him and said: "What good did you see in me that you saluted me?" The elder said to him: "It is just that I saw you toiling and you do not know you are toiling to no avail." The other said to him: "I was pricked in my conscience by your greeting and I learned that you are on God's side. Another monk, a bad one, met me and reviled me so I gave him a few blows [and put him] to death." The elder perceived that it was his disciple. The priest grasped his feet saying: "I will not let you go unless you make me a monk." Coming to where the [disciple-] monk was they picked him up and brought him into the church of the Mountain. [The brothers] were astounded when they saw the priest with [Abba Macarius] and they made [the priest] a monk; many pagans became Christians through him. Abba Macarius used to say: "A harsh word makes the good bad but a good [word] benefits everybody."

Macarius the Egyptian 40   They used to say of Abba Macarius that a robber entered his cell while he was away. When he came back to his cell he found the robber loading his goods onto a camel. Going into the cell, he took some of his goods and joined him in loading the camel. When they had loaded it the robber began beating the camel to make it get up but it did not rise. When Abba Macarius saw that it was not rising, he went into the cell and found a small hoe. He brought it out and put it on the camel, saying: "Brother, the camel is looking for this." The elder kicked it saying: "Get up," and it immediately got up and went a little way, following his instruction. Then it sat down again and did not get up until they unloaded all the goods; then off it went.

Macarius the Egyptian 41 [cf. 27]   Abba Aio asked Abba Macarius: "Tell me a saying." Abba Macarius said to him: "Flee from folk; remain in your cell; weep for your sins; take no delight in human conversation—and you are being saved."

Macarius the Egyptian S 1 [Guy 54–55; cf. Macarius the Egyptian 37] Abba Macarius used to say: "When I was young, a prey to *accidie* in my cell, I went out into the desert saying to my *logismos*: 'Whomsoever you meet, ask him for the grace of some benefit.' I found a child tending cattle and I said to him: 'What shall I do, child, for I am hungry.' 'Eat then,' he told me. Again I said I was eating and was still hungry. Again he said to me: 'Eat again then.' Again I said: 'I was eating and am still hungry.' Then he said to me: 'You are clearly an ass, abba, wanting to munch away all the time.' I went my way having reaped benefit."

MOSES

This Moses was an Ethiopian (i.e. black), a former slave who had been sent away by his master for thieving. He became a murderer and the chief of a robber band but he had a change of heart as a result of which he became an exemplary monk. He was slaughtered by the Mazics in 407 (aged seventy-five) having refused to flee from their attack.[87]

Moses 1 [18.17] Abba Moses of Petra was terribly embattled by *porneia*. No longer strong enough to remain in his cell he went and reported to Abba Isidore. The elder begged him to return to his cell but he would not accept that, saying: "Abba, I haven't the strength." So he took him and brought him up onto the housetop with him and said to him: "Look to the west." He looked and saw an innumerable host of demons; they were milling around together and shouting, ready for battle. Then Abba Isidore also said to him: "Look to the east." He looked and saw innumerable hosts of glorious holy angels. Then Abba Isidore also said: "Here, these are they who are sent by the Lord to help the holy ones; those in the west are they who are fighting against them. These who are on our side are the more numerous."

[87]See *HL* 19 and Cassian, *Conf.* 1 & 2.

When he had given thanks to God for this, Abba Moses took courage and returned to his own cell.

Moses 2 [9.7]   A brother once erred at Scete and a council was held. They sent for Abba Moses but he was unwilling to come. So the priest sent to him, saying: "Come, for the company is waiting for you." He got up and came; he took a basket with many holes, filled it with sand and carried it [with him]. Coming out to meet him, they said to him: "What is this, father?" and the elder said to them: "My sins are running out behind me and I do not see them—yet here I have come today to pass judgment on the faults of another!" They said nothing to the brother when they heard this, but forgave him.

Moses 3 [16.9]   Another time there was a council at Scete. Wanting to put him to the test, the fathers belittled him, saying: "Why does this Ethiopian come among us too?" but he kept quiet on hearing this. After they were dismissed they said to him: "Abba, were you not troubled just now?" "I was troubled but did not speak" [Ps 76.5], he said to them.

Moses 4 [15.43]   They used to say of Abba Moses that when he became a cleric and they put the stole on him, the archbishop said to him: "Look, you have become all white, Abba Moses." The elder said to him: "Maybe outside, my lord Pope, but what about inside?" The bishop wanted to put him to the test; so he said to the clergy: "When Abba Moses comes into the sanctuary, chase him away and follow him to hear what he says." The elder came in; they denounced him and chased him off, saying: "Get out, Ethiopian." Out he went, saying to himself: "They treated you rightly, ash-skinned black [man]; since you are not human, why come among humans?"

Moses 5 [13.4]   A directive was once issued at Scete: "Fast this week." It came about that some brothers from Egypt visited Abba Moses and he cooked them a little gruel. Seeing the smoke, his neighbors told the clergy: "Here, Moses has broken the directive of the fathers and cooked himself some gruel." "We ourselves will speak to him when he comes," they said. When Saturday came round, the clergy, well aware of the great discipline of Abba Moses, said to him before the company: "Oh Abba Moses, you have broken men's directive but fulfilled God's."

Moses 6 [2.19]   A brother visited Abba Moses at Scete asking him for a saying. The elder said to him: "Go and stay in a cell; your cell will teach you everything."

Moses 7 [2.20]   Abba Moses said: "He who flees from folk is like a bunch of ripe grapes, but he who is among folk is like an unripe grape."

Moses 8 [8.13]   The governor [of a province] once heard of Abba Moses and off he went to Scete to see him. When some folk reported the matter to the elder, he got up to run away into the marsh but they met him and said: "Tell us, old man, where is Abba Moses' cell?" "What do you want from him?" he said to them; "he is crazy." When the governor came into the church, he said to the clergy: "I am hearing things about Abba Moses and have come to see him and here an old man who was going into Egypt met us. We said to him: 'Where is Abba Moses' cell?' and he said to us: 'What do you want from him? He is crazy.'" The clergy were sad when they heard this; they said: "What sort of a person was this old man who said these things against the holy one?" "He was elderly, wearing old clothes, tall and black," they said, and the clergy said: "That is Abba Moses; he said those things so he would not meet you." The governor went his way having reaped great benefit.

Moses 9 [18.18]   Abba Moses used to say at Scete: "If we keep the commandments of our fathers, I warrant you in God's name that the barbarians will not be coming here. If we do not keep [them], this place is going to be devastated."

Moses 10 [18.18, continued]   Once when the brothers were sitting with him, he said to them: "Here the barbarians are coming to Scete today; but get up and run away!" They said to him: "And you, abba, are you not running away?" He said to them: "I have been waiting so many years for this day so that the saying of my Lord-and-master Christ might be fulfilled: 'All who take the sword shall be lost by the sword' [Mt 26.52]." They said to him: "Neither will we run away; we will die with you," but he said to them: "I have nothing to do with that; let each one decide for himself." There were seven brothers and he said to them: "Here are the barbarians, approaching the gate." In they came and killed them, but one of them fled behind some cord for fear and he saw seven crowns descending and crowning them.

Moses 11   A brother asked Abba Moses: "I see something before me and am not able to grasp it." The elder said to him: "Unless you become dead like those in graves you will not be able to grasp it."

Moses 12 [10.92]   Abba Poemen said that a brother asked Abba Moses: "In what way does a person make himself dead with respect to his neighbor?" The elder said to him: "Unless a person put it in his heart that he has already been three days[88] in a tomb, he cannot attain to this saying."

Moses 13 [6.27]   They used to say of Abba Moses at Scete that when he was about to arrive at Petra, he had exhausted himself travelling there and that he was saying to himself: "How can I collect my water here?" A voice came to him saying: "Come in and do not worry about anything," so in he went. Then some of the fathers visited him and he had only one small vessel of water; while he was boiling a few lentils it was used up. The elder was distressed so, while going in and out, he was praying to God and here a rain-cloud came over Petra itself and he filled all his vessels. After that they said to the elder: "Tell us why you were coming in and going out." The elder said to them: "I was pleading my cause before God, saying: 'You brought me hither and here I have no water so that your servants can drink,' and that is why I was coming in and going out, beseeching God until he sent us [water]."

[88]"Three years" in some mss.

Seven Chapters That Abba Moses Sent to Abba Poemen

He who observes them will be delivered from all chastisement
and will experience repose wherever he be staying, whether in the
desert or with brothers.

Moses 14 [I] Abba Moses said: "A person must die with respect to
his companion in order not to judge him in anything."

Moses 15 [II] He also said: "A person must mortify himself with
respect to every evil matter before departing from the body, so that
he wrong nobody."

Moses 16 [III] He also said: "If a person does not have it in his
heart that he is a sinner, God does not listen to him." The brother
said: "What does it mean to 'have it in his heart that he is a sinner'?" The elder said: "If one is carrying his sins he does not see his
neighbor's."

Moses 17 [IV] He also said: "If one's practice be not in accordance
with his prayer, he labors in vain." The brother said: "What is 'agreement between practice and prayer'?" The elder said: "No longer to do
the things we pray about, for when somebody abandons his desires,
then God is reconciled with him and receives his prayer."

Moses [IVb] A brother asked: "In all a person's toiling, what help is
there for him?" Said the elder: "It is God who helps, for it is written:
'God is our refuge and strength, a powerful help against the afflictions that find us'" [Ps 45.2].

Moses [V] The brother said: "And what of the fasts and vigils a person performs?" The elder said: "These cause the soul to be humbled,
for it is written: 'Behold my abasement and my toil and forgive all my
sins' [Ps 24.18]. If the soul bears these fruits God will have compassion toward it on their account."

Moses [VI] The brother said to the elder: "What is a person to do
in every temptation that comes upon him or at every *logismos* of

the enemy?" The elder said to him: "He ought to weep before the goodness of God that he might help him and he will soon experience repose, provided he intercede intelligently; for it is written: 'The Lord is my helper and I shall not fear what a person does to me' [Ps 117.6]."

Moses [VII] The brother asked: "Here a person is beating his slave for a sin he committed; what shall the slave say?" The elder said: "If the slave be a good one he will say: 'Have mercy on me for I have sinned.'" The brother said to him: "He says nothing else?" The elder said: "No, for from the moment he lays the blame on himself and says 'I have sinned' his master immediately has compassion on him. The bottom line in all this is: not to judge one's neighbor. When the hand of the Lord killed all the first born in the land of Egypt there was not a house there in which no one had died" [Ex 12.29–30]. The brother said to him: "What does this discourse mean?" The elder said to him: "If we took the trouble to see our sins we would not see the sins of a neighbor. It is folly for a person who has his own dead to leave it and go and weep for his neighbor's. To die with respect to your neighbor, that is to carry your sins and not to be anxious for every [other] person that this one is good, that one wicked. Do evil to nobody nor keep any evil in your heart against anyone. Do not belittle a wrong-doer; do not be influenced by one who wrongs his neighbor and do not rejoice with one who does wrong to his neighbor. Do not slander anybody but say: 'God knows each one.' Do not agree with one who slanders; neither rejoice with him in his slandering nor hate him who slanders his neighbor—and this is 'judge not [that you be not judged' Lk 6.37]. Do not be at enmity with anybody and do not foster enmity in your heart; do not hate one who is at enmity with his neighbor—and this is peace. Console yourself with this: there is labor for a short while then repose for eternity, by the grace of the divine Word. Amen."

MATOES

Matoes 1 [7.16]   Abba Matoes said: "I prefer some light activity that lasts to one that is onerous at first and soon broken off."

Matoes 2 [15.41]   He also said: "The nearer a person gets to God, the more he sees himself as a sinner; for when the prophet Isaiah saw the Lord, he began to declare himself wretched and impure" [Is 6.5].

Matoes 3   He also said: "When I was younger I used to say to myself: 'Perhaps I will do some good deed one day,' but now, having grown old, I see that I do not have one good deed in me."

Matoes 4 [10.49]   He also said: "Satan does not know by which passion the soul is worsted. He sows, but he knows not whether he will reap; he sows some people with *porneia*, others with slanderous *logismoi*, and likewise with the rest of the passions; and to whatever passion he notices a soul inclining, he fires it up."

Matoes 5   A brother visited Abba Matoes and said to him: "How were the people of Scete doing more than the Scripture [required of them by] loving their enemies more than themselves?" Abba Matoes said to him: "Until now I do not love the one who loves me as [I love] myself."

Matoes 6   A brother asked Abba Matoes: "What shall I do if a brother visits me and it is a fast day or at an early hour, for I am perplexed?" The elder said to him: "If you are perplexed but eat with the brother, you do well. But if you eat when you are not expecting anybody, you are following your own will."

Matoes 7   Abba James said: "I visited Abba Matoes and told him that, when I returned, I wanted to visit the cells. 'Greet Abba John on my behalf,' he said to me. So I came to Abba John and said to him: 'Abba Matoes greets you,' and the elder said to me: 'Behold Abba Matoes, a true Israelite in whom there is no guile' [cf. Jn 1.47]. When a year had passed, visiting Abba Matoes again, I communicated the greeting of Abba John to him and the elder said to me: 'I am not worthy of what the elder said; but know this: when you hear an elder esteeming a neighbor above himself, he has achieved a great stature, for this is perfection: to esteem one's neighbor above oneself.'"

Matoes 8 [5.6]   Abba Matoes used to say: "A brother came to me and told me that slandering is worse than *porneia*. 'That is a hard saying,' I said, so the brother said to me: 'What do you want the case to be then?' I said: 'Slandering is bad, but cured quickly, for the slanderer often repents, saying: 'I spoke badly,' but *porneia* is physical death.'"

Matoes 9 [15.42]   Abba Matoes once went from Raïthou to the district of Magdala, his brother with him. The bishop took the elder and made him a priest. While they were eating together the bishop said: "Forgive me, abba; I know you did not want this thing, but I presumed to do it so I could be blessed by you." The elder humbly said to him: "Certainly my *logismos* had little wish for it; but what troubles me is that [now] I have to separate from the brother who is with me, for I cannot bear offering all the prayers alone." The bishop said: "If you know that he is worthy, I will ordain him." Abba Matoes said to him: "I do not know whether he is worthy but I know one thing: he is better than me," and [the bishop] ordained him too. Both of them died without having ever approached an altar to offer the Eucharist. The elder used to say: "I have faith in God that I do not have much to answer for on account of the ordination, since I do not offer the Eucharist. Ordination is for the blameless."

Matoes 10   Abba Matoes said: "Three elders went to Abba Paphnutius (known as Cephalas) to ask him for a saying and the elder said to them: 'What do you want me to say to you: something spiritual or physical?' 'Spiritual,' they said to him. The elder said to them: 'Off you go then: love affliction more than repose, dishonor more than esteem, and giving rather than receiving.'"

Matoes 11 [1.34, N 330]   A brother asked Abba Matoes: "Tell me a saying," and he said to him: "Go and beseech God to give you sorrow in your heart and humility. Be always aware of your sins and do not judge others but be inferior to everybody. Have no friendship with a child, no relationship with a woman, no heretic as your friend. Disassociate yourself from loose talk; master your tongue and your belly, [refraining] from any more than a little wine. If somebody speaks to you about any matter whatsoever, do not argue with him. If he speaks well, say: 'Yes'; if he speaks badly, say: 'You know what you are talking about,' and do not contend with him about what he said; this is humility."

Matoes 12 [10.179]   A brother asked Abba Matoes: "Tell me a saying." He said to him: "Cut off from yourself all contentiousness in every matter. Weep and lament, for the time has drawn near."

Matoes 13 [11.79]   A brother asked Abba Matoes: "What am I to do?—for my tongue is troubling me. When I go among folk I am unable to restrain it: I pass judgment on them in every good deed and am reproving them; what am I to do?" In response the elder said: "If you cannot restrain yourself, run away and be alone—for this is a weakness. He who lives among brothers ought not to be a square peg but a round one, so he can turn toward everyone. It is not on account of virtue that I live alone but of weakness; they are strong ones, those who come into the presence of folk."

MARK THE DISCIPLE OF ABBA SILVANUS

Mark 1   They used to say of Abba Silvanus that he had a disciple at Scete whose name was Mark. He was immensely obedient and he was a scribe. The elder loved him for his obedience. He had eleven other disciples and they were troubled that he loved that one more than them. The elders were saddened on hearing of this. The elders came to him one day, reproaching him. He led them out and knocked at each cell saying: "Come, brother so-and-so, I need you," and not one of them followed him right away. He came to Mark's cell and knocked, saying: "Mark . . . " and he at once came leaping out on hearing the elder's voice—and he sent him on an errand. Then he said to the elders: "Where are the rest of the brothers, fathers?" Going into [Mark's] cell he examined his quaternion and found that he had set his hand to [write] an *omega* but, on hearing the elder he had not turned the pen to complete it. So the elders said: "Since God loves him, let us too love him whom you love."

Mark 2 They used to say of Abba Silvanus that once when he was walking around with the elders at Scete he wanted to demonstrate the obedience of Mark, his disciple, and why he loved him. Seeing a small boar, he said to him: "Do you see that little antelope, my son?" "Yes, abba," he said." "And its horns, how plausible they are?" "Yes, abba," he said; the elders were astounded at his answer and were edified by his obedience.

Mark 3 [14.12]   Once the mother of this brother Mark came down to see him and came in great style. The elder went out to her and she said to him: "Abba, tell my son to come out so I may see him." The elder went in and said to him: "Come out so your mother can see you." He was wearing tatters and was blackened from the cookhouse. Coming out in obedience, he closed his eyes and said to them: "Good health, good health, good health!" but he did not see them nor did his mother recognize that it was he. So again she sent to the elder saying: "Abba, send me my son so I may see him," and he said to Mark: "Did I not tell you: 'Go out so your mother can see you?'" "I went out in accordance with your instruction, abba," Mark told him, "but please do not tell me to go out once again—so I do not disobey you." The elder went out and said to her: "It was he who met you and said: 'Good health,'" and when he had consoled her, he dismissed her.

Mark 4 Another time [Silvanus] happened to come out of Scete and travel to Mount Sinaï where he stayed. The mother of Mark sent adjuring [Silvanus] with tears for her son to come out so she could see him, and the elder gave him leave. As he was preparing his sheepskin to come out he came to greet the elder and—burst into tears. He did not come out.

Mark 5 [18.20]   They used to say of Abba Silvanus that when he wanted to go into Syria his disciple Mark said to him: "Father, I do not want to go away from here and I will not let you go away. Wait here for three days," and the third day he died.

MILES

Miles 1 [19.13]   Once when Abba Miles was passing through a place, he saw a monk being held by somebody for having committed murder. The elder approached and, having questioned the brother, learned that he was being falsely accused. He said to those who were detaining him: "Where is the murder victim?" They showed him; he approached the murder victim and told everybody to pray; then he stretched out his hands to God and the dead man arose. [The elder] said to him in the presence of all: "Tell us who it was that murdered you." "I went into the church and gave money to the priest," he said, "but he rose up and strangled me; then he took me and threw me down at the abba's monastery. I beg you: let the money be recovered and be given to my children." Then the elder said to him: "Go to sleep until the Lord comes and raises you up."

Miles 2 [7.17]   Another time, while he was living in Persian territory with two disciples, two sons of the king who were full brothers went out hunting as was their custom. They cast nets over a large area, as much as forty miles, so that, if anything were found caught in the nets, they could kill it with spears. The elder was discovered with his two disciples and when they saw him, hairy and looking formidable, they were flabbergasted. They said to him: "Tell us whether you are a man or a spirit." He said to them: "I am a sinful

GIVE ME A WORD

man, come out to weep for my sins, and I worship Jesus Christ the son of the living God." They said to him: "There is no god other than the sun, the fire, and the water"—which they revered—"so come and sacrifice to them." But he said to them: "Those are creatures and you are deluded; but I urge you to turn about and come to know the true God, the creator of everything." They said to him: "You mean the condemned and crucified one is true God?" "Yes," said the elder, "the one who crucified sin and slaughtered death; I am saying he is the true God." After they had tortured him and his disciples they tried to force them to sacrifice. They beheaded the two disciples after torturing them severely. When they had severely tortured the elder for some days, later on, using their skills, they placed him between them and then shot arrows at him, one from in front, the other from the rear. The elder said to them: "Since you are of one mind to shed innocent blood, tomorrow, in a twinkling of an eye, at this time, your mother shall be dispossessed of her children and deprived of your love; for you are going to shed each other's blood with your own spears." Disregarding what he said, they went out hunting next day. When a deer ran out from the nets they mounted their horses and ran to overtake her. They threw their spears at it and pierced each other in the heart and they died, as the elder had said to them, cursing them. And they died.

MOTIOS

This is probably none other than Matoes.

Motios 1 [8.14, first half only; attributed to Matoes]   A brother asked Abba Motios: "If I go and stay in some place, how do you want me to conduct myself there?" The elder said to him: "If you are living somewhere, do not be wanting to make a reputation for yourself [saying]: 'I do not come out for the *synaxis*' or: 'I do not eat at an *agapē*,' for these create a hollow reputation and later on you will have trouble, for people go running to where they find such things." So the brother said to him: "What then shall I do?" The elder said: "Wherever you are staying, keep in step with them all and what you see the devout persons of whom you are sure doing, do that and you will experience repose. When you are equal with them, that is humility. When people see you not stepping out of line, then they regard you as the equal of all and no one will trouble you."

Motios 2 Abba Isaac, the disciple of Abba Motios (these both became bishops) recounted that the elder built a monastery at Heraclaeum and that, when he departed from there, he came to another place and built again there. By the operation of the devil there was a brother there who was at enmity with him and who tormented him. The elder arose and retreated to his own village. He made himself a monastery and shut himself up in it. Some time later the elders of the place he had abandoned came out, took the brother who had caused him distress and came to beg him to let them take him back to his monastery. When they approached [the place] where Abba Sores was they left both their sheepskins with him and the brother who had caused distress. When they knocked, the elder set up a ladder, looked down and recognized them. "Where are your sheepskins?" he said. "They are over here with this brother," they said. When he heard the name of the brother who had caused him distress, for joy the elder took an axe and broke down the door. He ran out to where the brother was; first he prostrated himself then embraced him and brought him into his cell. He entertained them for three days and himself too (which he was not accustomed to do) then he arose and went with them. Afterwards he became a bishop, for he was a wonder-worker. The blessed Cyril made Abba Isaac, his disciple, a bishop.

Megethius

Megethius 1   They used to say of Abba Megethius that he came out of his cell and if a *logismos* came upon him to withdraw from the place he would not return to his cell. Nor did he ever possess any of this world's material goods other than one needle with which he would split the palm-fronds. He made three baskets a day [to defray the cost] of his food.

Megethius 2 [14.10, in part]   They used to say of the second Abba Megethius that he was extremely humble. Trained by Egyptians, he had met many elders, both Abba Sisoes and Abba Poemen. He was living by the river at Sinaï. One of the holy ones happened to visit him and, as he told us himself, he said to him: "How do you live in this desert, brother?" He said: "I fast every second day and consume one loaf." And he told me: "If you will listen to me, eat half a loaf each day." He did so and found repose.

Megethius 3   Some of the fathers asked Abba Megethius: "If some cooked food is left over to next day, do you want the brothers to eat [it]?" The elder said to them: "If it is spoiled it is not good for the brothers to be obliged to eat it and get sick: throw it away. But if it is good and one throws it away out of wantonness, then prepares something else, that is bad.

Megethius 4 [N 238, 10.165]   He also said: "At first when we were brought together with each other we used to speak of [spiritual] benefit, confirming each other. We became as choirs, choirs [of angels] and we were going up to heaven. But now we meet together and come to slandering one another—and down we go."

MIOS

Mios 1 [14.9]   Abba Mios of Beleos said: "Obedience for obedience; if someone pays attention to God, God pays attention to him."

Mios 2 [15.47]   He also said of a certain elder[89] at Scete that he was a former slave and that he gained an extraordinary ability in discrimination. He used to go to Alexandria each year bringing his earnings to his masters. They would meet him and prostrate themselves before him. The elder would put water in the bowl and bring it so he could wash his masters' feet, but they would say to him: "No father, do not embarrass us." But he would say to them: "I am acknowledging that I am your slave and am grateful that you set me free to be a slave for God. For my part, I wash your feet, and you: you receive my earnings." But they would strive not to accept [them] and he would say to them: "If you do not want to accept them, I am staying here, slaving for you." They were in awe of him, so they would let him do what he wanted to do. They would send him on his way with honor and many goods so he could distribute alms on their behalf. He became eminent and beloved at Scete on this account.

Mios 3 [10.176]   Abba Mios was asked by a soldier whether God accepted repentance. After he had instructed him in many words the elder said to him: "Tell me, dear one, if your mantle is torn, do you throw it out?" "No," he said; "I sew it up and use it." The elder said to him: "So if you are sparing of your own clothing, will not God be sparing of his own creation?"

MARK THE EGYPTIAN

Mark the Egyptian [9.6]   They used to say of Mark the Egyptian that he remained for thirty years never coming out of his cell. The priest was in the habit of coming and celebrating the holy Eucharist

[89]Named "Abba Olympius" in 15.47.

for him, but when the devil saw [Mark's] virtuous patient endurance, he contrived to condemn him by putting him to the test. He
arranged for somebody possessed of a demon to go to the elder,
ostensibly for prayer. Before anything was said, the possessed one
called out to the elder saying: "Your priest has the odor of sin; do
not let him come to you any more." But inspired by the Spirit [Mark]
said to him: "My son, everybody rejects uncleanness; but you have
brought it to me, for it is written: 'Judge not that you be not judged'
[Mt 7.1]. Nevertheless, even if he be a sinner, the Lord will save him,
for it is written: 'Pray for one another that you might be healed' [Jas
5.16]." On saying this he offered a prayer, chased the demon out of the
fellow, and sent him away whole. When the priest came as usual, the
elder received him with joy and, when the good God saw the innocence of the elder, he showed him a sign. When the cleric was about
to take up his position before the Holy Table, as the elder recounted
it: "I saw an angel of the Lord coming down from heaven. He placed
his hand on the head of the cleric and the cleric became a pillar of
fire. Astonished at the sight, I heard a voice saying to me: 'Fellow,
why have you wondered at this matter? If an earthly emperor does
not allow his grandees to stand dirty in his presence and not in fine
array, how much more so will the Divine Power purify the ministers
of the Holy Mysteries standing before the Heavenly Glory?'" It was
because he did not condemn the cleric that Mark the Egyptian, the
noble martyr of Christ who became great, was deemed worthy of
this spiritual gift.

MACARIUS THE CITIZEN OF ALEXANDRIA

*Born at the end of the third century like his namesake "The
Egyptian," Macarius became known as "the city-dweller" because
he came from the city of Alexandria, and maybe also because he
retained something of the urban culture. He sold candies in his
youth and probably retained throughout his life the characteristics*

still to be observed in the young merchants who people the streets of Cairo today: their politeness, dynamism, and care-free nature, but also their audacity and even their calculating. Converted and baptized c. 330, Macarius became a monk at Nitria, and subsequently the priest at The Cells where he died 393/394 approaching 100. There is much confusion between the two persons of this name.

Macarius of Alexandria 1   Abba Macarius the citizen once went to cut palm-fronds, his brothers with him. On the first day they said to him: "Come and eat with us father," he went and ate. Again the next day they spoke to him about eating but he did not want to [eat]. He said to them: "You need to eat, my sons, because you are still flesh; but I do not want to eat now."

Macarius of Alexandria 2 [10.46]   Abba Macarius visited Abba Pachomius of the Tabennesiotes, and Abba Pachomius asked Abba Macarius: "When there are brothers who are out of order, is it good to correct them?" Abba Macarius said to him: "Correct [them] and judge aright those who are under your authority, but judge nobody who is not, for it is written: 'Do you not judge those who are inside [the fellowship]? But God judges those who are outside [it]'" [1 Cor 5.12–13].

Macarius of Alexandria 3   Abba Macarius once spent three months visiting a brother every day and not once did he find him not praying. "Here is an earthly angel," he used to say in wonder.

N—*Nu*

NIL

Although they are attributed to Nil, a disciple of John Chrysostom and superior of a monastery at Ancyra in Galatia, the following sayings are extracts from the Treaty on Prayer by Evagrius, whose writings became suspect in certain quarters.

Nil 1   Abba Nil said: "Whatever you do in revenge to a brother who has done you wrong will all become an obstacle for you at the time of prayer."

Nil 2   He also said: "Prayer is the offshoot of gentleness and absence-of-anger."

Nil 3   He also said: "Prayer is the remedy for grief and despondency."

Nil 4   He also said: " 'Go sell what you possess and give to the poor' [Mt 19.21]. Take the cross and deny yourself [Mt 16.24] so you can pray without distraction."

Nil 5   He also said: "Whatever you endure as a monk,[90] you will find the fruit of it in the time of prayer."

Nil 6   He also said: "If you long to pray as one should, do not grieve your soul; otherwise, you are running in vain."

Nil 7   He also said: "Do not desire your situation to be what seems good to you, but what pleases God, and you will be untroubled and thankful in your prayer."

[90]Lit. "philosophizing."

Nil 8   He also said: "Blessed is the monk who considers himself 'the offscouring of all things'" [1 Cor 4.13].

Nil 9   He also said: "The monk who loves *hesychia* remains unwounded by the darts of the enemy, but he who involves himself with multitudes receives wounds continually."

Nil 10   He also said: "Let the servant prepare himself for scourges who is negligent of the works of his master."

NISTEROS

There is considerable confusion about persons of this name and about its spelling.

Nisteros 1 [8.15]   Abba Nisteros the Great was walking in the desert with a brother when they saw a dragon—and fled. The brother said to him: "Are you afraid too, father?" The elder said: "I am not afraid, my son, but it was good for me to run away since I would not have been able to run away from the spirit of vainglory."

Nisteros 2 [1.18]   A brother asked an elder: "What good activity is there, that I could practice and live in it?" The elder said: "God knows what is good, but I heard that one of the fathers questioned Abba Nisteros the Great, the friend of Abba Antony, saying to him: 'What good work is there, that I might do [it]?' and he said to him: "Are not all undertakings equal? For the Scripture says: 'Abraham was hospitable and God was with him' [cf. Gen 18.2ff]; Elijah loved *hesychia* and God was with him; David was humble and God was with him. So whatever you observe your soul wishing to do for God, do it—and keep a watch on your heart."

Nisteros 3   Abba Joseph says to Abba Nisteros: "What am I to do about my tongue for I cannot control it?" The elder said to him: "So when you speak, do you experience repose?" "No," he said to him, and the elder said: "If you do not experience repose, why do you speak? Better to keep quiet; and if a conversation is taking place, hear a great deal rather than speak."

Nisteros 4   A brother saw Abba Nisteros wearing two tunics and he asked him: "If a poor man comes and asks you for a garment which one will you give him?" In reply he said: "The better one." The brother said: "And if another one comes and asks you, what would you grant him?" "Half the other one" the elder said, and the brother said: "And if another asks of you, what would you give [him]?" He said: "I would cut the remaining part, give him half and gird my loins with the rest." Again [the other] said: "And if somebody seeks that of you too?" and the elder said: "I will grant him the rest then go and stay somewhere until God sends and covers me, for I do not seek it of anybody else."

Nisteros 5 [11.91, N 264]   Abba Nisteros said: "In the evening and at dawn the monk ought to take stock: 'Of the things that God wills, what have we done and what of the things that God wills not have we done?'—and thus to investigate his own entire life; for Abba Arsenius lived in this way. Endeavour to stand before God each day without sin. Pray to God as though you are in his presence, for he truly is present. Do not make rules for yourself; judge nobody. It is foreign to the monk to swear, to commit perjury, to lie, to curse, to deride, to laugh. He who is honored or praised beyond his worth is severely punished."

NISTEROS THE COENOBITE

Nisteros the Coenobite 1 [1.19]   Abba Poemen used to say of Abba Nisteros: "As was the brazen serpent that Moses made for the healing of the people [cf. Num 21.9] so was this elder. He excelled in virtue and healed all [who came] while maintaining silence."

Nisteros the Coenobite 2 [15.46]   Abba Nisteros was asked by
Abba Poemen: "Where did you obtain this virtue of not speaking
or intervening whenever a difficulty arises in the coenobion?" He
replied: "Forgive me, abba: when I first entered the coenobion, I said
to my *logismos*: 'You and the ass are one; as the ass is beaten and does
not speak; is reviled and does not answer back, so should you be,' as
the Psalmist says: 'I have become like a beast of burden for you and
I am always with you'" [Ps 72.22–23].

NICON

Nicon [16.30; cf. Macarius the Egyptian 1, N 740]   A brother
asked one of the fathers: "How does the devil bring temptations
upon the holy ones?" The elder said to him: "There was one of the
fathers named Nicon living at Mount Sinaï and here somebody went
into the tent of a Pharanite and, finding his daughter there alone,
fell [into sin] with her. Then he said to her: 'Say that Abba Nicon
the anchorite did this to me.' When her father came and learnt [of
it] he took his sword and came down upon the elder. The elder
came out when he knocked and [the father] pulled out the sword
to kill him; but his hand became withered. The Pharanite went to
the church and told the priests; they sent for the elder and he came.
They inflicted many wounds on him and wanted to throw him out,
but he begged them, saying: 'Leave me here for God's sake so I can
repent.' They excommunicated him for three years and made an
injunction that no one was to visit him. He passed three years coming on Sunday and repenting; he would entreat everybody saying:
'Pray for me.' Some time later the one who had committed the sin
and had imputed the temptation to the anchorite became possessed
of a demon. He confessed before the church: 'I committed the sin; I
told her falsely to accuse the servant of God.' The entire community
went out and apologized to the elder, saying: 'Forgive us, abba.' He
said to them: 'As for forgiving, it is forgiven you; as for staying, I am

staying here with you no longer because there was not found even one of you who had the discretion to take my part,' and he went away from there." The elder said to the brother: "You see how the devil brings trials upon the holy ones."

NETRAS

Netras [10.50]   They recounted of Abba Netras, the disciple of Abba Silvanus, that, when he was living in his cell on Mount Sinaï, he acted with moderation toward himself in physical necessities; but when he became bishop at Pharan, he restricted himself with harsh austerity. His disciple said to him: "Abba, you did not lead an ascetic life like this when we were in the desert," and the elder said to him: "There it was desert, *hesychia*, and poverty; and I wanted to govern my body so that I would not fall sick and go looking for that which I did not have. But now it is the world and there are many resources. If I fall sick here, there is somebody to help me so I do not lose the monk."[91]

NICETAS

Nicetas [17.33]   Abba Nicetas used to tell of two brothers who met and wished to live together. One of them thought to himself: "Whatever my brother wants, I will do it." Likewise the other one thought: "I will do the will of my brother." They lived for many years, very lovingly, but when the enemy saw, he set out to separate them. Standing before the gate, he appeared to one of them as a dove, to the other as a crow. Then one [brother] said to the other: "Do you see that dove?" and he said: "It is a crow." They began to quarrel,

[91]10.50 ends: "But now we are in the world and there are many temptations; therefore I cause the body to waste away in order not to lose the monk. If I fall sick here, there is somebody to care for me"—which may be nearer to the original; cf. the story of Apphy, above.

each saying something different. They rose up and began fighting, even to the shedding of blood (to the utter delight of the enemy) and were separated. After three days, they came to themselves and returned to their senses. They prostrated themselves to each other, each one of them confessing what he thought the bird they had seen was. Recognizing the aggression of the enemy, they remained unseparated until death.

Ξ—*Xi*

Xoios

Xoios 1 A brother asked Abba Xoios: "If I find myself somewhere and I eat three loaves, is it a lot?" The elder said to him: "Did you come to the threshing floor, brother?" He then said: "If I drink three cups of wine, is it a lot?" He said to him: "If there were no demon it would not be a lot; if there is, it is a lot, for wine is foreign to monks living a godly life."

Xoios 2 [12.17] One of the fathers used to say of Abba Xoios the Theban that he once went to Mount Sinaï and as he was coming away from there a brother met him on the way. Sighing deeply, he began saying to the elder: "We are distressed by a drought, abba." The elder said to him: "Why are you not praying and interceding with God?" The brother told him: "We are praying and entreating and it does not rain." Said the elder: "You surely are not praying fervently; do you want to know that this is the case?" He stretched out his hands to heaven in prayer and it immediately rained. The brother was terrified when he saw it; he fell face down and did him homage but the elder fled. The brother reported what had happened to everyone; they glorified God when they heard it.

Xanthias

Xanthias 1 Abba Xanthias said: "The thief on the cross was justified by one word, and Judas, numbered with the apostles, lost all his labor in one night and descended from heaven to Hades. So let nobody boast of doing well, for all who trusted in themselves fell."

Xanthias 2 [19.20]   Abba Xanthias once went up from Scete to Terenouthis and there where he broke [his journey] they brought him a little wine as he was exhausted from his ascetic lifestyle. When some people heard of him they brought one possessed of a demon to him. The demon began abusing the elder and saying: "You have brought me to this wine-bibber?" The elder did not want to expel [the demon] but because of his insult he said: "I trust in Christ that I will not finish this cup before you come out." As the elder began drinking the demon cried out saying: "You are burning me, you are burning me," and before he had finished, the demon came out by the grace of Christ.

Xanthias 3 [N 434]   The same [elder] said: "The dog is better than I am for it has love and does not come to judgment."

O—*Omicron*

OLYMPIUS

Olympius 1 [11.109]   Abba Olympius said: "A priest of the pagans came down to Scete; he came to my cell and slept [there]. Seeing the monks' way of life, he said to me: 'Living like this, do you not see any [visions] from your God?' 'No,' I said to him, and the priest said to me: "And yet when we perform sacred rites for our god he hides nothing from us but reveals his mysteries to us. You who perform such labors: all night vigils, *hesychia*, spiritual disciplines, you say 'we see nothing?' You must certainly have evil *logismoi* in your hearts if you see nothing—and that is what separates you from your God. And for that reason his mysteries are not revealed to you.' Off I went and reported the priest's words to the elders. They were amazed, saying: 'That is indeed so: impure *logismoi* separate God from man.'"

Olympius 2 [5.50]   Abba Olympius of The Cells was embattled by *porneia* and his *logismos* said to him: "Go and take a woman." He got up, puddled some clay and formed a woman. Then he said to himself: "Here is your woman: you need to work a great deal to feed her," and work he did, laboring mightily. A day later he puddled some more clay and formed himself a daughter. Then he said to his *logismos*: "Look, your woman has given birth; now you need to work even more so you can feed and clothe your child." So doing, he wore himself out and he said to his *logismos*: "I do not have the strength to endure the labor any longer," and [his *logismos*] said to him: "If you do not have the strength to undergo the labor, then do not go looking for a woman." When God saw his labor, he took the battle away from him and he experienced repose.

ORSISIUS

*Orsisius was the second successor after Pachomius at the head
of the Pachomian communities. These and the piece attributed
to Psenthaisios (below) are the only Pachomian elements in
APalph.*

Orsisius 1 [15.60]   Abba Orsisius said: "Unbaked brick set in a
foundation near to a river does not last one day, but it lasts like
stone if it is baked. Likewise a person with a carnal mentality and
not purged by the fire of the word of God like Joseph [Ps 104.19, *LXX*
only] falls apart when he proceeds to govern. For there are many
temptations for such people in the midst of folk. A person aware of
his own limitations does well to flee from the burden of authority;
but they who are firm in the faith are immoveable. If one wants to
speak of the most holy Joseph himself, he will say that he was not
earthly. Many times he was tempted, and in what a country, where
there was not a trace of godliness at that time! But the God of his
fathers was with him and drew him out of all affliction; and now he
is with his fathers in the Kingdom of Heaven. As for ourselves, knowing our own limitations, let us fight the good fight; for in that way we
will only just be able to escape the judgment of God."

Orsisius 2 [11.78]   He also said: "I think that if a person does not
guard his own heart well, he forgets and disregards everything he
has heard; thus the enemy finds a place in him and overthrows him.
Likewise, a lamp that has been prepared and is shining is gradually
extinguished if it be neglected and not provided with oil; and then
darkness overcomes it. And not only that: it can also happen that a
mouse coming by will seek to eat the wick. This it cannot do before
the oil is consumed; but if it sees that there is not only no light but
no heat of fire either, then, in its desire to pull out the wick, it over-
turns the lamp. If it is an earthen lamp, it is broken; but if of bronze,
it is prepared for use again by the householder. Likewise, little by
little, the Holy Spirit recedes from the neglectful soul until finally its

warmth is extinguished, and then the enemy, devouring the fervor of the soul, destroys the body by iniquity. Yet if a person is well disposed toward God and has simply been overpowered by negligence, God the compassionate, by sending him fear of [God] and the recollection of retribution, prepares him to be vigilant and to keep a very strict watch on himself henceforth until his visitation."

Π—*Pi*

Poemen

Abba Poemen occupies by far the largest place in the collections of sayings. About three hundred items either quote what he is alleged to have said or make mention of him in some way. But it is very difficult to reconcile the various data provided by these items with each other, especially the chronological data. Derwas Chitty opined that there were two persons of this name:[92] one whom Rufinus encountered in 370,[93] who had known Antony, Ammonas, Pior and Pambo; and a second Poemen who came with his companions to be monks at Scete toward the end of the fourth century. These left Scete in 407 to take refuge at Terenouthis. This Poemen became the more famous; it is to him that most of the apophthegms are attributed. Yet in spite of some apparently insuperable chronological difficulties, there are those who insist that there was only one Poemen—and that it was in his circle that the apophthegmatic tradition was engendered and developed, hence his name, Poemen, 'the shepherd' (pastor in Latin). "With Abba Poemen the school of desert spirituality reached its apogee and it is with him that the genre of the apophthegm flourished," wrote Dom Lucien Regnault.[94]

Poemen 1 [11.55]   When Abba Poemen was young, he once went to an elder to ask him about three *logismoi*, but when he got to the elder, he forgot one of the three and returned to his own cell. As he

[92]Chitty, *The Desert a City*, 69–71.
[93]Rufinus, *HE* 2.8.
[94]Regnault, *Les Sentences*, 220.

reached out his hand for the key to open [his cell] he remembered the *logismos* he had forgotten. He left the key and returned to the elder. The elder said to him: "You were quick in coming, brother," and [Poemen] explained to him: "As I reached out my hand for the key I remembered the word I was looking for and did not open [the cell]; that is why I returned,"—and the length of the journey was very great. The elder said to him: "A shepherd [*poimēn*] of flocks you are and your name will be spoken throughout Egypt."

Poemen 2 [16.11]   Paesios, the brother of Abba Poemen, maintained contact with some people outside his cell and Abba Poemen was not in favor of this. He got up, went to Abba Ammonas, and said to him: "My brother Paesios maintains contact with some people and I have no repose." Abba Ammonas said to him: "Are you still alive, Poemen? Go, remain in your cell and put it into your heart that you have already been a year in the tomb."

Poemen 3 [10.53]   Some priests of the district once came to the monasteries where Abba Poemen was. Abba Anoub went in and said to him: "Let us invite the priests here today." He was standing for a long time [while] Abba Poemen gave him no answer; he went out in sorrow. Those who were sitting near to [Abba Poemen] said to him: "Abba, why did you not give him an answer?" Abba Poemen said to them: "This has nothing to do with me, for I am dead and a dead person does not speak. They are not to think that I am in here with them."

Poemen 4 [17.11]   There was an elder in Egypt before the coming of those associated with Abba Poemen who was well known and highly respected. When those associated with Abba Poemen came up from Scete, people abandoned the elder and came to Abba Poemen—who was troubled and said to his brothers: "What are we to do for this great elder, for folk have brought affliction upon us by leaving him and attaching themselves to us who are nothing? How can we sooth the elder?" He said to them: "Make a little food, get a *sextarius* of wine, and let us go to him and eat together; perhaps we will be able to soothe him like that." So they took up the victuals and went off. When they knocked at the gate he heard his disciple saying: "Who are you?" and they said: "Tell the abba: 'It is Poemen wanting to be blessed by you.'" When the disciple reported this to the elder, he made it clear to them, saying: "Get away; I have no time [for you]," but they stayed [out there] in the heat, saying: "We are not going away until we are deemed worthy [to be received] by the elder." Then, seeing their patience and humility, the elder was pricked in his conscience and opened to them. In they went and ate with him. While they were eating, the elder began to say: "In truth, it is not just the things I have heard of you, for I have witnessed one hundred times as much in what you do." He became their friend from that day on.

Poemen 5 [8.16]   The governor of that country once wanted to see Abba Poemen but the elder would not receive him. So he arrested the son of [the elder's] sister on the pretext that he was a malefactor and threw him into prison, saying: "I will release him if the elder come and intercede for him." [The elder's] sister came weeping to his door but he did not give her any answer. She reviled him, saying: "Hard-hearted one, have mercy on me for he is my only child." He sent someone to say to her: "Poemen has not engendered children," and with that, she went away. When the governor heard, he sent saying: "If [the elder] just say the word I will release [the nephew]," but the elder fired back: "Examine him according to the laws and, if he deserves to die, let him die; if not, do what you will."

Poemen 6 [9.10]   A brother in a coenobion once slipped up. Now there was an anchorite in those parts who had not emerged for a long time. The abba of the coenobion went to him and told him about the brother who had slipped up. "Expel him!" he said. When he came out of the coenobion, the brother went into a wadi and was weeping there. Some brothers who happened to be on their way to [see] Abba Poemen heard him weeping. They went in and found him in great distress; they begged him to [let them] take him to the elder but he was unwilling, saying: "I am going to die here." When they got to Abba Poemen they reported [this] to him. When he had exhorted them, he sent saying: "Tell him: 'Abba Poemen is calling you.'" The brother came to him and, when the elder saw him so afflicted, he got up and embraced him; with a smile, he invited him to eat with him. Abba Poemen sent one of his brothers to the anchorite saying: "Hearing about you, I have wanted to see you for many years, but on account of the reluctance of us both we have not met each other. But now, by the grace of God, an occasion presents itself; take the trouble to come here so we can see each other," for he used not to come out of his cell. On hearing this he said: "Unless God convinced the elder, he would not have sent to me." Up he got and came to him. They embraced each other joyfully then sat down; Abba Poemen said to him: "Two men were in a place and each had a corpse. One of the men left his own corpse and went to weep for the other's." The elder was pricked in his conscience by this tale when he heard it and recalled what he had done. He said: "Poemen is high as the heaven; I am as low as the earth."

Poemen 7 [19.14]   Many elders once visited Abba Poemen and here there was [also] some relative of Abba Poemen with a child whose face was turned backwards by [devilish] machination. Seeing the number of elders, [the child's] father took the child and sat outside the monastery, weeping. One elder happened to go out and, when he saw him, said to him: "Why are you weeping, fellow?" "I am a relative of Abba Poemen," he said, "and see what an affliction has befallen this child! We wanted to bring him to the elder but we were afraid. He does not want to see us; now, if he learns that I am here, he will send and chase me away. But, seeing that you were here, I presumed to come. If it please you, abba, have pity on me; take the child inside and intercede for him." The elder took the child and went in; but he acted shrewdly. He did not bring him to Abba Poemen immediately but, beginning with the least of the brothers, he said: "Make the sign [of the cross] over the child." When he had had them all sign in order, finally he brought [the afflicted child] to Abba Poemen. He was unwilling to sign it, but they begged him, saying: "Do as [we] all did, father." He heaved a sigh, stood up, and prayed, saying: "O God, heal your creature, so that it be not dominated by the enemy." Signing [the child] he healed it forthwith and gave it back to its father, sane and sound.

Poemen 8 [10.54]   A brother once left the area where Abba Poemen was for another country and encountered a certain anchorite there; he was a person of charity and many people were resorting to him. The brother told him about Abba Poemen and, when he heard of his virtue, he longed to see him. Some time after the brother had returned to Egypt, the anchorite got up and came to Egypt from abroad [and went] to that brother who had once visited him, [the brother] having told him where he was staying. [The brother] was amazed and very happy when he saw him. The anchorite said to him: "Of your charity, take me to Abba Poemen." He brought him to the elder and told him about [that anchorite], saying: "He is a great one, a person of much charity, highly respected in his country. I told him about you and he came desiring to see you." So [Abba Poemen] received him with joy; they embraced each other and sat down. The stranger began speaking from the Scriptures about spiritual and heavenly matters, but Abba Poemen turned his face away and did not give him an answer. When he saw that [the elder] was not speaking with him, he went out sorrowing and said to the brother who had brought him: "I made this entire trip abroad in vain; I came to the elder and he does not even want to speak with me." The brother went in to Abba Poemen and said to him: "Abba, it was on your account that he came, this great one who enjoys such esteem in his own place; why did you not speak with him?" The elder said to him: "He is from on high and speaks heavenly things; whereas I am from below and speak earthly things. If he had spoken to me about passions of the soul I would have answered him; [but] if of spiritual matters—I don't know those things." The brother went out and said to him:

"The elder does not readily speak from Scripture; but, if somebody speaks to him about passions of the soul, he will answer him." So, pricked in his conscience, [the anchorite] went in to the elder and said to him: "What am I to do, abba, for the passions of the soul are lording it over me?" Turning his attention to him, the elder rejoiced and said to him: "Now you are welcome; now I will open my mouth concerning these things and fill it with good tidings" [cf. Ps 80.11]. [The anchorite] reaped great benefit; he said: "This is indeed the true way," and he returned to his own country giving thanks to God for having been deemed worthy to meet such a holy person.

Poemen 9   The governor of the region was once detaining a person from Abba Poemen's village; they all came begging the elder to go and get him out, but he said: "Let me be for three days, then I will come." So Abba Poemen interceded with the Lord saying: "Lord, do not grant me this concession or they will not allow me to stay in this place." So the elder came begging the governor, but he said to him: "You are begging on behalf of a thief, abba?" and the elder rejoiced that he did not receive a concession from him.

Poemen 10   Some people recounted that Abba Poemen and his brothers were once working at making ropes but went no further because they could not buy thread. A person who was dear to them explained the situation to a devout merchant, but Abba Poemen never wanted to accept anything from anybody for the disturbance [it caused]. But the merchant, wishing to do something for the elder, pretended he needed ropes; he brought his camel and took [what they had made]. When the brother heard what the merchant had done, he came to Abba Poemen and, wanting to praise him, said: "No doubt, abba, he took them without really needing them in order to do something for us." When Abba Poemen heard that he took [the ropes] without needing them he said to the brother: "Go, hire a camel and bring them [here], for if you do not bring them, Poemen is not going to stay here with you. I am not wronging a man who is not in need so that he pays the penalty and receives my profit." Off went the brother and, with great toil, brought [the ropes] back; otherwise the elder was going away from them. When he saw [the ropes] he rejoiced as though he had found great treasure.

Poemen 11   The priest at Pelusium once heard that some brothers were often in the city, taking baths and neglecting themselves. He came to the *synaxis* and took their habits away from them; but subsequently his heart struck him and he repented. Intoxicated with his *logismoi*, he came to Abba Poemen carrying the brothers' albs and reported the matter to the elder. The elder said to him: "Do you yourself not have anything of the old man in you? Have you put him off?" The priest said: "I have my share of the old man." The elder said to him: "So you see, you too are like the brothers, for if you share even a little bit of the oldness, you are in subjection to sin just the same." The priest then went off, called the brothers, apologized to the eleven of them, clothed them with the monastic habit, and dismissed them.

Poemen 12 [10.57] [cf. Sisoes 20]   A brother asked Abba Poemen: "I have committed a serious sin and I want to repent for three years." The elder said to him: "It is a long time." "For a year, then?" said the brother to him, and again the elder said to him: "It is a long time." They who were present began saying: "How about forty days?" and again he said: "It is a long time," but he said: "I am telling you that if a person repent with his whole heart and go not on to commit the sin again, even in three days God will receive him."

Poemen 13   He also said: "The mark of the monk becomes apparent in temptations."

Poemen 14 [5.7]   He also said: "Just as the guardsman of the emperor stands by his side, always at the ready, so must the soul be at the ready against the demon of *porneia*."

Poemen 15 [10.58]   Abba Anoub asked Abba Poemen about the unclean *logismoi* that a person's heart generates and about vain desires. Abba Poemen said to him: "'Shall the axe boast without the one who hews with it?' [Is 10.15] And you, do not set your hand to them[95] and they are impotent."

Poemen 16 [4.32]   Abba Poemen also said: "If Nebuzar-adan the chief cook had not come, the temple of the Lord would not have been burnt [2 Kg 25.8ff], which means to say: if the relaxation of gluttony had not come into the soul, the mind would not have fallen in the battle with the enemy."

Poemen 17 [4.33]   They used to say of Abba Poemen that, when he was summoned to eat against his will, he would come in tears, in order not to disobey his brother and grieve him.

Poemen 18 [10.65]   Abba Poemen also said: "Do not live in a place where you see some who are jealous of you; otherwise you will make no progress."

Poemen 19 [4.34]   Some folk reported to Abba Poemen that a certain monk did not drink wine and he said to them: "Wine has nothing whatever to do with the monks."

Poemen 20 [10.59]   Abba Isaiah asked Abba Poemen about unclean *logismoi* and Abba Poemen said to him: "Just as with a chest filled with clothes, [which] rot away in time if a person abandon it, so it is with the *logismoi*. If we do not physically perform them, in time they disappear or rather rot away."

Poemen 21 [10.60]   Abba Joseph asked the same question and Abba Poemen said to him: "Just as if somebody put a snake and a scorpion into a jar and seal it, these will certainly die in the course of time, so too will the evil *logismoi* engendered by the demons expire through patient endurance."

Poemen 22 [10.66]   A brother came to Abba Poemen and said to him," I sow my field and give to charity from it." The elder said to

95or: "do not give them space or delight in them"

him: "You do well." Off he went with zeal and increased his charitable giving. Abba Anoub heard tell of this, and he said to Abba Poemen: "Do you not fear God, speaking to the brother like that?" but the elder kept silent. Two days later, Abba Poemen sent [for] the brother and said to him in the hearing of Abba Anoub: "What did you say to me the other day, for my mind was somewhere else?" The brother said to him: "I said that I sow my field and give to charity from it," but Abba Poemen said to him: "For my part I thought you were speaking of your brother the worldling. If it is you who are carrying out this work, this is not monks' work." He was sad when he heard this and said: "I know no other work, only this one; I am unable *not* to sow my field." When he had left, Abba Anoub prostrated himself, saying: "Forgive me." Said Abba Poemen to him: "I too knew from the beginning that it is not monks' work, but I spoke to his *logismos* and gave him zeal to progress in charity. Now he has gone off in sorrow and is going to do the same again."

Poemen 23 [10.68]   Abba Poemen said: "If a person sin and deny it, saying: 'I have not sinned,' do not condemn him, or you will cut off his eagerness. But if you say to him: 'Do not be disheartened, brother, and do not despair of yourself but be on your guard in future,' you rouse his soul to repentance."

Poemen 24 [10.71]   He also said: "Experience is good for it renders a person more tried and tested."

Poemen 25 [10.72]   He also said: "A person who teaches but does not do what he teaches is like a spring that waters and washes everybody but is unable to cleanse itself."

Poemen 26 [3.24]   Once when Abba Poemen was passing by in Egypt he saw a woman sitting in a sepulcher, weeping bitterly, and he said: "If all the delights of this world came [her way] they would not change her soul from sorrow. So too ought the monk to have sorrow in himself all the time."

Poemen 27 [10.75]   He also said: "There is a person who seems to keep silent, while his heart is passing judgment on others: such a person is speaking all the time. There is another person who is speaking from dawn to dusk yet maintains silence: I mean, he says nothing that is not beneficial."

Poemen 28 [10.81]   A brother came to Abba Poemen and said to him: "Abba, I have many *logismoi* and am in danger from them." The elder took him out into the open air and said to him: "Inflate your chest and hold the winds" [Prov 30.4], but he said: "I cannot do that." The elder said to him: "If you cannot do that, neither can you prevent the *logismoi* from coming: your [task] is to withstand them."

Poemen 29 [10.76]   Abba Poemen said: "If there are three together, one effectively practicing *hesychia*, one sick and offering thanksgiving, the other looking after [them] with a pure *logismos*, the three are of one undertaking."

Poemen 30 [18.22]   Abba Poemen said: "It is written: 'As the hart desires the springs of water, so longs my soul after you, O Lord' [Ps 41.2]. Because the harts in the wilderness consume many snakes and the poison burns them, they long to come to the waters. They drink and are cooled from the poison of the snakes. Likewise are the monks living in the desert burned by the poison of the wicked demons and they long to come to the springs of water on Saturday and Sunday, to the Body and Blood of our Lord, that is, in order to be cleansed from the bitterness of the evil one."

Poemen 31 [10.61]   Abba Joseph asked Abba Poemen: "How ought one to fast?" and Abba Poemen said: "I would like the person who eats every day to stop a little short of eating his fill." Abba Joseph said to him: "Did you not fast every second day when you were young, abba?" "Indeed for three and four days and even a whole week," the elder said, "but the elders, being capable themselves, tested all these things and concluded that it was good to eat each day, but in small quantity. And they handed the 'royal road' down to us because it is light" [cf. Num 20.17, 21.22, Mt 11.30].

Poemen 32 [11.58]   They used to say of Abba Poemen that when he was about to go to the *synaxis*, he would sit examining his own *logismoi* for one hour and then come out.

Poemen 33 [10.82]   A brother asked Abba Poemen: "A legacy has been left to me; what shall I do with it?" The elder said to him: "Go away and come in three days then I will tell you." He came as he had directed him and the elder said to him: "What am I to say to you, brother? If I say to you: 'Give it to a church,' they will have banquets there; if I say: 'Give it to your relative,' there is no reward for you; but if I tell you: 'Give it to the poor,' you will have no worries. Do whatever you like; this is not my business."

Poemen 34 [18.23]   Another brother asked him: "What is the meaning of 'Never repay evil with evil'?" [cf. Rom 12.17]. Abba Poemen said to him: "This passion works in four ways: first, in the heart; second, in the sight; third, in the tongue; fourth, in not doing evil in response to evil. If you can purge your heart, it does not come to the sight. If it comes to the sight, take care not to speak of it. If you do speak of it, quickly prevent yourself from rendering evil for evil."

Poemen 35 [1.20]   Abba Poemen said: "Being on the alert, paying attention to oneself, and discretion—these are three guiding virtues of the soul."

Poemen 36 [15.50]   He also said: "The working tools of the soul are: to prostrate oneself in the presence of God, not to measure oneself, and to throw your own will behind you." [cf. Mk 8.33, etc.]

Poemen 37 [16.12]   He also said: "Whatever trouble comes upon you, victory over it is to remain silent."

Poemen 38   He also said: "All physical repose is an abomination to the Lord."

Poemen 39 [3.26]   He also said: "Sorrow works two ways: it labors and protects" [cf. Gen 2.15].

Poemen 40 [10.83]   He also said: "If a *logismos* comes upon you concerning the essential needs of the body and you attend to it once, then it comes back a second time and you attend to it—if it comes a third time, pay no attention to it, for it is impotent."

Poemen 41 [15.53]   He also said that a brother asked Abba Alonius: "What is 'to be set at naught' [Mk 9.12]?" and the elder said: "To rank yourself lower than the beasts and to know that they are free from condemnation."

Poemen 42 [4.36]   He also said: "If a person remember the saying that is written: 'By your words you shall be justified, and by your words you shall be condemned' [Mt 12.37], he would choose rather to keep silent."

Poemen 43 [2.24]   He also said: "The beginning of evils is distraction."

Poemen 44 [7.20]   He also said that Abba Isidore, the priest of Scete, once spoke to the people, saying: "Brothers, was it not for adversity that we came to this place? Now there is no longer adversity, so for my part I am packing up my sheepskin and going off to where there is adversity and there I will find repose."

Poemen 45 [10.86]   A brother said to Abba Poemen: "If I see something, do you want me to speak of it?" The elder said: "It is written: 'He that gives an answer before he hears—it is folly and shame to him' [Prov 18.13]. Speak if you are asked; otherwise, keep silent."

Poemen 46 [cf. John Colobos 34]   A brother asked Abba Poemen: "Can a man trust himself to one activity?" and the elder said to him: "Abba John Colobos said: 'I want to partake a little of all the virtues.'"

Poemen 47 [4.37]   The elder also said: "A brother asked Abba Pambo if it is a good thing to praise one's neighbor, and he said to him: 'It is better to keep silent.'"

Poemen 48 [11.62]   Abba Poemen also said: "If somebody makes a new heaven and a new earth [Rev 21.1], he cannot be free of concern."

Poemen 49 [15.48; cf. 21.43]   He also said: "A person is as much in need of humble-mindedness and of the fear of God as he is of the breath that comes out of his nose."

Poemen 50 [3.28]   A brother asked Abba Poemen: "What am I to do?" and the elder said to him: "When Abraham entered the Promised Land, he bought himself a sepulcher, and through the tomb he inherited the land" [Gen 23.4–10]. The brother said to him: "What is 'a tomb'?" and the elder said to him: "A place of weeping and sorrow."

Poemen 51 [13.6]   A brother said to Abba Poemen: "If I give my brother a little bread or something else, the demons denigrate the deed as being done to please men." The elder said to him: "Even if it is done to please men, let us give the brother what he needs," and he told him this parable: "There were two men, both farmers, living in one city. One of them sowed and reaped a small crop of poor quality, while the other neglected to sow and reaped nothing. When there is a famine, which of the two will be found to live?" "The one who reaped a small crop of poor quality," the brother replied. Said the elder to him: "So it is also with us; let us too sow a little even if it be of poor quality so that we do not die by famine."

Poemen 52 [10.88]   Abba Poemen also said that Abba Ammonas said: "One person spends all his time carrying an axe and does not find out how to bring down a tree, while another person, experienced in felling, brings the tree down with a few strokes." He said that the axe is discretion.

Poemen 53 [1.22]   A brother asked Abba Poemen: "How ought a person to live his life?" The elder said to him: "Let us consider Daniel; that no accusation was found against him other than in the way he served the Lord his God" [Dan 6.5–9].

Poemen 54 [10.89]   Abba Poemen said: "A person's will is a brazen wall [cf. Jer 1.18] and an immoveable rock between him and God. If a person abandons it, he too says: 'In my God I will leap over the wall' [Ps 18.30–31]. But if [self-] justification combine with the will, a person is in a bad way."

Poemen 55 [15.54]   He also said that one day the elders were sitting down eating, and Abba Alonius stood there, waiting on them. They praised him when they noticed him, but he gave no response whatsoever. One of them took him aside and said to him: "Why did you not respond to the elders when they were praising you?" Abba Alonius said to him: "Had I responded to them, I would have been found to be one who accepted praise."

Poemen 56 [8.19]   He also said: "Folk talk at great length but achieve very little."

Poemen 57 [4.39]   Abba Poemen said, "Just as smoke chases out the bees and then the sweetness of their labor is taken, so does bodily repose chase the fear of God away from the soul and destroy all its good labor."

Poemen 58 [13.5]   A brother visited Abba Poemen in the [first] two weeks of Lent. After confessing his *logismoi* and attaining repose, he said to him: "I was almost prevented from coming here today." "What for?" the elder said to him. The brother said: "I thought that because of Lent, [the door] would not be opened to me." Abba Poemen said to him: "We were not taught to shut the wooden door but rather the door of the tongue."

Poemen 59 [2.25]   Abba Poemen also said: "One must flee from the things of the body, for when one is close to the war against the body he is like somebody standing above a very deep pit. Whenever it seems fit to his enemy, he easily throws a person down. But if that person be some distance from bodily matters, he is like one far removed from the pit, so that even if the enemy drag him along to throw him down, even while [the enemy] is dragging and coercing him, God sends him help."

Poemen 60 [1.23] He also said: "Affliction, confinement, and fasting:[96] these are the working tools of the monastic life, for it is written: 'If there were these three men: Noah, Job, and Daniel, I would live, says the Lord' [cf. Ezek 14.14]. Noah represents indifference to material goods, Job toil, Daniel discretion. If there are these three practices in a person, the Lord is dwelling in him."

Poemen 61 [15.57] Abba Joseph recounted: "While we were sitting with Abba Poemen, he named Agathon *abba*, and we said to him: 'He is too young; why are you calling him *abba*?' Said Abba Poemen: 'Because his mouth has caused him to be called *abba*.'"

Poemen 62 [5.9] A brother once came to Abba Poemen and said to him: "What am I to do, father, for I am afflicted by *porneia*? I went to Abba Ibistion you see and he said to me: 'You ought not to let it linger with you.'" Abba Poemen said to him: "The deeds of Abba Ibistion are up in heaven with the angels and it is hidden from him that you and I are subject to *porneia*. If a monk master his belly and his tongue and [tolerate] voluntary exile, be assured: he will not die."

Poemen 63 [Poemen 164 is identical] Abba Poemen said: "Teach your mouth to say what is in your heart."

Poemen 64 [9.9] A brother asked Abba Poemen: "If I see my brother's fault, is it good to conceal it?" The elder said to him: "Whenever we conceal our brother's fault, God conceals ours, and whenever we expose the brother's, God exposes ours."

---

[96]*APsys* 1.23 has "Poverty, affliction, and discretion" here, which accords better with what follows. cf. Poemen 36.

Poemen 65 [11.59]   Abba Poemen also said that somebody once asked Abba Paisios: "What am I to do with my soul, for it is insensitive and does not fear God?" and he said to him: "Go and attach yourself to a person who fears God, and from your contact with that person he will teach you too to fear God."

Poemen 66 [1.24]   He also said: "If a monk conquers two things, he can become free of the world." "What are they?" said the brother and the elder said: "Repose of the flesh and vainglory."

Poemen 67 [10.91]   Abraham, Abba Agathon's abba, asked Abba Poemen: "Why are the demons doing battle with me so?" and Abba Poemen said to him: "Are the demons doing battle with you? The demons do not battle with us as long as we are following our own wills, for our wills have become demons; it is they that oppress us so that we fulfill them. Do you want to see with whom the demons do battle? It is with Moses and those like him."

Poemen 68 [1.21]   Abba Poemen said: "God gave this way of life to Israel: to refrain from what is contrary to nature, that is, from anger, bad temper, jealousy, hatred, slandering a brother, and the rest of the things [pertaining] to the old way of life."

Poemen 69 [13.7]   A brother asked Abba Poemen: "Tell me a saying." The elder said to him: "The foundation of the undertaking that the fathers stipulated is grief." Again the brother said to him: "Tell me another saying." The elder replied: "Apply yourself to handiwork as much as you are able, in order to perform deeds of mercy with it, for it is written: 'Almsgiving and faith purge sins'" [Prov 15.27a]. "What is faith?" the brother said and the elder said: "Faith is to live in humble-mindedness and to perform [deeds of] mercy."

Poemen 70 [17.27 & 23a]   A brother asked Abba Poemen: "If I see a brother whom I have heard is at fault, I do not want to bring him into my cell; but if I see an excellent brother, I rejoice with him." The elder said to him: "If you do a small favor to the excellent brother, do twice as much for the other because he is the one who is sick. There was an anchorite named Timothy in a coenobion. The higoumen heard a rumor about a certain brother concerning a temptation and he asked Timothy about him: he advised [the higoumen] to expel the brother. When he had expelled him, the temptation that had afflicted the brother now afflicted Timothy, to the point that he was in danger. Timothy wept before the Lord, saying: 'I have sinned, forgive me.' There came a voice to him saying: 'Timothy, do not think I did this to you for any other reason than because you despised your brother in his time of temptation.'"

Poemen 71 [cf. Poemen S 17]   Abba Poemen said: "The reason why we are subject to so many temptations is that we do not stand by our name and our order, as the Scripture says. Do we not see that the Savior granted repose to the Canaanite woman who acknowledged her name [Mt 15.27]? Abigail too, how when she said to David: 'The sin is in me' he heard her and loved her [1 Sam 25.24]? Abigail personifies the soul, David the Divinity; therefore, if the soul blame itself before the Lord, the Lord loves it."

Poemen 72 [3.25]   Abba Poemen was once passing through the region of Diolcos together with Abba Anoub, and when they came to the sepulchers they saw a woman cruelly beating [her breast] and weeping bitterly. They stopped and considered her; then, moving on a little, they met someone, and Abba Poemen asked him: "What ails that woman that she is weeping bitterly?" He said to him: "Her husband has died; her son and her brother too." In response Abba Poemen said to Abba Anoub: "I tell you, unless a person put to death all the desires of the flesh [Col 3.5, Eph 2.3] and acquire that grief, he cannot be a monk. Her entire life and mind are in grief."

Poemen 73 [15.51]   Abba Poemen said: "Do not measure yourself, but attach yourself to someone who lives a good life."

Poemen 74   He also said that if a brother visited Abba John Colobos he accorded him the charity of which the Apostle speaks: "Charity is long-suffering and is kind" [1 Cor 13.4].

Poemen 75   He also said of Abba Pambo that Abba Antony said of him that he made the Spirit of God dwell in him by fearing God [1 Cor 3.16].

Poemen 76 [4.40]   One of the fathers told this about Abba Poemen and his brothers: "While they were living in Egypt, their mother wanted to see them and was not able to do so. She kept careful watch when they were coming to church and confronted them; but they saw her, turned back, and shut the gate in her face. She cried out at the gate, weeping with much wailing and saying: 'Let me see you, my beloved children.' When he heard her, Abba Anoub went in to Abba Poemen and said: 'What are we to do about that old woman weeping at the gate?' Standing inside, [Abba Poemen] heard her weeping with much wailing, and he said to her: 'Why are you shouting like that, old woman?' She shouted much more when she heard his voice, weeping and saying: 'I want to see you, my children; what does it matter if I see you? Am I not your mother? Did I not nurse you? Now I am all white haired, and when I heard your voice I was troubled.' The elder said to her: 'Do you want to see us in this world or in the next?' She said to him: 'If I do not see you here, will I see you there?' He said to her: 'If you steel yourself not to see us here, you shall see us there,' so she went her way rejoicing and saying: 'If indeed I am to see you there, I do not want to see you here.'"

Poemen 77   A brother asked Abba Poemen: "What is meant by 'high things' [Rom 12.16]?" "Righteousness," the elder said to him.

Poemen 78   Some heretics once came to Abba Poemen and began slandering the Archbishop of Alexandria, [alleging] that he derived his ordination from priests, but the elder remained silent; he called for his brother and said: "Set the table, have them eat, then send them on their way in peace."

Poemen 79   Abba Poemen said that a brother who was living with brothers asked Abba Bessarion: "What am I to do?" and the elder said to him: "Keep silent and do not measure yourself."

Poemen 80   He also said: "Do not attend with your heart to one in whom your heart does not have confidence."

Poemen 81   He also said: "If you hold yourself in low esteem you will experience repose wherever you are staying."

Poemen 82   He also said that Abba Sisoes used to say: "There is a shame that has the sin of a lack of fear."

Poemen 83   He also said: "Having your own way, taking repose, and being accustomed to these things are what cast the man down."

Poemen 84   He also said: "If you are given to silence you will experience repose in every place, no matter where you reside."

Poemen 85   He also said of Abba Pior that every day he started all over again.

Poemen 86   A brother asked Abba Poemen: "If a person be caught up in some fault then refrain from it, is he pardoned by God?" The elder said to him: "Will the God who instructed men to do this not rather do it himself? For he instructed Peter: 'Until seventy times seven'" [Mt 18.22].

Poemen 87   A brother asked Abba Poemen: "Is it good to pray?" The elder said to him: "Abba Antony said: 'This directive comes from the person of the Lord saying: 'Comfort my people says the Lord, comfort [them]'" [Is 40.1].

Poemen 88   A brother asked Abba Poemen: "Can a person maintain all his *logismoi* and not concede one of them to the enemy?" The elder said: "There is such a person who has ten and concedes one."

Poemen 89   There was a great practitioner of *hesychia* on Mount Athlib and robbers came upon him. The elder cried out; his neighbors heard and arrested the robbers. They sent them to the governor and he threw them into jail. The brothers were grieved, saying: "They were betrayed through us." They got up, went to Abba Poemen, and reported the matter to him. He wrote to the elder saying: "Reflect on the first betrayal and where it came from, then you will see the second [one]. For if you had not been betrayed from within the first time, you would not have committed the second betrayal." When he heard Abba Poemen's letter (for he was renowned in all that country and used not to come out of his cell) he got up, came into the city, got the robbers out of jail, and publicly freed them.

Poemen 90 [10.78]   Abba Poemen said: "He is not a monk who complains of his lot; he is not a monk who strikes back; he is not a monk who is given to anger."

Poemen 91   Some of the elders visited Abba Poemen and said to him: "If we see the brothers dozing off at the *synaxis*, are we to nudge them so they be watchful at the vigil?" but he said to them: "For my part, if I see a brother dozing off, I put his head on my knees and give him repose."

Poemen 92 [cf. 10.63]   They used to say of one brother that he was embattled by the demon of blasphemy but was ashamed to speak of it. When he heard of great elders he visited them in order to confess [his condition], but when he arrived he was ashamed to confess. He often visited Abba Poemen; the elder perceived that he had *logismoi* and it saddened him that the brother was not confessing it. On one occasion as he was sending him on his way he said to him: "Look, you have been coming here so long with *logismoi* to confess to me and when you come you do not want to speak of them. All at once, off you go, still afflicted by them. So tell me, my son: what is the matter?" He said to him: "The demon is battling me into blaspheming God and I was ashamed to speak of it"—and once he had told him the matter he was immediately relieved. The elder said to him: "Do not be troubled my son; when this *logismos* comes, say: 'I have no part in this: your blasphemy be on your own head, Satan. My soul wants no part in this business,' for everything to which the soul does not subscribe is of short duration." The brother went away healed.

Poemen 93   A brother asked Abba Poemen: "It seems to me that wherever I go, I find succor." The elder said to him: "Even those who [have] sword in hand have God being merciful to them in this age. So if we are courageous, he deals with us in his mercy."

Poemen 94   Abba Poemen said: "If a person blame himself, he will be steadfast everywhere."

Poemen 95   He also said that Abba Ammonas said: "There is a person who spends a hundred years in his cell and does not learn how one should live in a cell."

Poemen 96   Abba Poemen said: "If a person measure up to the Apostle's saying: 'To the pure all things are pure' [Titus 1.15], he sees himself as inferior to all creation." The brother said: "How can I regard myself to be inferior to a murderer?" The elder said to him: "If a person measure up to this saying and he see somebody committing murder, he says: 'This fellow only did this one sin: I am murdering every day.'"

Poemen 97   The brother put the same question to Abba Anoub that he had asked Abba Poemen and Abba Anoub said to him: "If a person measure up to this saying and he observe the shortcomings of his brother, he makes his [own] righteousness swallow them up." The brother said to him: "What is his righteousness?" "Always to blame himself," the elder replied.

Poemen 98   A brother said to Abba Poemen: "If I fall into grievous sin, my *logismos* devours me and accuses me [saying]: 'Why did you fall?'" The elder said to him: "At whatever time a person fall into a misdeed and say: 'I sinned,' it is done with, immediately."

Poemen 99 [10.70; cf. 4.27]   A brother asked Abba Poemen: "Why do the demons persuade my soul to be with one who is superior to me and cause me to despise one who is inferior?" The elder said to him: "This is why the Apostle said: 'In a great house there are not only vessels of gold and of silver but also of wood and of clay. If a man therefore purges himself from all these, he shall be a useful vessel, of value to his own master, ready for every good work' [cf. 2 Tim 2.20–21]."

Poemen 100 [cf. 4.27]   A brother asked Abba Poemen: "Why am I unable to speak freely with the elders about my *logismoi*?" The elder said to him: "Abba John Colobos said: 'The Enemy rejoices over no one more than over those who do not reveal their *logismoi*.' "

Poemen 101 [7.19; cf. 4.29]   A brother said to Abba Poemen: "My heart fails me if I encounter a little adversity." The elder said to him: "Are we not amazed at Joseph who, when he was a seventeen-year-old youth, endured temptation to the end [Gen 37–40] and God glorified him? Do we not see that Job too did not abandon patient endurance right to the end [Job 2.10] and that his trials were not strong enough to shake his hope in God?"

Poemen 102 [10.74]   Abba Poemen said: "[Living in] the coenobion requires three practices: one is humility, one obedience, and one motivation—which is a spur to the work of the coenobion."

Poemen 103   A brother asked Abba Poemen: "When I was having a difficult time I asked one of the holy ones for something I needed and he gave it to me in charity. If God supports me too, shall I give what he gave me to others in charity, or shall I rather give it to him who gave it to me?" The elder said to him: "The right thing to do in the eyes of God would be for it to be given back to him, for it is his." The brother said to him: "But what if when I take it to him he does not want to accept it and says: 'Go and give it in charity to whom you will,' then what am I to do?" The elder said to him: "The matter is really in his own hands. If somebody provide you with something of his own free will and without your asking him, that thing is yours. But if you ask [for something] either of a monk or of a worldling and he is unwilling to take it back, this is the verdict: that (with his knowledge) you give it away in charity on his behalf."

Poemen 104 [15.58] They used to say about Abba Poemen that he never wanted to make his comment on the saying of another elder; he would rather altogether commend him.

Poemen 105 Abba Poemen said: "Many of our fathers were courageous in spiritual discipline, but in subtlety of *logismoi* through prayer, only one here and there."

Poemen 106 Once when Abba Isaac was sitting with Abba Poemen, the crowing of a cock was heard and he said to him: "There are [chickens] here, abba?" but in reply he said to him: "Isaac, why do you oblige me to speak? You and your like hear them; to the vigilant they are of no concern."

Poemen 107 They used to say that if any folk came to Abba Poemen, he would first send them to Abba Anoub for he was older. But Abba Anoub would say to them: "Go to my brother Poemen, for he has the gift of speaking." But if Abba Anoub was sitting there, near to Abba Poemen, Abba Poemen would not speak at all in his presence.

Poemen 108 [14.13] A worldling who led a very devout life came to see Abba Poemen; there were other brothers there too with the elder, asking to hear a saying. Abba Poemen said to the faithful worldling: "Say something to the brothers," but he excused himself, saying: "I came to learn." But at the elder's great insistence he said: "I am a worldling, a greengrocer and a merchant. I buy wholesale and sell retail; I buy cheap and sell for much. I certainly do not know how to speak from Scripture but I will tell you a parable. Somebody once begged his friend, saying: 'Since I have a desire to see the king, come with me.' The friend said to him: 'I will come halfway with you.' To another friend he said: 'Come on, you take me to the king,' but he said to him: 'I will take you as far as the king's palace.' He spoke to a third [friend]: 'Come with me to the king,' and he said: 'I am coming; I will go to the palace; I will stand and speak [on your behalf] and I will usher you into the king's presence.'" "What is the meaning of the parable?" they asked him, and he said: "The first friend is spiritual discipline, which leads you halfway; the second is purity, which gets as far as heaven; the third is charitable alms-giving, which brings you confidently before God the king"—and the brothers went their way edified.

Poemen 109   A brother was living outside his own village and for many years he did not go up to the village. He used to say to the brothers: "Here, I have not gone up to the village for how many years but you go up once in a while." They told Abba Poemen about him and the elder said: "I used to go up by night and circle the village so that my *logismos* would not boast of my not going up."

Poemen 110   A brother asked Abba Poemen: "Tell me a saying," and he said to him: "When there is fire beneath the cauldron, a fly cannot touch it nor can any other of the reptiles; but, when it is cold, then they alight on it. So it is with the monk too: as long as he is engaged in spiritual works, the enemy finds no opportunity to bring him down."

Poemen 111 [cf. 4.14]   Abba Joseph used to say of Abba Poemen that he said: "This is the directive written in the Gospel: 'Let him who has a cloak sell it and buy a sword' [Lk 22.36], meaning: let him who enjoys repose abandon it and embrace the narrow way" [Mt 7.14].

Poemen 112 [9.21]   Some of the fathers asked Abba Poemen: "If we see a brother sinning, do you want us to reprove him?" The elder said to them: "For my part, even if I am obliged to go that way and I see him sinning, I pass him by and do not reprove him."

Poemen 113 [9.22]   Abba Poemen said: "It is written: 'Bear witness to that which your eyes have seen' [Prov 25.8], but I say to you that even if you touch it with your hands, do not bear witness. For one brother was deceived in some such thing: he saw his brother as though he were sinning with a woman. Deeply embattled, he went up and nudged what he thought to be them with his foot, saying: 'Just stop it now; how much longer?' and here *they* were found to be sheaves of wheat. That is why I said to you that even if you touch it with your hands, you are not to reprove."

Poemen 114 [5.11]   A brother asked Abba Poemen: "What am I to do, for I am embattled by *porneia* and in prey to anger?" The elder said to him: "This is why David said: 'I smote the lion and throttled the bear' [cf. 1 Sam 17.35], meaning: 'I cut off anger and wore down *porneia* by toil.'"

Poemen 115 [17.13]   He also said: "There is no greater love to be found than for somebody to lay down his life for his neighbor [cf. Jn 15.13]. For if somebody hears a bad word, one that wounds him that is, and is capable of uttering something like it himself but struggles not to say it, or if someone is being browbeaten and bears it without paying [his adversary] back, such a person is laying down his life for his neighbor."

Poemen 116 [cf. 4.28]   A brother asked Abba Poemen: "What is a hypocrite?" The elder said to him: "A hypocrite is one who teaches his neighbor something to which he has not attained himself, for it is written: 'Why do you notice the speck in your brother's eye when here there is a joist in yours?'" etc. [Mt 7.3–4].

Poemen 117 [10.67]   A brother asked Abba Poemen: "What is it 'to be angry with his brother without a cause'"? [Mt 5.22]. and he said: "All the conceit with which your brother arrogantly treats you and your getting angry with him is being angry with him without a cause. Even if he tear out your right eye and cut off your right hand and you get angry with him, it is your being angry with him without a cause. But if he would separate you from God, then get angry with him."

Poemen 118 [3.29, 3.30]   A brother asked Abba Poemen: "What am I to do about my sins?" The elder said to him: "One who wishes to redeem his sins redeems them by weeping, and he who wishes to acquire virtues acquires them by weeping. Weeping is the way Scripture and our fathers passed down to us, saying: 'Weep! For there is no other way but that one'" [cf. Jas 4.9].

Poemen 119   A brother asked Abba Poemen: "What is repentance for sin?" and the elder said: "Not to do it in future. That is why the righteous were called spotless: because they abandoned sins and became righteous."

Poemen 120   He also said: "The wickedness of folk is concealed behind them."

Poemen 121   A brother asked Abba Poemen: "What am I to do about these disturbances that are troubling me?" The elder said to him: "Let us weep before the goodness of God in all our adversity until he deal with us in his mercy."

Poemen 122   The brother also asked him: "What am I to do about the unprofitable affections that beset me?" He said: "The death rattle is upon a man who is clinging to affections for this world. Neither approach them nor touch them and they will detach themselves of their own accord."

Poemen 123   A brother asked Abba Poemen: "Can a person be dead?" He said to him: "If he incline toward sin, he becomes one who is dying; if he incline to what is good, he will live and perform it."

Poemen 124   Abba Poemen said that the blessed Abba Antony said: "The most a person can do is to charge himself with his own fault before the Lord and to expect temptation until his last breath."

Poemen 125 [cf. 4.9]   Abba Poemen was asked: "To whom is that verse addressed that is written: 'Take no thought for the next day'?"

[Mt 6.34]. The elder said to him: "It was said to a person in temptation who was losing heart so that he not worry, and saying: 'How long am I to be in this temptation,' but rather that each day he say: 'Today!'" [cf. Heb 3.13].

Poemen 126 b [10.55]   He also said: "To teach one's neighbor is [the work] of a healthy person, free of passions; for what is the point of building a house for somebody else and destroying one's own?"

Poemen 127 [10.56]   He also said: "What is the point in anyone's taking up a trade without learning it?"

Poemen 128 [353D]   He also said: "All excesses[97] are of the demons."

Poemen 129   He also said: "When a man is about to build a house he assembles all the necessary materials so that he may be able to erect the house and he assembles different kinds of things. So too let us take a little of all the virtues."

Poemen 130   Some of the fathers asked Abba Poemen: "How did Abba Nisteros have such patience with his disciple?" Abba Poemen said to them: "If it had been I, I would have put the pillow under his head too." Abba Anoub said to him: "And what would you have said to God?" "I would have said: 'You said: "first remove the joist from your own eye, then you will be able to see to remove the speck from your brother's eye'"" [Mt 7.5], said Abba Poemen.

Poemen 131   Abba Poemen said: "Being hungry and drowsy do not allow us to see these finer points."

Poemen 132   He also said: "Many became powerful but few without irritating."

Poemen 133   He also said with a sigh: "All the virtues entered this house except for one, and without that one, a person can barely keep

[97]*hypermetra.*

upright." So they asked him what it was and he said: "That a person blame himself."

Poemen 134   Abba Poemen often said: "We do not need anything other than an alert intelligence."

Poemen 135   One of the fathers asked Abba Poemen: "Who is it who says: 'I am a sharer with all those who fear you'?" [Ps 118.63]; and the elder said: "It is the Holy Spirit who is speaking."

Poemen 136   Abba Poemen said that a brother asked Abba Simon: "If I come out of my cell and, finding a brother diverting himself, I divert myself together with him; or if I find him laughing and I laugh together with him, then I am unable to experience repose if I go into my cell." The elder said to him: "If you come out of your cell, find people laughing and you laugh with them or talking and you talk [too] then you go into your cell, do you expect to find yourself as you were?" The brother said: "What am I to do?" and the elder replied: "Keep your guard up, inside and outside."

Poemen 137   Abba Daniel said: "We once visited Abba Poemen and we ate together. After we had eaten together he said to us: 'Go and repose yourselves a little, brothers,' so off went the brothers to repose a little and I remained to speak with him alone; I got up and came to his cell. Seeing me coming toward him he disposed himself as though he were sleeping. That was how the elder operated: he did everything in secret."

Poemen 138   Abba Poemen said: "If you see things or hear rumors, do not tell them to your neighbor, for it is the stirring up of war."

Poemen 139   He also said: "Run away the first time; run away the second time; the third time, become a sword."

Poemen 140   Abba Poemen also said to Abba Isaac: "Assuage the weight of your righteousness a little and you shall experience repose during your few [remaining] days."

Poemen 141 A brother visited Abba Poemen and while some [brothers] were sitting with him he praised another brother for his hatred of evil. Abba Poemen said to the one who had spoken: "What then is hatred of evil?" The brother was astounded and could not find an answer. He got up and prostrated himself before the elder, saying: "Tell me what hatred of evil is." Said the elder: "Hatred of evil is this: if somebody hated his [own] sins and held his neighbor to be in the right."

Poemen 142 A brother who was visiting Abba Poemen said to him: "What am I to do?" The elder said to him: "Go and live with somebody who says: 'What do I want?' and you will experience repose."

Poemen 143 [3.31] Abba Joseph recounted that Abba Isaac said: "I was once staying with Abba Poemen and I saw that he was in a trance. As I was very familiar with him, I prostrated myself before him and besought him saying: "Tell me where you were." Under coercion he said: "My *logismos* was where Saint Mary the *Theotokos* stood. She was weeping at the cross of the Savior [Jn 19.25] and I was wishing [I could] weep like that all the time."

Poemen 144 [10.64] A brother asked Abba Poemen: "What am I to do about this weight that is oppressing me?" The elder said to him: "Small and large vessels are equipped with girdles so that, when there is no favorable wind, they attach the tow-rope and the girdles to their chests and haul the vessel a little until God sends a wind. But if they learn that a storm is getting up, they hasten to attach [the vessel] to a pile so that it may not be tossed about. 'A pile' is to find fault with oneself."

Poemen 145 A brother asked Abba Poemen about the abuses arising from *logismoi* and the elder said to him: "This business is like a man who has fire on his left and a vessel of water on the right. If the fire burns, he takes water from the vessel and puts it out. Fire is the enemy's seed; water, to cast oneself into the presence of God."

Poemen 146   A brother asked Abba Poemen: "Is it better to speak or to remain silent?" The elder said to him: "He who speaks in a godly manner does well; he who remains silent in the same way, likewise."

Poemen 147   A brother asked Abba Poemen: "How can a person avoid speaking ill of his neighbor?" The elder said to him: "We and our brothers are two portraits. Whenever a man regards himself and finds fault [with what he sees] his brother will be found honorable in his eyes. But when he seems fine to himself he finds his brother inferior in his sight."

Poemen 148 [10.87]   A brother asked Abba Poemen about *accidie* and the elder said to him: "*Accidie* is present at every beginning and there is no passion worse than this. But if a person recognize it for what it is, he experiences repose."

Poemen 149   Abba Poemen said: "We see three physical activities in the case of Abba Pambo: no food until evening every day, silence, and a great deal of handiwork."

Poemen 150 [10.85]   He also said that Abba Theonas used to say: "Even if somebody acquire virtue, God does not endow the grace of it on him alone, for he knows that he was not trusting in his own toil. But if he go to his colleague, then it stays with him."

Poemen 151 [10.69]   A brother asked Abba Poemen: "I want to enter and live in a coenobion," The elder said to him: "If you want to enter a coenobion, unless you can be unconcerned in every contact and about every matter, you cannot perform the tasks of the coenobion, for you do not even have authority over the water bottle [there]."

Poemen 152   A brother asked Abba Poemen: "What am I to do?" He said: "It is written: 'I will proclaim my iniquity and concern myself with my sin'" [Ps 37.19].

Poemen 153 [5.8] Abba Poemen said: "A person must not mention these two *logismoi* or think of them in his heart: *porneia* and backbiting. If he wishes to give them any consideration whatsoever in his heart, he will reap no benefit; but if he is made angry by them he will experience repose."

Poemen 154 The brothers of Abba Poemen said to him: "Let us go away from this place, for the monasteries of this place are disturbing us and we are losing our souls. Here too the children's crying prevents us from practicing *hesychia*." Abba Poemen said to them: "You want to get away from here because of the angels' voices?"

Poemen 155 Abba Bitimios asked Abba Poemen: "If somebody is annoyed with me, I apologize to him, and he is not reconciled, what am I to do?" The elder said to him: "Take two more brothers with you and apologize to him and, if he is not reconciled, take another five. If he is not reconciled by them, take a priest. If he is not reconciled by this, calmly pray to God to convince him and do not worry" [Mt 18.15–18].

Poemen 156 Abba Poemen said: "Teaching [your] neighbor is like reproving him."

Poemen 157 He also said: "Do not fulfill your [own] will; rather accept the obligation to humble yourself before your brother."

Poemen 158 A brother asked Abba Poemen: "I have found a place that offers complete repose for the brothers; do you want me to stay there?" The elder said: "Stay in a place where you do your brother no harm."

Poemen 159 [11.61] Abba Poemen said: "These three things are of capital usefulness: that you fear the Lord; that you pray to God without ceasing; and that you do good to your neighbor."

Poemen 160 A brother said to Abba Poemen: "My body has become feeble but my passions are not becoming feeble." The elder said to him: "The passions are prickly thorns."

Poemen 161 [3.27]   A brother asked Abba Poemen: "What am I to do?" The elder said to him: "At the time of God's visitation, what do we have to worry about?" "About our sins," the brother said to him, so the elder said to him: "Let us then go into our cells and remaining there, let us recall our sins—and the Lord will go along with us in everything."

Poemen 162   A brother on his way to the marketplace asked Abba Poemen: "What do you wish me to do?" The elder said to him: "Become the friend of one who coerces himself and you will sell your wares in tranquility."

Poemen 163   Abba Poemen said: "Teach your mouth to say what is in your heart."

Poemen 164 [11.57]   Abba Poemen was asked about defilements and he replied: "If we hold firm to our practice and are attentively vigilant we shall not find any defilement in ourselves."

Poemen 165   Abba Poemen said: "Since the third generation at Scete and since Abba Moses the brothers have not progressed any further."

Poemen 166 [15.56]   He also said: "If a person maintains his [monastic] status he is not disturbed."

Poemen 167 [10.93]   A brother asked Abba Poemen: "How should I remain in my cell?" He said to him: "The visible aspect of staying in one's cell consists of handiwork, eating once a day, keeping silence, and meditating. But secretly to make progress in one's cell is to tolerate laying the blame on oneself in every place where you go and not to be negligent of the times for *synaxeis* or for secret [prayers]. If a slack time occurs in your handiwork, attend the *synaxis* and discharge it with an untroubled mind. Finally, keep good company and eschew bad company."

Poemen 168   A brother asked Abba Poemen: "If a brother has a little money from me, do you want me to ask him for it?" The elder said to him: "Ask him once." The brother said to him: "Then what should I do, for I cannot repress my *logismos*." The elder said to him: "Let your *logismos* wither away: just do not trouble your brother."

Poemen 169 Some of the fathers happened to visit the villa of a person who loved Christ, and Abba Poemen was of their number. While they were eating, some meat was put out and they all ate except for Abba Poemen. Aware of his discretion, the elders were amazed that he was not eating. When they got up they said to him: "You are Poemen and you acted like that?" In reply the elder said to them: "Forgive me, fathers; you ate and nobody was offended. But if I had eaten, since many brothers come to be with me, they would have been hurt, saying: 'Poemen ate meat and we do not eat [it]?'"—and they were amazed at this discretion.

Poemen 170 Abba Poemen said: "I am telling you, I am being thrown into the place where Satan is thrown."

Poemen 171 The same [elder] said to Abba Anoub: "'Turn away your eyes that they not see vanity' [Ps 118.37], for letting things go destroys souls."

Poemen 172 Paisios was once fighting with his brother while Abba Poemen was sitting there, fighting until the blood ran down from their heads and the elder said nothing to them whatever. Abba Anoub came in and, when he saw them, he said to Abba Poemen: "Why did you let the brothers go on fighting and not say anything to them?" Said Abba Poemen: "They are brothers; they will make peace again." Said Abba Anoub: "What is this? You saw how they carried on and you say: 'They will make peace again?'" Abba Poemen said to him: "Get it into your heart that I was not a party to what is going on here."

Poemen 173 A brother asked Abba Poemen: "There are brothers living with me; do you want me to direct them?" "No," said the elder; "first perform the [monks'] task and, if they wish to live, they will see for themselves." The brother said to him: "But they themselves want me to direct them, father." The elder said to him: "No; be an example to them, not a law-giver."

Poemen 174   Abba Poemen said: "If a brother visits you and you seem to be reaping no benefit from his coming, search your thoughts; find out what kind of *logismos* you were entertaining before his coming, then you will realize the reason why you reaped no benefit. If you do this with a humble mind and intelligently you will be blameless with respect to your neighbor, bearing your own shortcomings. For if a person conduct himself devoutly while remaining [in his cell] he will not transgress at all, for God is before him. I am of the opinion that one acquires the fear of God from remaining [in one's cell]."

Poemen 175   He also said: "A person who has a youth living with him and, experiencing any passion of the Old Man for him whatsoever, still keeps him [living] with him—such a person is like a man who has a field devoured by worms."

Poemen 176 [10.77]   He also said: "Wickedness does not in any way eliminate wickedness; so if a person treats you wickedly, do him some good—to eliminate wickedness by doing good."

Poemen 177   He also said: "When David was fighting with the lion he seized it by the throat and immediately killed it [1 Sam 17.35]. If we seize our own throat and belly we shall (with the help of God) conquer the invisible lion."

Poemen 178   A brother asked Abba Poemen: "What am I to do? Affliction comes upon me and I am disturbed." The elder said: "Violence causes both small and great to be disturbed."

Poemen 179   They used to say of Abba Poemen that he was staying at Scete with two of his brothers and the younger one was troubling them. He said to the other brother: "This young fellow is our undoing; get up and let us be gone from here." Out they went and left him. Realizing that they were a long time gone he saw them in the distance. He started to run after them, crying out. Abba Poemen said: "Let us wait for the brother, for he is in adversity." When he caught up with them [the brother] prostrated himself, saying: "Where are you going and [why are you] leaving me alone?" The elder said to him: "Because you trouble us; that is why we are going away." He said to them: "Yes, yes, let us go together wherever you like." When the elder saw that there was no guile in him, he said to his brother: "Let us go back brother, for he does not want to do these things; it is the devil that does them to him." They turned round and came [back] to their place.

Poemen 180   The higoumen of a coenobion asked Abba Poemen: "How can I acquire fear of God?" Abba Poemen said to him: "How can we acquire fear of God when we have paunches of cheese and pots of pickles inside us?"

Poemen 181   A brother asked Abba Poemen: "Abba, there were two men, one a monk, one a worldling. In the evening the monk was of a mind that he would throw off the monastic habit at dawn, while the worldling was of a mind that he would become a monk, but they both died that night; what is to be thought of them?" The elder said: "The monk died a monk, the worldling a worldling; they went off as what they were."

Poemen 182 [18.21]   Abba John who was exiled by [the Emperor] Marcian used to say: "Coming from Syria, we once visited Abba Poemen and we wanted to ask him about hardness of heart. The elder did not know Greek and there was no interpreter to hand. Perceiving our dismay, the elder began speaking in the Greek tongue, saying: 'The nature of water is soft, that of rock is hard; but a [dripping] vessel hung above a rock pierces the rock, drop by drop. Likewise, the word of God is soft but our heart is hard. When a person often hears the word of God, his heart is opened to fear God.'"

Poemen 183   Abba Isaac visited Abba Poemen and saw him pouring a little water over his feet. As he was quite familiar with him, he said to him: "How is it that some used severity and treated their bodies harshly?" Abba Poemen said to him: "We were not taught to slay the body but to slay the passions."

Poemen 184   He also said: "These three injurious factors I am unable to suppress: food, clothing, and sleep, but we can partially suppress them."

Poemen 185   A brother asked Abba Poemen: "I eat a lot of vegetables." "That is not good for you," said the elder; "eat your bread and a few vegetables—and do not be going to your father's place to get what you need."

Poemen 186   They used to say of Abba Poemen that if there were some elders sitting before him speaking of some [other] elders, if they were to name Abba Sisoes, he would say: "Leave the matter of Abba Sisoes aside, for what we know of him is more than words can describe."

Poemen S 1 [Guy 29]   He also said: "Teach your heart to keep a watch over what your tongue teaches."

Poemen S 2[98] [Guy 29–30, 10.30]   A brother asked Abba Poemen: "I am damaging my soul being with my abba; shall I stay with him?" Now the elder was aware that he was being damaged; he was amazed at him asking if he should still stay [there]. The elder said: "Stay if you want to"—he went off and stayed. Then he came again and said: "I am damaging my soul," and the elder did not say "Come away." A third time he came and said: "I really am not staying any longer." Abba Poemen said to him: "Now here you are being saved; off you go and stay [there] no more." So the elder would say: "Does a man who sees that his soul is being damaged need to ask? He asks about secret *logismoi* and it is for the elders to scrutinize them. It is not necessary to ask about flagrant sin, but to cut it off immediately."

---

[98]S2 is almost the same as Poemen 52, q.v.

Poemen S 3 [Guy 30]   Abba Poemen said that Abba Paphnutius was a great one and he used to take refuge in small acts of worship.

Poemen S 4 [15.49, Guy 30]   A brother asked Abba Poemen: "How ought I to be in the place where I am living?" The elder said to him: "Have the mentality of an alien in the place where you are living so you do not seek to advance your own opinion—and you will experience repose."

Poemen S 5 [Guy 30]   He also said: "This voice cries out to a man until his last breath: 'Turn around today.'"

Poemen S 6 [Guy 30]   The same [elder] said: "David wrote to Joab: 'Continue the war and you will capture the city and overthrow it' [2 Sam 11.25]. So the city is the enemy."

Poemen S 7 [Guy 30]   He also said: "Joab said to the people: 'Be bold and be as sons of power and we shall go to war for the people of our God' [Cf. 2 Sam 13.28 at the end]. We are such as they."

Poemen S 8 [Guy 30]   He also said: "If Moses had not led the sheep to a fold, he would not have seen what he saw at the bush" [Ex 3.1–2].

Poemen S 9 [Guy 30]   A brother asked Abba Poemen: "How is it that you are now in this place?" He said: "I wanted for myself and my brothers to finish our course at Scete, but look—here we are."

Poemen S 10 [Guy 30]   He also said: "How can a man teach his neighbor that which he has seen but against which he set no guard?"

Poemen S 11 [Guy 30; cf. Anoub 1]   He also said: "A person living with his neighbor ought to be like a pillar of stone: insulted but not getting angry, revered without becoming haughty."

Poemen S 12 [Guy 30]   He also said: "A person cannot know the exterior [enemies], but when those within rise up, if a person do battle with them, he casts them out."

Poemen S 13 [Guy 30]   He also said: "Not to foresee something impedes us from progressing toward excellence."

Poemen S 14 [Guy 30]   He also said: "Do not entrust your conscience to somebody in whose heart you do not have confidence."

Poemen S 15 [Guy 30]   Abba Poemen said: "Let me tell you: in the place where there is war, there I am campaigning."

Poemen S 16 [Guy 30]   Abba Poemen heard of somebody who fasted for six days because he was angry. The elder said: "He has learnt how to endure six days but he has not learnt to cast out anger."

Poemen S 17 [Guy 30–31]   Abba Poemen said: "We are in such trouble because we are not taking care of our brother whom the Scripture stipulated we are to take in. Or do we not see the Canaanite woman who followed the Savior, crying and beseeching for her daughter to be healed—and that the Savior looked with favor on her and healed [her daughter]?" [Mt 15.21–28].

Poemen S 18 [Guy 31; cf. 11.63]   Abba Poemen said: "If the soul distance itself from every argumentative person, from human intercourse and disturbance, the Spirit of God will come upon it and that which is sterile will be able to bring forth."

Poemen S 19 [Guy 31; cf. Poemen 81, 4.38 & 9.11]   A brother asked Abba Poemen: "How ought they to be who are in a coenobion?" The elder said to him: "He who lives in a coenobion ought to regard all as one, holding his mouth and his eyes in check; then he will experience repose and be without a care."

Poemen S 20 [Guy 31]   Concerning the servants of Shimei [1 Kg 2.39–40] Abba Poemen said: "They are material possessions that bring their own reward: for these destroy those who possess them."

Poemen S 21 [Guy 31]   A brother asked Abba Poemen: "What am I to do about my sins?" The elder said to him: "Weep on your own;

for both the release from sin and the achievement of virtues come about through mourning."

Poemen S 22 [Guy 31]   He also said: "To weep is the path delivered to us by Scripture and by our fathers."

Poemen S 23 [Guy 31; Poemen 143 is identical]   A brother visiting Abba Poemen said to him: "What am I to do?" The elder said to him: "Go and associate with someone who says: 'What do I want?' and you will experience repose."

PAMBO

Pambo died in the presence of Melania the elder in 373, aged seventy. He was one of the first companions of Amoun in the desert of Nitria. He was a priest and he had known Antony and Macarius;[99] Poemen speaks of him three times.[100]

Pambo 1   There was [an elder] called Abba Pambo and of him it was said that for three years he interceded with God saying: "Do not glorify me on earth"—and God so glorified him that nobody could stare him in the face on account of the glory his face possessed.

Pambo 2 [10.94; cf. *HL* 14]   Two brothers once came to Abba Pambo and one of them asked him: "Abba, after fasting for two days I eat a pair of loaves; am I saving my soul or being led astray?" The other said: "Abba, I gain two *keratia* per day by the labor of my hands. I keep a little back for my food and give the rest to charity; am I being saved or going to be lost?" But the elder did not give them an answer, much though they pleaded with him. Then after four days, just as they had to leave, the clergy pleaded with them, saying: "Do not be disturbed, brothers; God will provide your reward. Such is the custom of the elder; he is not in a hurry to speak without the assurance

[99]*HL* 10.
[100]Poemen 47, 75 & 150.

of God." So they went in to the elder and said to him: "Abba, pray for us." He said to them: "Do you want to leave?" "Yes," they said, and attributing their practices to himself, writing on the ground he began saying: "Pambo is fasting two days and eating a pair of loaves; but is it by this that he becomes a monk? No. Pambo earns two *keratia* and gives them to charity, but is it by this that he becomes a monk? Not yet." He said to them: "Works are good, but if you keep your conscience [clear] with respect to your neighbor, in that way you are being saved." Reassured, they went away with joy.

Pambo 3 [14.14]   Four [monks] from Scete dressed in skins once came visiting Pambo the Great and they each made known the virtue of his companion in his absence. The first one fasted a great deal; the second was indifferent to possessions, the third very charitable. Of the fourth one they told him that he had been obedient to an elder for twenty-two years. Abba Pambo answered them: "I tell you that the virtue of this one is greater, for each one of you has obtained whatever virtue he possesses by [doing] his own will, while he, having suspended his own will, does the will of somebody else. Such persons are confessors if they hold fast to the end."

Pambo 4 [3.32]   The archbishop of Alexandria, Athanasius of sacred memory, invited Abba Pambo to come down from the desert to Alexandria. He came down and, seeing a woman of the theater there, broke down in tears. When those who were there with him sought to know why he wept, he said: "Two things have moved me: first, her destruction; secondly, that I do not make such an effort to please God as she makes to please shameful men."

Pambo 5 [cf. Pambo 8, *HL* 10.6]   Abba Pambo said: "By the grace of God, since I renounced [the world] I have not regretted a word I have spoken."

Pambo 6 [cf. Isaac of The Cells 12]   Again [Abba Pambo] used to say: "The monk ought to wear the sort of clothing that, if he threw it out of the cell for three days, nobody would take it."

Pambo 7 [17.14]   Abba Pambo was once travelling with some brothers in parts of Egypt. When he saw some worldlings sitting there he said to them: "Get up and embrace the monks so you may be blessed, for they are continually speaking with God and their mouths are holy."

Pambo 8 [1.25, *HL* 10.6]   They said of Abba Pambo that as he was dying, at the moment of death, he said to the holy men who were present: "From the time I came to this place in the desert, built my cell and dwelt in it, I do not recall eating bread except what came from my hands nor have I repented of anything I said until this moment. And yet I am going to God as one who has not even begun to serve him."

Pambo 9 [*HL* 10.7]   There was this that set him above many [others]: if he were asked about a phrase in Scripture or some spiritual matter, he did not answer immediately, but would say he did not know the answer. And if he were pressed further, he would not give an answer.

Pambo 10   Abba Pambo said: "If you have a heart you can be saved."

Pambo 11 [4.86]   The priest of Nitria[101] asked: "How ought the brothers to be living?" "In great asceticism," they said: "and guarding their conscience with respect to their neighbor."

Pambo 12 [cf. Silvanus 12]   They used to say of Abba Pambo that, as Moses received the likeness of the glory of Adam when his face was glorified, so too did the face of Abba Pambo shine like lightning, and he was like an emperor sitting on his throne. Abba Silvanus and Abba Sisoes were similarly distinguished.

Pambo 13   They used to say of Abba Pambo that his face never smiled. One day the demons wanted to make him laugh. They tied a

---

[101] *APsys* 4.86 begins: "They used to say of Abba Pambo, Abba Bessarion, Isaiah, Abba Paisios and Abba Athre that a priest of the Mountain [of Nitria] asked them when they had met with each other . . ."

wing to a log and carried it along, making a disturbance and crying:
"A wing, a wing!"—and Abba Pambo laughed when he saw them.
The demons began to dance, calling "Ha ha! Pambo has laughed!"
but in reply he said to them: "I did not laugh; I derided your feeble-
ness when it takes so many of you to carry the wing."

Pambo 14   Abba Theodore of Phermē asked Abba Pambo: "Tell
me a saying." With a great deal of effort he said to him: "Go and be
merciful to everybody, Theodore, for mercy finds freedom of speech
in the presence of God."

PISTOS

*In this passage, taken from the works of Isaiah of Scete [30, 6A],
pistos is not a proper noun but an adjective affirming the cred-
ibility of the person who is the narrator. This passage really ought
to be filed under Sisoes (see below).*

Pistos [15.60]   Abba Pistos recounted: "Seven of us anchorites went
to Abba Sisoes who was living on the island of Clysma, begging him
to say something to us. 'Forgive me,' he said, 'for I am a simple fellow, but I paid a visit to Abba Ōr and also to Abba Athre; Abba Ōr
had been sick for eighteen years. I prostrated myself before them
[requesting them] to say something to me. Abba Ōr said: "What have
I to say to you? Go your way and do whatever you see. God is with
him who exerts and coerces himself in all things." Now Abba Ōr and
Abba Athre were not from the same region but there was great peace
between them right until they departed from the body. The obedience of Abba Athre was great and great was the humble-mindedness
of Abba Ōr. I spent a few days with them observing them and I saw
a great wonder that Abba Athre worked. Somebody brought them
a small fish and Abba Athre wanted to prepare it for Abba Ōr, the
elder. He had the knife and was cutting the fish when Abba Ōr called
him. He left the knife in the middle of the fish and did not cut the rest

of it. I was amazed at his great obedience [and] that he did not say: "Wait until I cut the fish." I said to Abba Athre: "How did you come by such obedience?" and he said: "It is not mine; it is the elder's," and he took me aside, saying: "Come and see his obedience." He cooked the little fish, deliberately spoiling it; then he presented it to the elder who ate it without speaking. [Abba Athre] said to him: "Good is it, elder?" and he answered: "It is very good." After that he brought him a little [fish] that really was good and he said: "I spoiled it, elder," and he replied: "Yes, you did spoil it a little." Then Abba Athre said to me: "Did you see that the obedience is the elder's?" I went away from them to observe whatever I saw to the best of my ability.' This is what Abba Sisoes told the brothers. One of us begged him: 'Of your kindness do you yourself say something to us.' He said: 'He who is consciously aware that he does not count fulfils all the Scripture.' Another of us also said to him: 'What is voluntary exile [*xeniteia*], father?' and he said: 'Keep silent and say: "I have nothing to do with this" wherever you go—that is voluntary exile.' "

PIOR

According to an apophthegm that is only known in Latin, Pior became a monk and a disciple of Antony at a very young age. For many years he lived a solitary life between Scete and Nitria, making a new start every day [Poemen 85].

Pior 1   Having worked at the harvest for somebody, the blessed Pior reminded him that he should receive his wage; but he procrastinated and [Pior] went off to his dwelling. When the season called for it, he harvested for him again and, diligently though he worked, that one gave him nothing so off he went to his dwelling. The third year came round; the elder accomplished his customary task and went away having received nothing. But the Lord prospered the house of that man; he went around the monasteries in search of the holy one, bringing his wage. As soon as he found him he fell at his feet and gave it to him saying: "The Lord has given it to me." But [Pior] entreated him to donate it to the priest at the church.

Pior 2 [4.42]   Abba Pior he used to eat walking around. When somebody enquired: "Why do you eat like that?" he said: "I do not want to treat food as work, but as incidental."[102] To somebody else who had asked about it he replied: "[It is] so that my soul may not experience any physical pleasure even when I am eating."

Pior 3 [9.13]   Once there was a council at Scete concerning a brother who had transgressed; the fathers were talking, but Abba Pior remained silent. Later on he got up and went out; he took a sack, filled it with sand, then carried it over his shoulder. He put a little sand in a basket and carried it in front of him. When he was asked by the fathers what this was meant to be, he said: "This sack with a lot of sand in it is my transgressions, for they are many. I have left them behind me so I am not distressed about them and weep. And here are my brother's few transgressions in front of me; by going on about them, I am passing judgment on him. I should not act so, but rather carry my own [sins] before me and worry about those, beseeching God to forgive me." When they heard this, the fathers said: "Truly, that is the way of salvation."

PITYRION

The following is an extract from HME *15.*

Abba Pityrion, the disciple of Abba Antony, used to say: "He who would drive out demons will first have to enslave his passions. Whatever passion one masters, he drives out the demon of it. There is a demon associated with wrath," he said; "if you are in control of wrath, the demon of [wrath] has been driven out—and so it is with each passion."

[102]There is a word-play here: *ergon / parergon.*

PISTAMON

Pistamon [6.15]   A brother asked Abba Pistamon: "What am I to do, for I am troubled when I go selling my handiwork?" In reply the elder said: "Both Abba Sisoes and the others used to sell their handiwork; there is no harm in it. But when you are selling, state the price of the item once, then if you wish to lower the price a little it is up to you. This way you will experience repose." The brother spoke to him again: "If I have what I need from somewhere, do you want me to concern myself with handiwork?" In reply the elder said: "Even if you do have what you need from somewhere, do not abandon your handiwork. Do what you are able, only do not be troubled."

PETER THE PIONITE

Peter the Pionite lived at The Cells and may have been the disciple of Abba Lot. The meaning of "Pionite" is unclear.

Peter the Pionite 1 [4.43]   They used to say of Abba Peter the Pionite at The Cells that he did not drink wine. When he grew old, the brothers used to dilute a little wine and beg him to accept [it]. He would say: "Believe me, I regard this as a condiment,"[103] and he blamed himself for [drinking] the diluted wine.

Peter the Pionite 2 [11.65]   A brother said to Abba Peter, [the disciple] of Abba Lot: "My soul is at peace when I am in my cell but, if a brother visit me and speak about external matters, my soul is troubled." Abba Peter told him that Abba Lot used to say: "Your key opens my door." The brother said to him: "What is this saying?" and the elder said: "If somebody visits you, you say to him: 'How are you? Where have you come from? How are the brothers? Were they hospitable to you or not?'—and then you open the brother's door and you hear things you do not want to hear." "That is how it is," he said,

[103]or perhaps "spiced [wine]"—meaning a medicament.

"so what shall somebody do if a brother comes to him?" The elder said: "Complete sorrow is what teaches;[104] one cannot be protected where there is no sorrow." "When I am in my cell," said the brother: "sorrow is with me, but if someone come to me or I come out of the cell, I do not find it." The elder said: "It is not yet at your disposal but as if it were on loan, for it is written in the Law: 'When you acquire a Hebrew slave, six years shall he serve you; the seventh year you shall send him away, a free man. If you give him a wife and she bear children in your house and he not want to be set free on account of his wife and children, you shall bring him to the door of the house. You shall pierce his ear with an awl and he shall be your slave forever' [cf. Ex 21.2–6]. The brother said: "What does this passage mean?" Said the elder: "If a man labor away at something to the best of his ability, at whatever time he seeks it for his own need, he will find it." He said to him: "Of your kindness explain this to me." The elder said: "Not even a bastard son remains in servitude to somebody, but the legitimate son does not leave his father."

Peter the Pionite 3   They used to say of Abba Peter and Abba Epimachus that they were colleagues at Raïthou. While they were eating at the church the [other brothers] urged them to come to the table of the elders. Very reluctantly Abba Peter went there—alone. When they got up Abba Epimachus said to him: "How did you dare to go to the table of the elders?" But he answered: "If I had sat with you, the brothers would have urged me as an elder to be the first to bless [the food] and I would have been as one greater than you. But now when I went to be with the fathers I was the least of them all and [became] more humble in *logismos*."

Peter the Pionite 4   Abba Peter said: "We must not be swelled up with pride when the Lord does something through us—but rather be thankful that we were found worthy to be called [to serve] by him." He used to say it was advantageous to think like that with respect to every virtue.

---

[104]*in luctu omnino doctrina est*, "there is teaching in all sorrow," *P&J*.

Paphnutius

*This name, the Egyptian equivalent of Theophorus, "God-bearing,"
occurs frequently in the early monastic literature.*

Paphnutius 1 [9.14]   Abba Paphnutius said: "Travelling the road I
happened to lose my way in the fog and found myself near a village. I
saw some persons having shameful relations with each other. I stood
there interceding for my sins and here there came an angel bearing
a sword and said to me: 'Paphnutius, all they who pass judgment on
their brothers will perish by this sword. However, because you did
not pass judgment but humbled yourself before God as though you
had committed the sin, for this reason your name has been inscribed
in the book of the living.'"

Paphnutius 2 [17.15]   They used to say of Abba Paphnutius that he
drank wine reluctantly. Once when he was travelling he came upon
a band of robbers drinking wine. Now the robber-chief recognized
him and was aware that he did not drink wine, but seeing that he was
quite exhausted, he filled the cup with wine and, sword in hand, said
to the elder: "I will kill you if you do not drink it." Now [the elder]
realized that [the robber-chief] meant to fulfil the commandment
of God, consequently he wanted to win him over; so he accepted
[the wine] and drank it. Then the robber-chief apologized to him,
saying: "Forgive me, abba, I have distressed you," and the elder said:
"I have faith in God that, on account of this cup, he will have mercy
on you now and in the age to come." Said the robber-chief to him: "I
have faith in God that from now on I will do no harm to anybody,"
and the elder won over the entire band by abandoning his will for
the Lord's sake.

Paphnutius 3   Abba Poemen said that Abba Paphnutius used to
say: "Throughout the days of the life of the elders I visited them twice
a month (I was twelve miles distant from them). I used to tell them
about my every *logismos* and they would say nothing to me other

than this: 'Wherever you go, do not measure yourself and you will experience repose.'"

Paphnutius 4 There was a brother with Abba Paphnutius at Scete embattled by *porneia* and he would say: "If I took ten wives I would not satisfy my lust." The elder would exhort [him] saying: "No, my son: it is a battle [waged by] the demons," but he was not persuaded; he went to Egypt and took a wife. Some time later the elder happened to go up to Egypt and he met him carrying baskets of tiles. The elder did not recognize him but [the brother] said to him: "I am your disciple so-and-so." When the elder saw him in so dishonorable an estate he wept, saying: "How could you abandon that honorable estate and arrive at this dishonorable one? Did you really take the ten wives?" With a sigh he said: "In fact I took one and I am at my wits' end to keep her in bread." Said the elder to him: "Come back with us," and he said: "Is there repentance, abba?" "There is," he said, and he left all and followed him. He came into Scete and, from his experience, he became a tried and tested monk.

Paphnutius 5 A *logismos* came to a brother residing in the desert of the Thebaid: "Why stay [here] accomplishing nothing? Get up and go to a coenobion; there you shall accomplish something." He got up and came to Abba Paphnutius, telling him of the *logismos*. The elder said to him: "Go and stay in your cell; offer one prayer at dawn, one in the evening, and one at night. Eat when you are hungry, drink when you thirst, sleep when you are tired; stay in the desert and do not be swayed by [the *logismos*]." He came to Abba John too and told him what Abba Paphnutius had said. Abba John said: "Do not offer a prayer at all; just stay in your cell." He got up and came to Abba Arsenius and told him everything. [That] elder said to him: "Hold on to what the fathers told you; I have nothing more than they had to say to you." Away he went, well convinced.

Paul of Thebes

This is not the Paul of Thebes whose Life, generally regarded to be fictitious, was written by Jerome.[105]

Paul of Thebes [19.15] One of the fathers recounted of a certain Abba Paul, originally from Lower Egypt but residing in the Thebaid, that he would hold asps, snakes, and scorpions in his hands [Lk 10.19] and cut them in two. The brothers prostrated themselves before him saying: "Tell us what kind of activity you undertook so that you acquired this spiritual gift." "Forgive me, fathers," he said; "if one acquire purity, everything is subject to him as it was to Adam when he was in Paradise before he contravened the commandment" [Gen 1.28].

Paul the Barber

Paul and his brother Timothy were barbers at Scete. One wonders what kept them so busy; presumably the Egyptian monks kept the hair short (cf. HME 8.59) and had to have frequent recourse to the barber.

Paul the Barber 1 [16.10] Abba Paul the Barber and his brother Timothy were residing at Scete and a difference of opinion often arose between them for various reasons. "How long are we going to carry on like this?" said Abba Paul, and Abba Timothy said to him: "Of your charity, bear with me when I oppose you and when you oppose me I too will bear with you." This they did and they experienced repose the rest of their days.

Paul the Barber 2 [11.64] The same Abba Paul and Timothy his brother were barbers at Scete and they were overwhelmed by the [rest of the] brothers. Timothy said to his brother: "What do we want

---

[105]Caroline White, trans., *Early Christian Lives* (London: Penguin, 1998), 75–84.

with this profession? Throughout the whole day we are not allowed to practice *hesychia*." In response, Abba Paul said to him: "The *hesychia* of the night is enough for us if our mind is keeping watch."

PAUL THE GREAT

Paul the Great 1 [7.21]   Paul the Great, the Galatian, said: "A monk who has a few necessities in his cell and comes out to worry is the plaything of the demons. I too have suffered from this."

Paul the Great S 1 [Guy 32]   Abba Paul said: "Follow Jesus."

Paul the Great 2 [cf. 15.52]   Abba Paul said: "I am immersed in a slough up to my neck and I cry out to God saying: 'Have mercy on me.'"

Paul the Great 3 [4.41]   They used to say of Abba Paul that he lived throughout Lent on a measure of lentils and a small pot of water, shut up [in his cell] with one mat, braiding and unravelling it until the feast.

PAUL THE SIMPLE

This Paul was a disciple of Antony; see HL 22 and HME 24.

Paul the Simple [18.26]   The blessed Abba Paul the Simple, the disciple of Abba Antony, told the fathers something like this: that once when he was in a monastery for a visitation and for the benefit of the brothers, after the usual conversation with each other they went into the holy church of God to offer the customary *synaxis*. Blessed Paul (he said) carefully observed each one of those going into the church [to see] in what spiritual state they were going in. For he had this spiritual gift accorded to him by God: he could see the state of each person's soul as we see one another's faces. All were going in with shining faces and a sparkling look, the angel of each one rejoicing on their account. "But I saw one," he said, "whose body was all shady and black, with a demon on either side, retaining him with a halter through the nostrils, pulling him between themselves. His holy angel was following at a distance, dismayed and distressed." Paul was sitting before the church, weeping and beating his breast many times with his hand, greatly lamenting the one who had appeared to him in this way. When the brothers saw the man's strange behavior and his sudden breaking into tears and weeping, they insisted that he tell them why he was weeping, for they feared that his behavior was a condemnation of everybody. They invited him to go into the *synaxis* with them, but he shook them off and declined. He sat outside in silence, severely regretting the one who had been shown to him like that. Not long afterwards the *synaxis* was accomplished, and as they were all coming out, again Paul examined each one, for he wanted to know in what state they were coming out. He saw that man who formerly had a body all shady and black coming out of the church with a shining face and a white body, the demons following a long way off while his holy angel stayed close to him, greatly rejoicing on his charge's behalf. Paul sprang up with joy and shouted out, blessing God and saying: "Ah, the unspeakable love of mankind and goodness of God!" At a run he mounted some high steps and said with a loud voice: "'Come and behold the works of God' [Ps 45.9a] how they are fearful and worthy of all admiration. Come and see him 'who wishes all to be saved and to come to awareness of the truth' [1 Tim 2:4]. 'Come let us worship and fall down before him' [Ps 94.6] and let us say: 'you alone can take away sins.'" They all came eagerly running together, wanting to hear what was being said. When they were all assembled Paul told them what had been seen by him, before they went into the church and again afterwards; and he asked the man to say why God had suddenly granted him such a transformation. Encouraged by Paul, the person told his story before them all, without dissimulation: "I am a sinful person," he said, "living in *porneia* for a long time until now. When I went into the holy church of God just now, I heard the Prophet Isaiah being read, or rather God speaking through him: 'Wash you, make you clean; put away the evil of your doings from before my eyes. Learn to do what is good; seek judgment. Though your sins be as scarlet, they shall be as white as snow; and, if you are willing and obedient to me, you shall eat the good of the land' [Is 1.16–19, *partim*]. And I, the sexual offender, was severely pricked in my conscience by the word of the prophet; groaning in my inner self I said to God: 'You are the God who came into the world to save sinners [cf. I Tim 1.15]. Do you now fulfil in me, the unworthy sinner, that which you have just proclaimed through your prophet. For here: from now on I give you [my] word; I guarantee and promise in my heart that I will no longer do any of [those] evil things. I will reject all iniquity and serve you from now on with a pure conscience. Today then, Lord-and-master, from this very hour, receive me who repent and fall before you, separating myself henceforth from every sin.'" Having given these undertakings, he said: "I came out of the church determined within myself never again to commit anything that is foul before the eyes of God." All those who were hearing began to cry out to God with a single voice saying: "'Lord how wonderful are your works; you have made them all in wisdom!' [Ps 103.24]" O Christians, may we then learn from the divine Scriptures and the holy revelations the whole goodness of God toward those who sincerely take refuge in him and turn away from their former misdoings by repentance. May we learn that God provides the good things he has promised without requiring satisfaction for past sins, and let us not despair of our salvation. Just as he promised through the Prophet Isaiah to wash those bogged down in sin and to make them white like wool and like snow [Ps 50.9], and to make us worthy of the benefits of the heavenly Jerusalem; so too does he also through the Prophet Ezekiel assure us with an oath that he will not destroy us: "As I live, says the Lord, I do not wish the death of a sinner, but that he might turn about and live" [Ezek 18.32, 33.11].

PETER OF DIOS

According to what is written in *The Life of Abba Antony,*[106] if ever Peter, the priest of those at Dios, prayed with other people, whilst he was obliged on account of his priesthood to stand in front, he stood behind, confessing in his humble-mindedness. This he would do without distressing anybody.

[106]Nothing like this is to be found in *VA* today.

P—*Rho*

The Roman

Comparison of the first item below with Arsenius 36 (above) reveals that "the Roman" is in fact Arsenius. Another version names the patient disciple of the second item as Peter.

The Roman 1 [10.110]   There once came and resided very near to the church at Scete a monk from Rome who had been a grandee of the palace; he had one servant to wait on him. When the priest noticed his weakness and learnt from what luxury he had come he sent him whatever God supplied and came to the church. After spending twenty-five years at Scete [this monk] gained the second sight and became famous. When one of the great Egyptians heard about him, he came to see him, expecting to find an intensified bodily discipline in him. He went in and embraced him; they offered a prayer and sat down. The Egyptian saw him wearing soft clothing [cf. Lk 7.25]. There was a mat with a fleece on it beneath him and a small pillow; his feet were clean, shod with sandals. When he saw these things he was offended because in that place there was no such way of life, but rather austerity. As the elder had second sight, he became aware that [the Egyptian] was offended and he said to the one who waited on him: "Make us a feast in honor of the abba today." There were a few vegetables and he cooked them; when the time arrived, they got up and ate. The elder had a little wine for his weakness too, so they drank. When evening fell they offered the twelve psalms then they went to bed; likewise in the night. When he got up at dawn the Egyptian said: "Pray for me," and out he went, none the wiser. When he had gone a little way, the elder (wishing to do him some good) sent and called him back then received him

again with joy. He enquired of him: "What country are you from?"
"I am Egyptian," he said. "From which city?" but he said: "I am not a
city-dweller." [The elder] said: "What was your work in the village?"
"Herdsman," he said. "Where did you sleep?" said the elder; "In the
field," he said. "Did you have bedding under you?" said the elder.
"Would I have bedding to put under me in the field?" he said. "But
how did you sleep," said the elder; "On the ground," he said. "What
were you eating in the field," the elder said, "or what wine used you to
drink?" and he replied: "Is there food and drink in the field?" "How
did you live then?" the elder said, and he said: "I would eat dry bread
with a little salted fish if there was any and water." "That is severe
hardship," the elder replied and continued: "Was there a bath house
in the village where you could wash?" "No," he said, "but we would
wash ourselves in the river when we wanted to." When the elder had
got all this from him and had learnt of his former way of life and
affliction, wishing to do him some good, he told him the nature of his
own former life in the world: "The wretched person you see is from
the great city of Rome where I became a grandee in the emperor's
palace." When he heard the beginning of the story, the Egyptian was
conscience-stricken and began listening carefully to what was being
said by him. He spoke to him again: "I abandoned Rome and came
to this desert. I at whom you are looking also possessed great houses
and much wealth. I turned my back on those and came to this little
cell. I at whom you are looking also had golden beds with valuable
bedding, in exchange for which God has given me this mat and a
fleece. My clothing too was very expensive, instead of which I now
wear these cheap clothes. Then again much gold was expended for
my nourishment: in its place God has given me these few vegetables
and a little cup of wine. The slaves dancing attendance on me were
many, while here, in exchange, God has prompted this elder to wait
on me. Instead of a bath, I pour a little water on my feet and [wear]
sandals on account of my weakness. Again, instead of musicians
with flutes and lute, I say the twelve psalms; likewise during the
night, instead of the sins I used to commit, I now offer my little act

of worship before taking repose. So I beg of you, abba, not to be offended by my weakness." The Egyptian came to himself when he heard this and said: "Ah me! It was from much adversity in this world that I came to be comfortable; and what I lacked then I now possess. But you came from being very comfortable into affliction; you came from high honor and much wealth to lowliness and poverty." He went his way having reaped much benefit. He became his friend and often visited him to receive benefit, for [the Roman] was a person with second sight, replete with the fragrance of the Holy Spirit.

The Roman 2 [16.26]   The same [elder] said: "There was an elder who had a fine disciple but that elder was so contemptuous that he threw the disciple out of the gate together with his sheepskin. The brother, however, just remained there, sitting outside. When the elder opened [the gate] and found him sitting [there] he prostrated himself before him, saying: "Father, the humiliation of your long-suffering patience has overcome my contempt. Come inside; from now on you are the elder and father, I the junior and the disciple."

RUFUS

Rufus 1 [2.35]   A brother asked Abba Rufus: "What is *hesychia* and what benefit is there in it?" The elder said to him: "*Hesychia* is remaining in a cell in fear and conscious awareness of God, refraining from rancor and arrogance. That kind of *hesychia* is the mother of all virtues; it protects the monk from the fiery darts of the enemy, preventing him from being wounded by them. Yes, brother, do acquire [*hesychia*], keeping in mind the exit at your death, for you know not at what hour the thief will come [Lk 12.39]. In a word: keep a watch on your own soul."

Rufus 2 [14.29, N 296]   Abba Rufinus said that one who resides in obedience to a spiritual father has a greater reward than one who retires by himself into the desert. He used to say that one of the fathers recounted: "I saw four orders in heaven. The first order:

a man who is sick and is giving thanks to God. The second order: one who practices hospitality and keeps at it, rendering service. The third order: one who pursues the desert [life], seeing nobody. The fourth order: he who resides in obedience to a father, subject to him for the Lord's sake. The one maintaining his obedience was wearing a crown of gold and a breastplate and he enjoyed greater distinction than the others." And he said: "I said to my guide: 'How is it that the one who is inferior to the others has greater distinction?' In answer he said to me: 'Whereas the one who practices hospitality does so of his own free will, just as the one residing in the desert has retired there of his own free will, he who is obedient has totally abandoned all his own wishes and depends on God and on his own father. It is for this reason that he received greater distinction than the others.'" Therefore, my sons, obedience practiced for the sake of the Lord is a fine thing. You have now partially heard some sketchy evidence of this admirable practice, my sons.

> O, obedience, salvation of all the faithful!
> O, obedience, mother of all the virtues!
> O, obedience, discoverer of the Kingdom!
> O, obedience, that opens the heavens and draws man up from earth!
> O, obedience, the nourishment of all the saints from which they drew sustenance, and through you were they made perfect.
> O, obedience, co-habitant of the angels!

ROMANUS

When Abba Romanus was about to die, his disciples gathered around him, saying to him: "How ought we to be governed?" The elder said: "I am not aware of having ever told one of you to do something unless I had first made a resolution not to be angry if he did not do what I said was to be [done], and in this way we lived in peace all our days."

Σ—*Sigma*

Sisoes

About fifty apophthegms are attributed to Abba Sisoes, plus the
seven uttered by "Tithoes." But there are at least two if not three
persons with this name. The earliest and most famous Sisoes left
Scete after Antony died to take up residence in the elder's hermit-
age together with Abraham, his disciple, later retiring to Clysma.
This may be that "Sisoes the Theban" mentioned in some items,
but there is also a "Sisoes of Petra"—clearly not the same Sisoes,
as we read of a brother who asked the one about a saying of the
other [Sisoes 36, below]. Yet the majority of the following items
probably refer to the original Sisoes (of Scete and Clysma)—who
left behind a very strong impression.

Sisoes 1 [16.13]   A brother who had been wronged by another
brother came to Abba Sisoes the Theban and said to him: "I have
been wronged by a brother and I want to be revenged," but the elder
entreated him saying: "No my son; do you rather leave the business
of revenge to God," but he said: "I will not rest until I revenge myself."
The elder said: "Let us pray brother." The elder stood up and said:
"Oh God, we no longer need you to look after us, for we are getting
our own revenge." The brother fell at the elder's feet when he heard
that, saying: "I will no longer take issue with my brother: forgive
me, abba!"

Sisoes 2 [4.45]   A brother asked Abba Sisoes: "What am I to do,
for I attend church; often there is an *agapē* and they detain me." The
elder said: "This is a difficult matter." His disciple, Abraham, said:
"If the attendance be on a Saturday or Sunday and a brother drink

three cups, that is not many, is it?" And the elder said to him: "Not many—provided Satan be not [there]."

Sisoes 3 [2.26]   Abba Abraham, the disciple of Abba Sisoes, said to him: "You have aged, father; let us go a little nearer to where there is habitation." Said Abba Sisoes to him: "Let us go to where there is no woman." His disciple said to him: "And where is there a place where there is no woman, other than the desert?" So the elder said: "Take me to the desert then."

Sisoes 4 [4.46]   Abba Sisoes' disciple often said to him: "Abba, get up; let us eat," and he would say: "Have we not eaten, my son?" He: "No, father," so the elder would say: "If we have not eaten, bring [something] and let us eat."

Sisoes 5 [4.47]   Abba Sisoes once confidently affirmed: "Take heart; here I have been for thirty years and am no longer pleading with God about sin. But this is what I say when I pray: 'Lord Jesus Christ, protect me from my tongue,' for every day even until now I fall because of it and commit sin."

Sisoes 6 [10.98]   A brother said to Abba Sisoes: "How is it that the passions do not recede from me?" The elder said: "Their instruments are inside you; give them their due and they will go away."

Sisoes 7 [20.5]   Abba Sisoes was once residing alone at the mountain of Abba Antony; as his attendant was taking his time in coming to him, he had not seen anybody for upwards of ten months. As he was walking about on the mountain, he came across a Pharanite hunting wild beasts. He said to him: "Where do you come from and how long have you been here?" "Truth to tell, abba, I have been on this mountain eleven months and I have not seen anybody but you," he said. When the elder heard this, he went into his own cell and smote himself, saying: "Here you thought you had accomplished something, Sisoes, and in fact you have not yet accomplished what this worldling has already done."

Sisoes 8 [4.44]   Once an offering took place on the mountain of Abba Antony and a *knidion*[107] of wine was there. Taking a small bottle and a cup, one of the elders brought [some wine] to Abba Sisoes. He gave it to him and he drank it. Likewise a second [cup] and he accepted it. He offered him a third, but [the elder] did not take it, saying: "Stop brother, or do you not know that it is Satan?"

Sisoes 9 [15.62]   One of the brothers visited Abba Sisoes at the mountain of Abba Antony and, while they were speaking, he said to Abba Sisoes: "Have you not now attained the stature of Abba Antony, father?" and the elder said: "How could I have attained the stature of the holy one? If I had one of the *logismoi* of Abba Antony I would have become all on fire. Yet I do know a person who, with great effort, can carry his *logismos*."

Sisoes 10 [14.15]   One of the Thebans once came to Abba Sisoes[108] wanting to become a monk, and the elder asked him if he had anybody in the world. "I have one son," he said, and the elder said to him: "Go and throw him into the river, then you will become a monk." After he set out to throw [his son into the river] the elder sent a brother to prevent him. The brother said: "Stop, what are you doing?"And he said: "The abba told me to throw him [in]," so the brother said to him: "The elder also said: "Do *not* throw him [in]," and leaving [his son] he came to the elder and became a well-tried monk on account of his obedience.

Sisoes 11 [15.63]   A brother asked Abba Sisoes: "Did Satan use to persecute those of old time like this?" The elder said: "More so nowadays, for his time has drawn nigh and he is troubled."

Sisoes 12 [19.18]   Abraham, the disciple of Abba Sisoes, was once tempted by a demon and the elder perceived that he had fallen. He got up, stretched his hands to heaven and said: "O God, whether you

---

[107]A measure of uncertain quantity.
[108]"one came to Abba Sisoes the Theban" in some mss.

want to or not, I am not letting you go until you heal him"—and he was healed immediately.

Sisoes 13 [15.65]   A brother questioned Abba Sisoes: "I observe that in my own case the memory of God remains with me." The elder said to him: "It is no great thing for your *logismos* to be with God, but it is great to see oneself as inferior to all creation; for that and physical toil are conducive to an attitude of humble-mindedness."

Sisoes 14 [20.7]   They used to say of Abba Sisoes that when he was at the point of death and the fathers were sitting with him, his face shone like the sun and he said to them: "Here Abba Antony has come," and a little later he said: "Here the chorus of the prophets has come." Again his face shone excessively and he said: "Here the chorus of the apostles has come." Then his face was doubly lit up and here he seemed to be talking with some people. The elders besought him saying: "With whom are you speaking, father?" and he said: "Here the angels have come to take me and I am begging to be allowed to repent a little." The elders said to him: "You do not need to repent, father," but the elder said to them: "I really do not know whether I have made a beginning"—and they all realized that he was perfect. Then his face suddenly shone like the sun again and they were all afraid. He said to them: "Here the Lord has come and he is saying: 'Bring me the choice vessel [cf. Acts 9.15] of the desert'"—and forthwith he gave up the spirit. There was something like a streak of lightning and the whole house was filled with perfume.

Sisoes 15 [8.20]   Abba Adelphios, Bishop of Nilopolis, came to visit Abba Sisoes at the mountain of Abba Antony. When they were about to leave, before they set out [the elder] made them eat something early in the morning—but it was a fast day. When he had laid the table there were brothers knocking [at the gate]. "Give them a little porridge," he said to his disciple, "for they are exhausted." Abba Adelphios said to him: "Wait a little so they do not say that Abba Sisoes is eating early in the morning." The elder heeded him but said to his disciple: "Go and give [it] to them." However, when they saw the porridge, they said: "Perhaps you have guests and perhaps the elder is eating with you too?" "Yes," said the brother. They began to be troubled and to speak like this: "God forgive you for allowing the elder to eat at this hour, or do you not know that he has to inflict himself with hard labor for many days?" The bishop heard them; he prostrated himself before the elder saying: "Forgive me, abba, for I thought in a human way, but you do what God wills." Abba Sisoes said to him: "Unless God glorifies somebody, people's glory is nothing."

Sisoes 16 [15.64] Some others visited him to hear something from him but he said nothing to them. Every time he would say: "Excuse me." Seeing his baskets, they said to Abraham his disciple: "What are you doing with these baskets?" "We sell them here and there," he said, and hearing this the elder said: "Sisoes eats from here and there." They derived much benefit on hearing this and joyfully went their way, edified by his humility.

Sisoes 17 [8.21] Abba Amoun of Raïthou asked Abba Sisoes: "When I am reading Scripture my *logismos* wants to compose a fine speech so I have an answer to questioning." The elder said to him: "There is no need for that; do you rather acquire for yourself from the purity of your mind the ability to 'take no thought' [Mt 6.25ff] and to speak."

Sisoes 18 [19.17] A worldling, together with his son, once visited Abba Sisoes at the mountain of Abba Antony and it came about that his son died on the way. [The parent] was not distressed: in faith he took [the son] to the elder and fell down with his son as though making a prostration in order to be blessed by the elder. Then the father got up, leaving the son at the elder's feet, and went out of the cell. Thinking that [the child] was making a prostration to him, the elder said to him: "Get up and go out," not realizing that he was dead. [The child] immediately got up and went out. His father was astounded when he saw him; in he went and did homage to the elder, reporting the matter to him. But the elder was saddened on hearing it, for he did not want that to happen. His disciple ordered [the parent] not to report it to anybody until the elder's death.

Sisoes 19   Three elders visited Abba Sisoes when they heard about him. The first one said to him: "Father, how might I be saved from the fiery river?" [Dan 7.10] but he did not answer him. The second one said to him: "Father, how may I be saved from the gnashing of teeth [Mt 8.12] and the worm that does not die?" [Mk 9.48]. The third one said to him: "Father, what shall I do, for the recollection of outer darkness is killing me ?" [Mt 8:12]. In answer the elder said to them: "I have no recollection of any of those things; but as God is compassionate I hope he will be merciful to me." The elders went their way in sorrow when they heard what he had to say. But the elder did not want to let them go away in sorrow. He recalled them and said to them: "You are fortunate my brothers; I envied you. The first among you spoke of the fiery river, the second of hell, the third of darkness. If your mind is dominated by such recollections, it is impossible for you to sin. What am I to do, I the hard-hearted one who am not even permitted to know whether there be a chastisement for people and, accordingly, am sinning all the time?" Prostrating themselves they said: "As we heard, so have we seen."

Sisoes 20 [cf. Poemen 12]   There were those who asked Abba Sisoes: "If a brother fall, should he not do a year's penitence?" "That is a hard saying," he said, but they said: "Six months then?" Again he said: "That is a long time." "For forty days?" they suggested, and again he said: "That is a long time." "What then?" they said; "if a brother fall and an *agapē* takes place right away, is he to come in to the *agapē*?" "No," said the elder; "he must repent for a few days. I have faith in God that if such a person repent wholeheartedly, God will accept him in three days."

Sisoes 21   Abba Sisoes once came to Clysma and some worldlings came to see him. They spoke a great deal but he answered them not a word. In the end one of them said: "Why are you bothering the elder? He is not eating; for that reason he cannot speak either." "Me, I eat when I have to," the elder replied.

Sisoes 22 Abba Joseph asked Abba Sisoes: "For how long ought a person to cut off the passions?" Said the elder to him: "You want to know how long?" "Yes," said Abba Joseph; so the elder said: "At whatever time a passion arises, cut it off immediately."

Sisoes 23 A brother asked Abba Sisoes of Petra about [his] way of life and the elder said to him: "Daniel said: 'I ate no desirable bread'" [Dan 10.3].

Sisoes 24 [20.6] They used to say of Abba Sisoes that he would always shut the door when he was staying in his cell.

Sisoes 25 Some Arians once came to Abba Sisoes at the mountain of Abba Antony and began speaking ill of the Orthodox; the elder answered them not a word. He summoned his own disciple saying: "Abraham, bring me the book of the holy Athanasius and read it." While they kept silence their heresy became apparent. He sent them on their way in peace.

Sisoes 26 Abba Amoun once came from Raïthou to visit Abba Sisoes at Clysma. Seeing him distressed at having left the desert, he said to him: "Why are you distressed, abba? What more could you accomplish in the desert now you have grown so old?" Turning a reproachful gaze upon him the elder said: "What are you telling me, Amoun? Was not the freedom of my *logismos* alone sufficient for me in the desert?"

Sisoes 27 Abba Sisoes was once residing in his cell when his disciple came knocking. "Get away, Abraham," the elder shouted; "do not come in for I have no time for the things of this world now."

Sisoes 28 A brother asked Abba Sisoes: "How did you leave Scete where you were with Abba Ōr to come and live here?" The elder told him: "When Scete began to be populated and I heard that Abba Antony had died I got up and came here to the mountain. When I found that conditions here were [conducive to] *hesychia* I stayed a short time." "And how long have you been here?" the brother said to him. "Seventy-two years," the elder told him.

Sisoes 29   Abba Sisoes said: "When there is somebody taking care of you, you do not have to give orders."

Sisoes 30 [cf. John Colobos 17, 17.10]   A brother asked Abba Sisoes: "If we are walking along the way and our guide goes astray, should we tell him?" "No," the elder said to him. "Should we let him lead us astray then?" said the brother. The elder said to him: "What else? Are you going to take a stick and beat him? I know some brothers who were walking along and their guide went astray in the night. They were twelve in number and they all knew they had gone astray; they were each one at pains not to say anything. At daybreak their guide learnt that they had strayed from the way. 'Forgive me,' he said to them; 'I have gone astray.' They all said: 'We too knew that but we kept silent.'" [The brother] was astounded when he heard this and [Abba Sisoes] said: "The brothers disciplined themselves not to speak [of it] until death," and he glorified God. The extent to which they had gone astray was twelve miles.

Sisoes 31   Once there came some Saracens who despoiled the elder and his brother. When they went out into the desert in search of something to eat the elder found some camel droppings; he broke them and found some barley seeds. He ate one seed and kept one in his hand. His brother came and found him eating; he said to him: "Is this love—that you found some food and are eating alone without calling me?" "I did you no wrong brother," said Abba Sisoes to him; "here is your share; I was holding it in my hand."

Sisoes 32   They used to say of Abba Sisoes the Theban that while he was staying at Calamon in Arsinoë a different elder was sick at the other lavra and he was distressed when he heard of it. He was fasting every second day and it was the day when he did not eat when he heard. He said to his *logismos*: "What shall I do? If I go, the brothers may well oblige me to eat; but if I wait until tomorrow perhaps he will die. Well, this is what I shall do: I will go and not eat." So off he went, fasting—fulfilling the commandment of God. He did not deviate from his godly way of life.

Sisoes 33 One of the fathers recounted that Abba Sisoes of Calamon, wishing to overcome [the need for] sleep, once suspended himself from the precipice of Petra. But an angel came and detached him, forbidding him to do that ever again or to deliver such a tradition to others.

Sisoes 34 One of the fathers asked Abba Sisoes: "If I am residing in the desert and a barbarian comes by wanting to kill me, shall I kill him if I am able?" "No," said the elder, "hand him over to God. For whatever temptation comes upon a person, let him say: 'It is on account of my sins that this has happened.' But if it is a good thing: 'This is by the providence of God!'"

Sisoes 35 A brother asked Abba Sisoes the Theban: "Tell me a saying," and he said: "What can I say to you? That I read the New Testament and return to the Old?"

Sisoes 36 The same brother asked Abba Sisoes of Petra [about] the saying Abba Sisoes the Theban told [them] and the elder said: "For my part I go to bed in sin and in sin I get up."

Sisoes 37 They used to say of Abba Sisoes the Theban that he used to run away to his cell when the congregation was dismissed. They used to say: "He has a demon," but he was performing the work of God.

Sisoes 38 A brother asked Abba Sisoes: "What am I to do, abba, for I have fallen?" The elder told him: "Get up again." "I got up," said the brother, "then I fell again." "Get up again and again," the elder said, so the brother said: "Until when?" "Until you are carried off either in the good or in the fallen state; for a person will go hence in the state in which he is found," the elder said.

Sisoes 39   A brother asked an elder: "What am I to do, for I am troubled about my handiwork? I like braiding rope but I am unable to work at it." The elder said: "Abba Sisoes used to say we ought not to work at some relaxing task."

Sisoes 40   Abba Sisoes said: "Seek out God; do not seek out where he dwells."

Sisoes 41   He also said: "Self-esteem and fearlessness often occasion sin."

Sisoes 42   A brother asked Abba Sisoes: "What am I to do?" He said to him: "What you are looking for is an intense silence and humility, for it is written: 'Blessed are they who remain in him' [Is 30.18]. In this way you will be able to stand."

Sisoes 43 [1.26]   Abba Sisoes said: "Be as of no significance, cast your will behind you, become unconcerned [cf. Mt 6.25] and you shall experience repose."

Sisoes 44   A brother asked Abba Sisoes: "What am I to do about the passions?" and the elder said: "Each one of us is tempted by his own desires" [Jas 1.14].

Sisoes 45   A brother asked Abba Sisoes: "Tell me a saying," but he said: "Why do you oblige me to speak in vain? Look here and do what you see [me doing]."

Sisoes 46   Abba Abraham, the disciple of Abba Sisoes, once went away on an errand. For days on end [the elder] would not be attended by anybody else, saying: "Can I let any man other than my brother become familiar with me?" and he accepted [nobody] until his disciple came, putting up with the inconvenience.

Sisoes 47   They used to say of Abba Sisoes that while he was sitting down he cried out with a loud voice: "O wretchedness!" His disciple said to him: "What is the matter, father?" The elder said to him: "I am looking for one man with whom to speak and I am not finding [one]."

Sisoes 48 Abba Sisoes once went out from the mountain of Abba Antony to the outer mountain of the Thebaid and dwelt there. Some Meletians were there, living at Calamon in Arsenoë. Hearing that he had gone to the outer mountain certain people desired to see him; but they were saying: "What shall we do? There are Meletians at the mountain. We know the elder is not harmed by them but maybe we who wish to meet the elder will fall prey to the temptation of the heretics." So in order not to encounter the heretics they did not go to see the elder.

Sisoes 49 They used to say of Abba Sisoes that he fell ill; there were elders sitting with him when he spoke to some [other] persons. "What are you seeing, abba?" they said to him, and he said to them: "I see some people coming for me and I am beseeching them to allow me a little time to repent." One of the elders said to him: "Even if they allow it, can you usefully repent at this stage?" The elder said to him: "If I cannot do that I can groan over my soul a little and that will suffice for me."

Sisoes 50 They used to say of Abba Sisoes that he fell ill when he came to Clysma. There was a knock at the door while he was sitting in his cell with his disciple. Being aware of this the elder said to Abraham his disciple: "Tell the one who knocked: 'It is I, Sisoes on the mountain; it is I, Sisoes in the valley,'" but he disappeared on hearing this.

Sisoes 51 Abba Sisoes the Theban said to his disciple: "Tell me what you see in me and I will tell you what I see in you." His disciple said to him: "You have a good mind but you are a bit hard." The elder said to him: "You are a good man but soft in the head."

Sisoes 52 They used to say of Abba Sisoes the Theban that he would not eat bread. At the Easter festival the brothers prostrated themselves [begging him] to eat with them. In reply he said to them: "I can do one thing: I can either partake of bread, or of the edibles you have prepared." "Eat bread alone then," they told him—and so he did.

SILVANUS

Originally from Palestine, Silvanus lived successively at Scete, Sinaï, and near Gaza. He had a number of disciples, among whom Zachariah, Zeno, Mark, and Netras are encountered in these pages.

Silvanus 1 [4.48]   Abba Silvanus and Zachariah his disciple once visited a monastery and [the brothers] obliged them to eat something before they set out. When they had come out, his disciple found water by the wayside and he wanted to drink. The elder said to him: "Today is a fast, Zachariah," but he said: "Were we not eating, father?" The elder said: "That eating was out of love [for the brothers]; but let us keep our own fast, my son."

Silvanus 2 [3.33]   The same [elder] was once sitting with some brothers when he went into a trance and fell on his face. After some considerable time he got up and began to weep. The brothers enquired of him: "What is the matter, father?" but he remained silent and went on weeping. But when they urged him to speak he said: "I was snatched away to the judgment and I saw many of our type going off to punishment and many worldlings going off into the kingdom." The elder was mourning and would not come out of his cell. If he was obliged to come out, he would hide his face in his cowl, saying: "Why do I want to see this transitory light that offers no advantage?"

Silvanus 3 [18.27]   Another time, Zachariah his disciple came in and found him in a trance, his hands stretched out to heaven; he closed the door and went out. Coming in about the sixth and the ninth hours he found him likewise. He knocked and went in about the tenth hour and found him in *hesychia*. "What was the matter today?" he said to him, and the elder said: "I was unwell today, my son." He however grasped [the elder's] feet and began to say: "I will not let go of you unless you tell me what you saw." "I was snatched away into heaven," the elder said to him, "and I saw the glory of God. I was standing there until now, but now I have been dismissed."

Silvanus 4 [11.68]   Once when Abba Silvanus was residing at Mount Sinaï, his disciple Zacharias went away on an errand and he said to the elder: "Release the water and irrigate the garden." Going out, he covered his face with his cowl and he could only see his own footsteps. A brother came visiting him at that time and, seeing him from a distance, observed what he was doing. When the brother came in to him he said: "Tell me, abba, why were you watering the garden like that, your face covered with the cowl?" The elder said to him: "It was so that my eyes might not see the trees and my mind be distracted from its work to them, my son."

Silvanus 5 [10.99]   A brother visited Abba Silvanus at Mount Sinaï; he saw the brothers working and said to the elder: "'Labor not for the meat which perishes' [Jn 6.27], for 'Mary has chosen the good part' [Lk 10.42]." The elder said to his disciple: "Zachariah, give this brother a book and put him in an empty cell." When the ninth hour came round, [the brother] was watching by the door to see whether they would send someone to invite him to eat. But as nobody invited him, he got up, came to the elder and said to him: "Did the brothers not eat today, abba?" "Yes," said the elder, and the brother said: "Then why did you not call me?" "Since you are a spiritual person," the elder said, "you do not need this food. But we, being physical [creatures], we want to eat; that is why we are working. But you 'have chosen the good part,' reading all day long, and you do not want to eat physical food." When he heard this, he prostrated himself saying: "Forgive me, abba," and the elder said to him: "Mary certainly needs Martha, and it is thanks to Martha that Mary gets the praise."

Silvanus 6 [11.70]   They once asked Abba Silvanus: "Father, what way of life did you practice to acquire this understanding?" and he answered them: "I never allowed a *logismos* that would anger God to enter my heart."

Silvanus 7   They used to say of Abba Silvanus that he secluded himself in his cell with some small chickpeas and he did a job on them—a hundred siftings of them.[109] Here there came a man from Egypt with an ass charged with loaves. He knocked at the cell and discharged them. The elder took the siftings, loaded them onto the ass, and sent him on his way.

Silvanus 8   They used to say of Abba Silvanus that Zachariah his disciple went out without him, took the brothers, and moved the fence of the garden to enlarge it. When the elder heard of this he took his sheepskin and went out, saying to the brothers: "Pray for me." When they saw him [leaving] they fell at his feet saying: "Tell us what is the matter, father." He said to them: "I am not coming in and I am not taking the sheepskin off me until you put the fence back in its original position." They moved the fence back and made it as it was before and so the elder returned to his cell.

Silvanus 9 [6.28]   Abba Silvanus said: "I am a slave and my master said to me: 'Do my work and I will feed you; do not ask where from; whether I possess it or steal it or borrow it, you are not to ask: only to work—and I will feed you.' So then, if I work, I eat out of my wage; if I work not, I am eating charity."

Silvanus 10 [21.36, N 117]   He also said: "Woe to that man whose reputation is greater than his performance."

Silvanus 11 [11.69]   Abba Moses asked Abba Silvanus: "Can a person make a fresh start each day?" and Abba Silvanus said: "If he is a real worker, a person can make a fresh start each day and each hour."

---

[109]The meaning is obscure here; maybe he picked them over a hundred times.

Silvanus 12 [cf. Pambo 12]   One of the fathers said that somebody once met Abba Silvanus and, having seen his face and body shining like an angel's, he fell face down. He used to say that others had acquired this spiritual gift.

SIMON

Simon 1 [8.22]   A governor once came to see Abba Simon, but he, when he heard, put on his belt and went up into a palm tree to prune it. Those who came shouted out: "Elder, where is the anchorite?" but he said to them: "There is no anchorite here," and they went away when they heard.

Simon 2 [8.23]   On another occasion another governor came to see him. The clergy took the initiative and said: "Abba, get ready, for the governor has heard of you and is coming to be blessed by you." "Yes," he said; "I am getting myself ready." Wearing his ragged old clothes he took bread and cheese in hand, got up, and sat down at the gate, eating. When the governor came together with his retinue and saw him, they reviled him, saying: "This is the anchorite of whom we heard?"—and they took off forthwith.

SOPATROS

Sopatros [14.16]   Somebody asked Abba Sopatros: "Give me a commandment, abba, and I will keep it." "Let no woman enter your cell," he said; "do not read apocryphal writings, and engage in no discussions concerning the likeness,[110] for this is not heresy, but hair-splitting and quibbling on both sides of the question. The whole of creation is incapable of comprehending this matter."

---

[110]This probably means Christological disputes.

SARMATAS

Sarmatas 1   Abba Sarmatas said: "I prefer one who has sinned, if he knows he has sinned and repents, to one who has not sinned and considers himself one who acts righteously.

Sarmatas 2   They used to say of Abba Sarmatas that, on the advice of Abba Poemen, he often undertook to fast for forty days and the days went by like nothing in his sight. So Abba Poemen came to him and said to him: "Tell me, what have you seen while enduring such toil?" "Not much," he said to him. Abba Poemen said to him: "I will not let you go unless you tell me." "I found out only one thing," he said: "that if I say to sleep: 'Go away,' away it goes; and if I say: 'Come,' come it does."[111]

Sarmatas 3   A brother asked Abba Sarmatas: "My *logismoi* are saying to me: 'Do not work: eat, drink, and sleep.'" The elder said to him: "Eat when you are hungry, drink when you are thirsty, and sleep when you are weary." In due course another elder came to the brother and the brother told him what Abba Sarmatas had said, then the elder said to him: "This is what Abba Sarmatas told you: 'When you are hungry to the limit and so thirsty you can bear it no longer, then eat and drink, and when you are weary from protracted vigils, then sleep. That is what the elder was telling you.'"

Sarmatas 4   The same brother also asked Abba Sarmatas: "My *logismoi* are telling me to go out and visit the brothers." The elder said to him: "Do not listen to them saying this. Just say: 'Look, I heard you first time; this time I cannot hear you.'"

[111] cf. Mt 8.9, Lk 7.8.

Serapion

Serapion 1 [17.34]   One day Abba Serapion was passing through a village of Egypt when he saw a whore standing at her dwelling. The elder said to her: "Expect me this evening; I want to come to you and spend this night at your side." "Very well, abba," she said in reply. She got herself ready and prepared the bed. When it was evening the elder came to her and as he entered the dwelling he said to her: "Did you get the bed ready?" "Yes, abba," she said. Closing the door he said to her: "Wait a little; we have a rule; [wait] until I first fulfill it," and the elder started his *synaxis*. Beginning with the Psalter, he offered a prayer at each psalm, beseeching God on her behalf, that she might repent and be saved. And God heard him: the woman stood by the elder, trembling and praying. The woman fell to the ground as the elder finished the entire Psalter. Starting the Apostle,[112] the elder recited a large part of it and so fulfilled his *synaxis*. The woman was pricked in her conscience; she realized that it was not to sin that he came to her, but to save her. She fell down before him saying: "Of your charity abba, take me to wherever I can be well-pleasing to God." Then the elder took her to a monastery for virgins and handed her over to the amma, saying: "Receive this sister but do not impose a yoke or a commandment on her as [you do] on the other sisters; rather give her whatever she wants and let her go where she wishes." When she had passed a few days she said: "I am a sinner; I want to eat [only] every second day." Then after a few days she said: "I have many sins; I want to eat [only] every fourth day." The some days later still she begged the amma of the monastery: "Since I gravely saddened God with my transgressions, of your charity, put me in a cell, seal it up, and pass me a little bread and some handiwork through a hole." The amma did so for her and she was well-pleasing to God for the remaining time of her life.

Serapion 2 [6.16]   A brother asked Abba Serapion: "Tell me a saying." The elder said: "What can I say to you? That you took the goods

---

[112]The book containing the Acts of the Apostles and the Epistles.

of widows and orphans and set them in this embrasure?"—for he saw that it was full of books.

Serapion 3 [11.71]   Abba Serapion said: "Just as the soldiers of the emperor standing before him cannot turn their attention to left or to right, so too if a person stand before God and rivet his attention on *his* presence, in fear of *him* all the time, no action of the enemy can terrorize him."

Serapion 4 [8.12; from Cassian, *Conf.* 18.11, attributed to Serapion]   When a brother visited Abba Serapion, the elder invited him to offer a prayer as usual but he declined, saying that he was himself a sinner and not worthy of the monastic habit. [The elder] wanted to wash his feet but he refused, using the same words. He obliged him to eat something and the elder began to eat too. He admonished him, saying: "My son, if you want to receive benefit, persevere in your cell, paying attention to yourself and to your handiwork. [Coming out] does not procure you such benefit as staying [inside]." He was piqued on hearing that and changed his face so much that he was not able to hide it from the elder, so Abba Serapion said to him: "Hitherto you were saying: 'I am a sinner' and accusing yourself of not even being worthy to live—and yet you became so angry when I lovingly admonished you? If you want to be humble, learn to tolerate courageously that which is said to you by others and do not apply meaningless words to yourself." The brother prostrated himself before the elder on hearing this and went his way having reaped great benefit.

Serinos

An Abba Serinos and his disciple Isaac once visited Abba Poemen [APsys 10.73]; Cassian relates two conferences of an Abba Serenus [Conf. 7 & 8].

Serinos 1   They used to say of Abba Serinos that he was a very hard worker and only ever ate two dried loaves. His colleague Abba Job (himself a great ascetic) came to him and said: "I maintain my practice in my cell but if I come out I fall in with the brothers." Abba Serinos said to him: "It is no great virtue if you maintain your practice in your cell, but it is when you come out of your cell."

Serinos 2   Abba Serinos said: "I have spent my time harvesting, sewing, braiding; and in all these [activities] I would not have been able to be fed if the hand of God had not fed me."

Spyridon

The following are extracts from Socrates, HE 1.12.

Spyridon 1   Concerning Spyridon, so great was the sanctity when he was a shepherd that he was deemed worthy to become a shepherd of men too. He was called to be bishop of one of the cities of Cyprus, Trimithus by name. Being a very modest person, he tended his sheep while holding the bishopric. Once in the middle of the night some thieves crept up to the sheepfold intending to steal some of the sheep. But God, who was saving the shepherd, saved the sheep too: the thieves were trussed up near the fold by an unseen force. At first light the shepherd came to the sheep and, finding [the thieves] with their hands [tied] behind their backs, he realized what had happened. He offered a prayer then released the thieves. He admonished and exhorted them at some length to pursue honest work rather than live from evil-doing. He gave them one ram and sent them on their way; calling out laughingly he said: "[The ram] is so you will not seem to have been up all night for nothing."

Spyridon 2   They also used to say that he had a maiden daughter who shared her father's piety, Eirene by name. Somebody who was known to her entrusted a valuable piece of jewelry to her, which she then hid in the ground for greater security; but then a little later she departed this life. Eventually he who had entrusted it to her came by. When he could not find the maiden, he applied to her father, Abba Spyridon, threatening and beseeching him by turns. As the elder regarded the other's loss as his own, he came to his daughter's tomb and besought God to show him the promised resurrection ahead of time—and he was not disappointed in his hope. The maiden promptly appeared to her father, alive—indicating the place where the jewelry lay—then departed again. The elder took the deposit and handed it over.

SAIO

This somewhat disreputable tale is not found anywhere else but in the Synagogē.

They used to say of Abba Saio and Abba Mouē that they cohabited; that Abba Saio was extremely obedient but very harsh. To try him the elder would say to him: "Go and steal." He would go and steal from the brothers out of obedience, giving thanks to the Lord for everything. The elder would take the pilfered goods and give them back in secret. Once when they were travelling he fainted away and the abba left him, exhausted. He came and said to the brothers: "Go and fetch Saio for he is lying in a state of collapse." They went and brought him [in].

SARAH[113]

Sarah 1 [5.13] They recounted of Amma Sarah that for thirteen years she continued to be fiercely embattled by the demon of *porneia*

[113]"When Amma Sarah leapt over a small stream while she was walking in the way a worldling saw her and laughed. Unaware that the grace of God had come upon her she said to the worldling: 'Be quiet: you are going to burst.' She turned round and saw him with his intestines spilled out. Stricken with fear she prayed saying: 'My Jesus, bring him back to life and I will never say such a thing again.'" Translated from a Latin text. José Geraldes Freire, ed., *A Versão Latina por Pascásio de Dume dos Apophthegmata Patrum*, 2 vols. (Coimbra, 1971), 1:157–333, item 80.2.

and she never prayed for the battle to be stayed, but would rather say: "Oh God, give me strength!"

Sarah 2 [5.14]   The same spirit of *porneia* once attacked her more vehemently, suggesting the vanities of the world to her. But she, without diminishing her fear of God or her spiritual discipline, went up to her rooftop one day to pray. The spirit of *porneia* appeared to her in bodily form and said to her: "Sarah, you have conquered me," but she said to him: "It is not I who have conquered you but Christ, my lord-and-master."

Sarah 3 [7.26]   They used to say of her that she spent sixty years living over the river and did not peer out to see it.

Sarah 4 [10.107]   Another time two elders, great anchorites, came to her from the district of Pelusium and as they were approaching they were saying to each other: "Let us take this old woman down a peg or two." They said to her: "See that your *logismos* be not lifted up, amma, and you say to yourself: 'Here there are anchorites coming to me who am a woman.'" Amma Sarah said to them: "I am a woman by nature but not in *logismos*."

Sarah 5 [10.108]   Amma Sarah said: "If I pray to God that everybody have confidence in me I will be at the door of each one, apologizing. But I shall rather pray that my heart be pure with everyone."

Sarah 6 [11.127]   She also said: "When I put my foot on the ladder to go up, I also set death in front of my eyes before I go up there."

Sarah 7 [13.19]   She also said: "It is good to give alms even for people. If a person [give alms] to please people, eventually it is pleasing to God as well."

Sarah 8   When some people from Scete visited Amma Sarah one day she handed them a basket of fruit. Leaving the good fruit aside, they ate the pieces that were spoiled. "You really are men of Scete," she said to them.

Syncletica

All the following sayings are extracted from the Life of this fourth-century Alexandrine saint [VS].[114]

Syncletica 1 [3.34, VS 60]   Amma Syncletica said: "It is a struggle and great toil at first for those who approach God, but then it is unspeakable joy. Just as they who want to light a fire are engulfed in smoke and reduced to tears at first, then in this way attain the desired object, so too must we ignite the divine fire within ourselves with tears and pains, for [Scripture] says 'Our God is a consuming fire'" [Heb 12.29].

Syncletica 2 [4.4, VS 24]   She also said: "We who have taken up this calling must maintain absolute self-control. It is true that self-control seems to be practiced by the worldlings too, but thoughtlessness[115] is present with it because they sin with all their other senses, for they look in an unseemly way and laugh in a disorderly manner."

Syncletica 3 [4.50, VS 80]   She also said: "Just as the most bitter medicines put poisonous animals to flight, so prayer with fasting puts a sordid *logismos* to flight" [cf. Ps 67.3].

Syncletica 4 [4.51, VS 95]   She also said: "Do not let the delight in worldly wealth delude you into thinking that it is of any use. They esteem the art of cooking for their pleasure, but you transcend their plentiful supply of victuals by fasting and cheap commodities, for the Scripture says: 'The soul abundantly supplied makes a joke of honeycombs' [Prov 27.7]. Do not stuff yourself with bread and you will not long for wine."

Syncletica 5 [6.17, VS 30]   The blessed Syncletica was asked whether indifference to possessions was a perfectly good thing. "It is a very

[114]PG 28:1488–1557; E. Bryson Bongie, trans., *The Life of the Blessed Syncletica* (Toronto, 1995).
[115]"... self control ... thoughtlessness": there is a play on the words *sōphrosynē / aphrosynē*—which could equally mean *chastity / unchastity*.

good thing for those who are capable of it," she replied, "for they who endure it are afflicted in the flesh but experience repose in the soul. Just as stiff garments are washed and whitened by being trodden on and vigorously twisted, so the strong soul also grows stronger through voluntary indigence."

Syncletica 6 [7.22, *VS* 94]   She also said: "If you happen to be in a coenobion, do not change your place for you will be severely harmed. Just as the bird that gets up from her eggs makes them infertile and barren, so too does the faith of a monk or a virgin who moves from place to place become chilled and die."

Syncletica 7 [7.23, *VS* 98]   She also said: "The ambushes of the devil are many. He did not shift a soul by penury? He brings up affluence as bait. He did not succeed with injuries and insults? He sets forth praise and glory. He was worsted by health? He makes the body sick. When unable to lead astray with pleasures, he endeavors to turn the soul aside through involuntary pains. He brings some very severe illnesses on demand to obfuscate those who through them became fainthearted in their love for God. But even if the body is lacerated and is burning up with gravest fevers and furthermore is vexed by unmanageable thirst, if you undergo these things, as you are a sinner call to mind the chastisement that is also to come, the eternal fire, the judicial punishments, and do not be fainthearted in present conditions but rejoice that God has regarded you and keep that saying of praise on your tongue: 'The Lord has chastened and corrected me but he has not given me over unto death' [Ps 117.18]. You were iron but cast off rust through fire. But if, on the other hand, you become ill when you are righteous, you are progressing from great to greater. You are gold but, through the fire, you become yet more approved. An angel was given to you [as a thorn] in the flesh [cf. 2 Cor 12.7]? Be glad! See whom you have come to resemble, for you have been considered worthy of Paul's part. Are you being tried by fever and chastened by cold? Well, the Scripture says: 'We went through fire and water then you brought us to a place of refreshment' [Ps 65.12].

You got to the first: wait for the second. As you practice virtue, cry out the words of holy David, for he says: 'Poor, in misery, and suffering am I' [Ps 68.30]. You will become perfect through this pair of afflictions, for he says: 'You have set me at large when I was in trouble' [Ps 4.1]. Let us rather be trained with respect to our souls in these exercises, for we see the adversary before [our] eyes."

Syncletica 8 [7.24, VS 99]   She also said: "If sickness troubles [us] let us not be sorrowful because, on account of the sickness and the weakness of the body, we are incapable of standing to pray or to sing out loud. All these things are aimed at purging our desires. For fasting and sleeping rough have also been prescribed for us on account of pleasures. So if illness took the edge off these no more need be said. This is the great *askēsis*: to persevere in sicknesses and to send up hymns of gratitude to God.

Syncletica 9 [7.25, VS 102]   She also said: "When you are fasting do not posit illness as a pretense, because those who do not fast often fell into the same kind of illnesses. Did you begin to do good? Do not hold back when the enemy blocks you, for he is himself negated by your patience. They who set out to sail unfurl the sails at first when they encounter a favorable wind, then when an adverse wind comes upon them the sailors do not discharge the ship because the wind is against them. They wait quietly for a while or wrestle with the storm, then sail on again. So it is with us; when an adverse wind is against us, let us complete our voyage without fear, having unfurled the cross instead of a sail."

Syncletica 10 [10.101, VS 37]   She also said: "They who amass palpable wealth by toil and dangers at sea, after they have acquired much, long for yet more. They consider what is in hand as nothing, straining to get that which is not in hand. But we neither possess anything of the things that are sought after, nor do we wish to acquire anything in our fear of God."

Syncletica 11 [15.68, Hyperechios 73–74]   She also said: "Imitate the Publican so you be not condemned with the Pharisee [Lk 18.14] and choose the gentleness of Moses in order to transform your flinty heart into springs of water" [Ex 17.6].

Syncletica 12 [10.104, VS 79]   She also said: "It is dangerous for somebody who has not been raised through the practical experience of life to undertake teaching. Just as somebody who had a house that was dilapidated would damage the guests he took in by the collapse of the building, so too those [teachers] who had not first built themselves up securely would bring to perdition those who came to them. They motivated the ascetics [who followed them] to salvation with words, but wronged them by the badness of their behavior."

Syncletica 13 [10.103, VS 64]   She also said: "It is good not to get angry, but if it happens, [Paul] did not allow you even the space of a day for the passion, for he said: 'Let not the sun go down [upon your wrath]' [Eph 4.26]. Would you wait until your whole span of time was setting? Why hate the person who grieved you? It is the devil, not he, who grieved you. Hate the illness, not the person who is ill."

Syncletica 14 [10.106, VS 26]   She also said: "Insofar as athletes make progress, so they encounter a greater opponent."

Syncletica 15 [10.105, VS 100]   She also said: "There is also an intensified *askesis* that is of the enemy, and his disciples practice it. How then are we to discriminate the godly and royal *askesis* from that which is tyrannical and demoniacal? Clearly it is a question of due proportion. Let there be one rule of fasting throughout your time. Do not fast four or five days in a row then break it next day with an abundance of provisions. Disproportion is destructive everywhere. Fast while you are young and in good health, for old age will come together with sickness. Whilst you are able, lay up treasure [cf. Mt 6.20] where food is concerned so you may experience repose when you are no longer able [to do so]."

Syncletica 16 [14.17, VS 100]   She also said: "When we are living in community, let us rather prefer obedience to *askesis*, for [*askesis*] teaches disdain while [obedience enjoins] humble-mindedness."

Syncletica 17 [14.18, VS 101]   She also said: "We must govern the soul with discretion and, when in a coenobion, not seek our own [well-being] nor serve our personal opinion but obey [our] father in the faith."

Syncletica 18 [18.28, VS 28]   She also said: "It is written: 'You are to be wise as serpents and harmless as doves' [Mt 10.17]. To be 'wise as serpents' is said [to warn] us not to be deceived by the assaults and techniques of the devil (for like quickly acquires a knowledge of like); 'harmless as doves' indicates the purity of the action."

Syncletica S 1 [Guy p. 34, VS 101]   Amma Syncletica said: "Many who are in the mountain behave as though they were in towns—and are lost. It is possible to be with many people yet to be alone in one's thought; also really to be alone and yet to be among many in one's mind."

Syncletica S 2 [Guy p. 34, VS 101]   She also said: "Those who commit faults in the world, even inadvertently, we throw into prison; and we imprison ourselves for our sins so that the voluntary gesture of our will may stave off future punishment."

Syncletica S 3 [Guy p. 34–35, VS 38]   She also said: "Just as treasure is found to be lacking once it is exposed, so virtue disappears when it becomes known and is noised abroad. And just as wax is melted before a fire, so too does the soul disintegrate and lose its vigor from being praised."

Syncletica S 4 [Guy p.35, VS 78]   She also said: "Just as it is not possible to be at once both plant and seed, so is it impossible for us to produce heavenly fruit with earthly glory lying all around us."

Syncletica S 5 [11.71, Guy p.35, *VS* 22]   She also said: "Children, we all want to be saved but we fall short of salvation through our own negligence."

Syncletica S 6 [11.73, Guy p.35, *VS* 25]   She also said: "Let us be on our guard for it is through our senses that thieves get in, even though we do not wish it. For how can a house not be blackened when there is smoke blowing around outside and the windows are open?"

Syncletica S 7 [11.74, Guy p.35, *VS* 45]   She also said: "We must arm ourselves against the demons, for they approach from without and are set in motion from within. The soul is like a ship: sometimes it is sunk by a mighty swell from without, sometimes from within because the bilge is overflowing. So too are we sometimes lost through sinful practices on the outside, sometimes defiled by *logismoi* within. So we must watch out for the attacks of the spirits from outside and drain off the impurities of the *logismoi* within."

Syncletica S 8 [11.75, Guy p.35, *VS* 46–47]   She also said: "We are never free of concern here, for the Scripture says: 'Let him who stands see that he does not fall' [1 Cor 10.2]. We are sailing in darkness, for it is said that our life is a sea by the sacred psalmist David [Ps 129.1]. But with the parts of the sea, some can be full of monsters while others are quite calm. We seem to be sailing in the calm part of the sea while the worldlings are in the danger-zones. We are sailing by day, travelling under the sun of righteousness, they by night, borne along as a result of ignorance. Yet it is often possible for the worldling who encounters a storm and peril, calling for help and keeping watch, to save his own craft—while we who are in calm waters can be sunk through negligence, having let go the rudder of righteousness."

Syncletica S 9 [15.66, Guy p.25, *VS* 56]   She also said: "Just as a ship cannot be built without nails, so is it impossible to be saved without humble-mindedness."

Syncletica S 10 [10.102, Guy p.35, *VS* 40]   She also said: "There is a sorrow that is beneficial and a sorrow that is destructive. Useful sorrow is to groan for one's own sins and for the ignorance of [one's] neighbors; [it serves us] not to fall short of the intended goal, but to attain the ultimate goodness. But there is a sorrow that is of the enemy, a totally unreasonable sorrow that has been called *accidie* by many people. It is necessary to scare this spirit away, especially by prayer and psalm-singing."

T—*Tau*

TITHOES

See the note on "Sisoes" above.

Tithoes 1 [12.13]   They used to say of Abba Tithoes that if he did not quickly lower his hands when he stood in prayer, his mind was rapt away on high. So if it happened that some brothers were praying with him he would make a point of quickly lowering his hands so that his mind would not be rapt away and stay that way.

Tithoes 2 [4.52]   Abba Tithoes said: "For us, voluntary exile [*xeniteia*] is a person being in control of his own mouth."

Tithoes 3 [11.67]   A brother asked Abba Tithoes: "How am I to keep a watch on my heart?" The elder said to him: "How will we keep a watch on our heart when our tongue lies open and our belly?"

Tithoes 4   Abba Matoes used to say of Abba Tithoes: "Nobody can find a reason to open his mouth against him in any matter; like pure gold lying in the balance, thus was Abba Tithoes."

Tithoes 5   Once when Abba Tithoes was residing at Clysma he thought carefully then said to his disciple: "Irrigate the palm trees my son," but he said: "We are at Clysma, abba." The elder said: "What am I doing at Clysma? Take me back to the mountain."

Tithoes 6 [cf. John Colobos 23]   Abba Tithoes was once sitting with a brother close by; but he did not know that and he sighed. He was not aware that a brother was close by for he was in a trance. He prostrated himself saying: "Forgive me brother; I have not yet become a monk, for I sighed in your presence."

Tithoes 7 [15.61]   A brother asked Abba Sisoes: "What kind of a road is it that leads to humility?" Said the elder to him: "This is the road leading to humility: continence, prayer, and esteeming oneself to be inferior to all creation."

TIMOTHY

Timothy [13.18]   Abba Timothy the priest asked Abba Poemen: "There is a woman in Egypt who plays the harlot and gives her earnings away in alms." In response the elder said: "She will not go on being a harlot, for the fruit of faith is apparent in her." Now it happened that the mother of Timothy the priest came to him and he asked her: "That woman, did she go on playing the harlot?" "Yes," she said, "and she has increased [the number of] her lovers too. But she has also increased her almsgiving." Abba Timothy reported [this] to Abba Poemen but he said: "She will not go on playing the harlot." Then the mother of Abba Timothy came again and said to him: "Do you know that that woman, the harlot, wanted to come with me so you might pray for her?" On hearing this he reported it to Abba Poemen and he said to him: "Then rather do you go and meet her." Abba Timothy went and met her; she was conscience-stricken and wept when she saw him and heard the word of God from him. "From this day I am going to attach myself to God and no longer play the harlot," she said to him. She entered a monastery forthwith and was well-pleasing to God.

Υ—Upsilon

Hyperechios

Hyperechios is a little-known fifth-century writer who composed a collection of 159 sayings, from which the following and some others are taken and to which the numbers refer.[116]

Hyperechios 1 [4.53, 66]   Abba Hyperechios said: "Just as a lion is fearsome to the wild asses, so is the well-tried monk to lascivious *logismoi.*"

Hyperechios 2 [4.54, 80a]   He also said: "For the monk, fasting is a bridle against sin. He who sets it aside finds himself [to be like] a horse in heat" [Jer 5.8].

Hyperechios 3 [4.57, 97]   He also said: "The kind of man who does not hold his tongue when he is angry will not master his passions either."

Hyperechios 4 [4.59, 144]   He also said: "It is good to eat flesh and to drink wine and not to eat the flesh of your brothers in backbiting."

Hyperechios 5 [4.60, 153]   He also said: "By whispering, the serpent expelled Eve from Paradise, and he who bites back at his neighbor is like it, for he ruins the soul of him who hears and does not keep his own safe."

Hyperechios 6 [6.18, 40–41]   He also said: "The monk's treasure is voluntary destitution; lay [it] up in heaven, brother [cf. Matt 6.19–20] for the ages of repose are limitless."

---

[116]Text in PG 79:1472–1489; F. Poswick, trans., *Collectanea Cisterciensia* 32 (Scourmont, 1970), 245–255.

Hyperechios 7 [11.76, 23b]   He also said: "Let your consciousness always dwell on the Kingdom of Heaven and soon you shall inherit it."

Hyperechios 8 [14.19, 59 & 139]   He also said: "Obedience is the monk's precious jewel. He who possesses it will himself be heard by God and will stand with confidence beside the Crucified One, for the crucified Lord was obedient unto death" [cf. Phil 2.8].

Φ—*Phi*

PHOCAS

Phocas 1   Abba Phocas of the coenobion of Abba Theognios the Jerusalemite used to say: "When I was residing at Scete there was an Abba James, a young man, at The Cells who had his physical father as his spiritual father too. At The Cells there are two churches: one for the Orthodox (where he communicated) and one for the schismatics. As Abba James possessed the spiritual gift of humble-mindedness [and] he was loved by everybody, both the church people and the schismatics. The Orthodox would say to him: 'See the schismatics do not deceive you and draw you into their communion, Abba James.' Likewise the schismatics would say to him: 'Abba James, so that you know, if you communicate with the dyophysites you will lose your soul, for they are Nestorians and they defame the truth.' Now Abba James was without guile; in the straitened circumstances from what was being said to him on either side he was at a loss what to do; so off he went to intercede with God. He hid himself away in *hesychia* at a cell outside the lavra, wearing his grave clothes as though he were about to die. (It is the custom of the Egyptian fathers to keep the *leviton* in which they received the sacred habit and the cowl until they die and then to be buried in them. They only wore them on Sunday for Holy Communion then take them off right away.) Away he went to that cell, interceding with God; he wore himself out with fasting, fell to the floor, and remained lying there. He used to say he suffered mightily from demons in those days, especially in his mind. When forty days had passed he saw a small child coming in to him, all joyful and saying to him: 'What are you doing here, Abba James?' Suddenly suffused with light and gaining

313

strength from the sight of him he said to him: 'Lord-and-master, you
know what is the matter. Some are saying to me: "Do not abandon
the church," while others are saying: "the dyophysites will lead you
astray," and I am quite confused. Not knowing what I should do I
came to do what I am doing.' The Lord answered him: 'You are good
where you are,' and forthwith, as soon as the word was spoken, he
was there before the doors of the holy church of the Orthodox of the
Council [of Chalcedon]."

Phocas 2   Abba Phocas also said: "When Abba James moved back
to Scete he was violently embattled by the demon of *porneia*. In
danger of capitulating, he came to me and explained his situation.
He said to me: 'In two days I am going off to such-and-such a cave. I
beg you for the Lord's sake to tell nobody, not even my father. Count
off forty days and when they are fulfilled, of your charity come to
me bringing Holy Communion. Bury me if you find me dead; if still
alive, let me receive Holy Communion.' Heeding these instructions
of his, I went to him when the forty days were fulfilled taking Holy
Communion, some ordinary white bread, and a little wine. Even as
I drew near to the cave I detected the great stench that was in fact
coming out of his mouth and I said to myself: 'The blessed one is at
rest.' But when I went in to him I found him half dead. He moved his
right hand a bit when he saw me and, as far as he was able, indicated
by the movement of his hand [his desire for] Holy Communion. 'I
have it,' I told him—so I wanted to open his mouth: but it was tightly
closed. I was at a loss what to do. Going out into the desert I found
a twig from a bush and, with great effort, I was just able to open his
mouth a little. I poured in some of the sacred Body and Blood after
making it as thin as possible. He gained strength from receiving Holy
Communion. A little later I damped some crumbs of ordinary bread
and offered it to him; a little later still, some more—as much as he
could take. In this way, one day later, by the grace of God he came
with me, making his way to his own cell, delivered with God's aid
from the destructive passion of *porneia*."

Felix

Felix [3.36]   Some brothers visited Abba Felix and they had some worldlings with them. They besought him to say something to them but the elder kept silent. As they went on beseeching him at some length he said to them: "You want to hear something?" "Yes, abba," they said, so the elder said: "There is nothing to say now. When the brothers used to ask the elders and would do what they said to them, God showed them how to speak. But nowadays when they ask but do not do what they hear, God has taken away the spiritual gift of speaking from the elders and they do not find anything to say—since there is no one doing [what they say]." The brothers sighed when they heard this and said: "Pray for us, abba."

Philagrius

Philagrius [6.19]   Among the holy ones there was a man named Philagrius. He was living in the desert of Jerusalem and he used to toil away to provide his own bread. When he was standing in the market place to sell his handiwork, here somebody had lost a purse containing a thousand pieces of gold. When the elder found it he stayed right where he was, saying: "The one who lost it is sure to come"—and here he came, weeping. Taking him aside the elder gave [the purse] to him. He detained him and wanted to give [the elder] part of [its contents] but the elder was reluctant. Then [the fellow] began to shout: "Come and see a man of God and what he has done!" but the elder quietly slipped away and went out of the city so he would not be exalted.

PHORTAS

Abba Phortas said: "If God wants me to live, he knows how to look after me. If he does not want it, what is the point of my living?" He accepted nothing from anybody, even though he was confined to bed, for he said: "If anybody ever brings me anything and not for the sake of God, then neither have I anything to give him nor does he receive a reward from God. For he did not offer [it] in the name of God, so the one who offered is shortchanged. They who are devoted to God and look to him alone must remain so devout that they do not consider it an outrage even if they are wronged thousands of times."

X—*Chi*

CHOMAI

Chomai [1.27]   They used to say of Abba Chomai that when he was about to die, he said to his sons: "Do not dwell with heretics; do not become acquainted with persons in authority. Do not let your hands be stretched out to gather in; let them rather be stretched out to give."

CHEREMON

They used to say of Abba Cheremon at Scete that his cave was forty miles from the church, and twelve miles from the marsh and water. Thus he took his handiwork to his cave carrying two water jars side by side, and stayed there in *hesychia*.

Ψ—Psi

PSENTHAISIOS

The following passage is an extract from the first Greek Life of St Pachomius, §25.[117]

Abba Psenthaisios, Abba Souros, and Abba Psoios said: "We reaped great benefit on hearing the discourses of our father Abba Pachomius and were inspired zealously to pursue good works. We were amazed on seeing the discourse of his practice while he remained silent; we said to each other: 'We used to think all the holy ones had been made like this by God, holy and inflexible from their mother's womb, not of their own free will—and that sinners were incapable of pious living because they were created like that.' But now we see the goodness of God clearly [displayed] in this our father. Though born of pagan parents, he has become so devoted to God and is invested with all the commandments of God. Thus are we all able to follow him just as he follows the holy ones, for this is what is written: 'Come unto me all who labor and are heavily laden and I will give you rest' [Mt 11.28]. Let us then die and live with this man, for he is leading us straight to God."

[117]Cf. Orsisius 1 & 2 above.

Ω—Omega

ŌR

Ōr 1 [3.37]   They used to say of Abba Ōr and Abba Theodore that when they were puddling clay for a cell, they said to each other: "If God were to visit us now, what would we do?" They abandoned the clay in tears and each withdrew to his own cell.

Ōr 2 [20.8]   They used to say of Abba Ōr that he neither lied nor swore nor cursed anybody and only spoke when it was necessary.

Ōr 3 [20.9]   Abba Ōr would say to Paul his disciple: "Make sure you never bring an alien discourse into this cell."

Ōr 4   Paul, the disciple of Abba Ōr, once went away to buy palm-fronds; he found that others had come before him and put down a deposit. Now Abba Ōr never put down a deposit on anything: he sent the price at the time of purchase and bought. His disciple went to another place for branches and the gardener said to him: "Somebody already gave me a deposit but he did not come—so do you take the branches." He took them, came to the elder, and reported this. The elder clapped his hands on hearing it, saying: "Ōr is not working this year," and he would not allow the branches inside until [the disciple] took them back to their place.

Ōr 5 [N 132]   Abba Ōr said: "If you see me entertaining a *logismos* against somebody, you know that it is because he has the same against me."

Ōr 6   In Abba Ōr's district there was a count, Longinus by name, who performed many a charitable deed. He besought one of the fathers who was visiting him to take him to Abba Ōr. The monk went to the elder singing the praises of the count: that he was a good man, doing many charitable works. After a moment's thought the elder said: "Yes, he is good," so the monk started to beg of him, saying: "Permit him to come to see you, abba." In answer the elder said: "He shall surely not cross this wadi and see me."

Ōr 7   Abba Sisoes asked Abba Ōr: "Say something to me." He said to him: "Do you have faith in me?" "Yes," he said, and [Abba Ōr] said to him: "Go on then, and whatever you see me doing, you do it too." "What do I see in you, father?" he said, and the elder said to him: "That my *logismos* is inferior to all people."

Ōr 8   They used to say of Abba Ōr and of Abba Theodore that they were making good beginnings and giving thanks to God all the time.

Ōr 9 [N 98, 21/15]   Abba Ōr used to say that humble-mindedness is the monk's crown.

Ōr 10 [N 300, 15.74]   He also said: "He who is honored or praised above his worth suffers great harm. But he who is not at all honored by folk will be glorified from on high."

Ōr 11 [N 299, 15.72]   He also said: "Whenever a *logismos* of conceit or pride comes upon you, search your conscience: have you kept all the commandments? Do you love your enemies and are you grieved at their defeat? Do you regard yourself as an 'unprofitable servant' [Lk 17.10], more sinful than all? And then do not think so highly of yourself either, as having accomplished all things well, for you know that such a *logismos* undoes everything."

Ōr 12 [N 305 & 659, 15.79]   He also said: "Do not blame somebody else in each temptation; blame only yourself, saying: 'This comes about because of my sins.'"

Ōr 13 [N 331, 15.73]   He also said: "Do not speak against your brother in your heart, saying: 'I am more vigilant and more ascetic,' but rather submit to the grace of Christ in the spirit of poverty and unfeigned love, lest you fall into a spirit of boasting and lose your toil, for it is written: 'Let him who thinks he stands take heed lest he fall' [1 Cor 10.12]. But be 'seasoned with salt' in the Lord" [Col 4.6].

Ōr 14 [N 320, 8.31]   He also said: "Either make a clean break with men or make a laughingstock of the world and of men by making yourself a fool in many ways."

Ōr 15 [N 592/19]   He also said: "If you slander your brother and your conscience troubles you, go, prostrate yourself before him, and say to him: 'I slandered you,' and make sure you are not led astray again; for slandering is the death of the soul."

POPULAR PATRISTICS SERIES

ST VLADIMIR'S SEMINARY PRESS
1-800-204-2665 • www.svspress.com